Fallen Order

Italy and Central Europe,
to 1644

HOLY ROMAN
EMPIRE

POLAND

Vistula

Elbe

Prague •
MORAVIA • Litomysl

Strasnitz
Nikolsburg
(Mikulov)
Vienna

AUSTRIA

Danube

Budapest
HUNGARY

Milan •

Po

Adige

Venice •

O T T O M A N   E M P I R E

Danube

Carcare •
Savona   • Genoa
Guiglia
Fanano   • Pieve di Cento
Pisa   Florence
Arno

Tiber

• Ancona

Adriatic Sea

• Norcia
Castro   • Narni
Moricone
Mentana   • Chieti
ROME   • Poli   • S. Salvatore
• Frascati

CORSICA

Naples • • Somma

Campi
Salentina

SARDINIA

*Tyrrhenian
Sea*

Bisignano •
Cosenza •

Cagliari

Palermo   Messina

SICILY

0   50   100   150 miles

0   50   100 150   200 km

N
W   E
S

FALLEN ORDER
A History

KAREN LIEBREICH

ATLANTIC BOOKS
London

First published in Great Britain in 2004 by Atlantic Books,
an imprint of Grove Atlantic Ltd

1 3 5 7 9 8 6 4 2

A CIP catalogue record for this book is available from the British Library.

ISBN
1 84354 073 8 (hardback edition)
1 84354 163 7 (trade paperback edition)

Printed in Great Britain by CPD, Ebbw Vale, Wales.

Atlantic Books
An imprint of Grove Atlantic Ltd
Ormond House
26–27 Boswell Street
London WC1N 3JZ

LIST OF CONTENTS

ACKNOWLEDGEMENTS

There are many people to thank. One of my greatest debts must be to the two Piarist archivists: Father Osvaldo Tosti, initially at the Florentine house who first welcomed me in and introduced me to the Order; and Father Claudio Vilá Palá who guided me through the wealth of the Roman archive with his gentle chuckle. Both men represented to me the best of priestly virtues. More recent thanks are due to Father Archivist Alcubierre and to Father Severino Giner Guerri.

I owe a huge debt of gratitude to Professor Anthony Pagden, now of UCLA, who rescued me from Florence; to Dr Kristian Jensen of the British Library, who translated Campanella's *Apologia* with me and won the argument over commas but nevertheless remained a friend; to Professor Gigliola Fragnito Broglia who came through with advice and help when it was most needed; to Adrian Levy for his advice and encouragement; to Beatrijs de Hartogh of the European University Institute for her continued support; to Sam Levy for research assistance; and to Michael Liebreich for his fraternal solidarity. I would also like to thank Chris Aujard for his help with cross-country skiing. On the translation front, rapid emergency consultations were generously provided by Andrea Casalotti for Italian and Leslie Winter and Paul Kriwaczek for Latin.

I would like to thank the European University Institute, the British

School at Rome and the Deutscher Akademischer Austausch Dienst for their financial support in the early stages of this research.

The librarians at the British School at Rome (even when covered in builders' dust during a major renovation), the European University Institute, the British Library and the London Library always went out of their way to help. It has been a great pleasure to work with Toby Mundy, Clara Farmer, Bonnie Chiang and the rest of the team at Atlantic Books. And last but not least, as always, my thanks to Jeremy, who has kept the computers working and all the home fires burning (and who would like me to mention his intellectual input too).

LIST OF ILLUSTRATIONS

The author and publishers are grateful to the following for permission to reproduce images: 4, British Library; 5, Ministero per i Beni e le attivà culturali – Foto Soprintendenza PSAD Siena & Grosseto; 9, 10, 15, akg-images, London; 16, Saskia Ltd., © Dr. Ron Wiedenhoeft.

A NOTE ON COINAGE
AND TIME

The Gregorian calendar was introduced by Gregory XIII in 1582 and was in use throughout Catholic Europe and the Netherlands (though not in England). Following this innovation, the New Year began on 1 January, although Florentines, along with some old-fashioned ecclesiastics, still used 25 March, the Annunciation (Ab Incarnatione), as the beginning of their year. Nearly all of the correspondence cited in this book uses the modern version.

Time was calculated from the first sound of the church bell ringing for Angelus, half an hour after sunset, which varied according to the seasons. In Rome, the Angelus would be rung at around five o'clock in the afternoon at the beginning of November, whereas in May it would be after 8 p.m. This would be zero hours – each hour thereafter was counted up to twenty-four. Where necessary an explanatory comment is provided.

Coinages, weights and measures present a labyrinth of complexity, since each state in Italy had its own system. Contemporaries spent a great deal of time trying to calculate the conversion rates. One of the fathers in Cesena on the Adriatic coast, south of Venice and equidistant from Bologna and Florence, tried to explain the situation in his region to the Roman headquarters:

I think I've already told you about these measures once before [he began impatiently]. One staro is half a rubbio; one starolo is half a staro; one quartarolo is half a starolo; five bernarde make a quartarola, or twenty bernarde make one staro. The scudo from here is worth four lire and four bolognini; the lire is two giulii, the bolognino is six quattrini, ten bolognini make a giulio or sixty quattrini ... If you would like me to clarify the accounts let me know. I think they are so clear anyone could follow them...[1]

For anyone who wishes to work out comparative values more precisely, a note at the end of this book contains conversion rates for some of the main states, and some monthly salaries for various jobs and careers in Rome.[2]

Financial references have, however, been kept to a minimum so complex calculations should not interfere with the main narrative of the book.

DRAMATIS PERSONAE

MELCHIORRE ALACCHI (1591–1642)

Born in Sicily. Arithmetic and calligraphy teacher, then novice master. Helped to found the Naples school and tried to establish schools in Venice and Sardinia. Sent on several pilgrimages.

FRANCESCO ALBIZZI (1593–1684)

Assessor of the Inquisition. Bitter enemy of the Piarists, friend of Sozzi and Cherubini. Appointed cardinal 1654.

AMBROGIO AMBROGI (1609–45)

Novice under Alacchi. Taught in Moravia 1631–5. Interested in mathematics and the teachings of Galileo, taught in Florence 1639. Left the order 1641 to become architect general in the papal army.

ANTONIO BARBERINI, CARDINAL SAN'ONOFRIO (1569–1646)

Urban VIII's brother. Capuchin friar.

FRANCESCO BARBERINI (1597–1679)

Most powerful papal nephew. Patron of the arts.

TADDEO BARBERINI (1603–47)

Papal nephew. Appointed commander-in-chief of the papal army 1630 and prefect of Rome 1631.

VINCENZO BERRO (1603–65)

Came to Rome 1625, novitiate under Alacchi. Headmaster in Naples until fell from grace. Last secretary to Calasanz. Author of *Notes on the Foundation*. Roman provincial 1659. Headmaster in Florence 1665.

JOSÉ DE CALASANZ (1557–1648)

Aragonese priest, founder of the Piarist Order, sanctified 1767. Created patron saint of all popular Christian schools in the world 1948.

TOMMASO CAMPANELLA (1568–1639)

Dominican, born in Stilo, Calabria. In prison 1599–1627. Philosopher, author of *City of the Sun, Apologia pro Galileo*, etc. Taught Piarist students at Frascati 1631. Fled from Rome to Paris 1634.

PIETRO CASANI (1572–1647)

The order's first novice master, respected right-hand man of Calasanz, frequently nominated assistant general, provincial or visitor. Author of several memos to the Vatican suggesting administrative reforms for the order. Proposed for beatification by the order 1982.

BENEDETTO CASTELLI (1578–1643)

A Benedictine father, specialist in hydraulics and professor of mathematics at Pisa. Later tutor to the papal nephew, Taddeo Barberini. Friend of Galileo. Not related to the Piarist provincial Francesco Castelli.

FRANCESCO CASTELLI (1583–1657)

Trained as a lawyer. Held many important positions as headmaster in various schools and provincial in northern Italy. Intellectually curious, he was responsible for many of the pedagogical initiatives of the order. Tough on trouble-makers, especially Alacchi. Killed in a knife fight.

GLICERIO CERUTTI, DELLA NATIVITÀ ([?]–1660)

Visitor to Naples, 1645. After Calasanz's death, headmaster of San Pantaleo. In 1659, while assistant general, burnt much of the Piarist archives.

STEFANO CHERUBINI, DEGLI ANGELI (1600–48)

Joined in 1617. Headmaster in Narni where he showed his excellent administrative skills. Transferred to run the Naples school 1627. Of noble origin, with excellent connections at the Vatican, where his father Laerzio and his brother Flavio were important lawyers. After his fall from grace in 1629, promoted ever upwards, becoming universal superior 1643.

POPE CLEMENT VIII, IPPOLITO ALDOBRANDINI (1536–1605)

Pope 1592–1605.

CARLO CONTI (1614–[?])

Studied under Campanella (1631), then sent via Nikolsburg to Florence to join the Galilean group. Poet. Left the order 1646.

GIOVAN FRANCESCO FIAMMELLI
([?]–post 1630)

Renowned Florentine mathematician who worked with Calasanz in the early years (1602–6), then moved to Bologna and later Florence to establish his own version of the Pious Schools. Author of *Il Principe difeso* (1604), a treatise on fortifications and *La riga matematica* (1605), an explanation of how to measure by eye.

GIOVANNI GARZIA CASTIGLIA (1585–1659)

Also known as Father Garzia of Castille. Headmaster of Frascati, 1626–31, assistant general 1632–43, Roman provincial 1640–1, general of the order 1656–9. Quiet and reserved.

NICOLÒ MARIA GAVOTTI (1606–73)

Born in Savona, Gavotti taught in Carcare and Naples where he met Cherubini. By 1639 he had become a bitter enemy of Calasanz. Forced to leave Naples for Genoa 1642. Nominated visitor to the province of Liguria 1643. Expelled from the order 1661.

VINCENZO MARIA GAVOTTI (dates unknown)

Brother of Nicolò. Joined the order in 1625, and followed in his brother's footsteps. Left the order 1648.

POPE GREGORY XV,
ALESSANDRO LUDOVISI (1554–1623)

Pope 1621–3.

SALVATORE GRISE (1610–42)

Joined the order in 1628. Galilean, pupil of Benedetto Castelli. Left the order 1641.

IGNAZIO GUARNOTTO, DI GIESÙ
(dates unknown)

Joined the order 1631. Hastily transferred from Naples to Genoa 1638. Ally of Cherubini. Left the order 1646.

POPE INNOCENT X,
GIOVANBATTISTA PAMPHILIJ (1574–1655)

Pope 1644–55.

GLICERIO LANDRIANI (1588–1618)

Related to San Carlo Borromeo, wealthy, generous and fervent in his religion. Joined the Piarists but died a few years later. The order presented him for beatification 1620.

FAMIANO MICHELINI,
FRANCESCO DI SAN GIUSEPPE (1604–65)

The most important Galilean Piarist, tutor to the Medici princes. Appointed to the chair of mathematics at the University of Pisa 1648. Author of *Trattato della direzione de' Fiumi* (1664).

ANGELO MORELLI, DI SAN DOMENICO
(1608–87)

Studied under Campanella (1631), then sent to Florence to join the Galilean group.

GIOVANNI MUZZARELLI ([?]–1643)

Florentine inquisitor, responsible for supervising Galileo's house arrest. Friend of Sozzi.

POPE PAUL V,
CAMILLO BORGHESE (1550–1621)

Pope 1605–21.

PAOLO OTTONELLI (1566–1626)

Captain in the Modenese army, married to Isabella de Montecuccoli, Countess of Polinago. When he was forty-two his wife died, having given him six children, and he joined the order, donating his worldly property to found the school at Fanano, of which he was then appointed headmaster. Friend of St Filippo Neri, cardinals and several popes.

SILVESTRO PIETRASANTA, SJ
(1590–1647)

Jesuit preacher and author of many works in rhetoric. Apostolic visitor, 1643–6.

GIOVAN ANTONIO RIDOLFI, DELLA NATIVITÀ
(dates unknown)

Joined the order 1632. Secretary to Pietrasanta. Left the order 1647, and became public teacher.

DOMENICO ROSA (dates unknown)

Painter and brother of Salvator. Joined the order 1629. Taught in Florence, 1634–8. Left the order after its suppression.

CLEMENTE SETTIMI, DI SAN CARLO
(1612–[?])

Galilean Piarist in Florence from 1634, secretary to Galileo. Left the order 1646 to become a private teacher.

MARIO SOZZI, DI SAN FRANCESCO
(1608–43)

Tonsured at twelve, in 1639 sent to Florence. Controversial character who frequently reported his colleagues to the Inquisition. Appointed vicar general of the order 1642.

PELLEGRINO TENCANI (1579–1640)

Headmaster in Norcia 1621–7. Administrator of the Nazarene College 1628–31. Headmaster in Moravia, then provincial, 1634–5. Assistant general 1636 until his death.

AGOSTINO UBALDINI (1601–[?])

Somasco, apostolic visitor 1643.

POPE URBAN VIII,
MAFFEO BARBERINI (1568–1644)

Pope 1623–44.

VINCENZO VIVIANI (1622–1703)

Pupil of Clemente Settimi, who became Galileo's secretary and first biographer. Member of the Accademia del Cimento in Florence. Published *Life of Galileo* 1654. Many Galilean publications on mathematics and hydraulics.

'Of great seriousness and commitment'

In 1643, after a failure by the Church hierarchy to deal with child abuse scandals amongst their members, a group of priests took control of the Order of the Clerics Regular of the Pious Schools.

It would be anachronistic to call this group a paedophile ring, but it is nevertheless true that a man accused of abusing the boys in his care was promoted to universal superior of a Catholic teaching order, supported by a small group of like-minded priests, and with the full complicity of the Inquisition and the pope himself. At a time of heightened religious awareness, sex with boys was clearly recognized as a grave sin.

The initial cover-up was ordered by no less a man than the patron saint of all Christian schools.

I arrived in Florence as a naive twenty-one-year-old student. I had been accepted for a doctorate at the European University Institute, a postgraduate hothouse established in the early flowering of enthusiasm for all things European. The supposed *crème de la crème* of the Continent's studenthood, strictly rationed according to nationality – four Danes, one Luxemburgeois, nine Italians – would study, research, live and sleep together, and create a common European home and culture.

My residence was initially a crumbling seventeenth-century palazzo on the northern outskirts of the city, where I faced the daunting prospect of inventing a doctoral thesis. The university itself was situated in a former abbey, the Badia Fiesolana, on the hillside overlooking Florence. Renovated by the Medici in the sixteenth century when it was already several hundreds of years old, it was a warren of buildings with a glorious covered cloister. Although the university overflowed into the church building itself when important dignitaries came to visit, religious services were still held by an order of monks called the Scolopi. The priest responsible for the Badia was a kindly communist, Ernesto Balducci, well-known throughout Italy for his social policy interventions and outspokenness on moral issues.

I had come to study educational reform in the seventeenth century and had no idea where to start. The Scottish professor who interviewed me suggested I talk to Father Balducci, whose religious order was of potentially major importance in the history of education, and whose archives were – he imagined – conveniently situated a short stroll across the cloisters.

Father Balducci was charm itself. He suggested that indeed his order had made very important contributions, not only to education, but to science and culture. Scolopi meant Scuole Pie or Pious Schools and the title could be anglicized into Piarists. As part of the Counter-Reformation, it had never come to England, but in Italy, Spain and central Europe the order's schools were renowned. Like many a foundation originally dedicated to the poor, the schools had eventually evolved into exclusive private academies. Famous former pupils included musicians such as Mozart, writers such as Victor Hugo, astronomers, patriots, kings, emperors, presidents and even a pope.[1] Balducci dwelt proudly on the order's pre-eminence in mathematics and other sciences, and told me that it had been closely linked to Galileo, with several of the fathers carrying out the experiments for the house-bound and blind scientist in his later years.

He did not, however, mention that the order was one of the earliest ever to be closed down by the pope, an unprecedented and dramatic step. And he did not mention why. No history of the order or of the Catholic Church reveals the reason for this suppression. It would take me years to discover it. While the documents themselves were silent, the secondary sources – mostly books written by the fathers themselves – would skim lightly over the order's closure. The online *Catholic Encyclopaedia*, for instance, one of the most commonly cited reference works on the Internet on this subject, skips blithely from 1612 when the Roman school moved to larger premises, to 1748 when the founder was beatified.[2] If the records were not pure hagiography, telling of the persecution of the blameless priests, and especially of the saintly founder, they blandly covered the closure with a remark about 'bureaucratic intrigue', 'administrative problems', 'accusations of incompetence' or 'internal dissent'. Where the Knights Templar, the first order to be suppressed back in the fourteenth century, had been closed down ostensibly for heresy (although more likely because of political intrigue), the Piarists seemed to have vanished quietly for no good reason.[3]

The order's regional archives were not held in the Badia, but in the centre of Florence, in an anonymous building around the corner from the Medici-Riccardi Palace, almost opposite Michelangelo and Brunelleschi's simple church of San Lorenzo. They were under the supervision of Father Osvaldo Tosti, a small round man with a surly manner, dressed in ash-strewn clerical black. He spoke no English, though he was fluent in Latin and Greek. At that time I had basic school Latin, no Greek, and two weeks of Italian classes at the University. Father Tosti had, however, spent several decades teaching deaf children before being assigned to archival work and as a result we managed a crude level of communication.

Stubbing out his cigar, the father led me through a labyrinth of identical corridors to two tiny rooms crammed floor to ceiling with a jumble of books and documents. He was doing his own research in the archive and had no time for general organization, dusting or conservation. He sat me down with the least difficult documents for a non-Italian speaker, lists of school boys dating from 1632 onwards. It was hunched over these rare and initially incomprehensible papers that I learned to read seventeenth-century Italian, occasionally slipping out to the elegant bars of Florence to order a *caffè macchiato*, before returning to the cramped little rooms to plough through the names and marginalia, puzzling over the abbreviations.

Each *elenco* or list was held in a little notebook compiled by the headmaster in November when the school year began. Sitting at his desk, looking out over the new intake, the priest scratched down each child's name, address, age, father's job and the class to which he was assigned. Later he would note the child's profession or further study after he had left school. I could see where, almost four centuries ago, he had dipped his quill in the ink and quickly wiped away the little blot that had fallen. I could see when he was probably irritated and pressed his nib too hard. I could see where he grew tired and fed up with inscribing the details of the ninety-four new boys in the lowest grammar class. Gradually, by force of repetition, I learned to crack the coded abbreviations. *Abb.o* was *abbaco* or arithmetic, *manc.* was *mancarono*, absent. *Ill.o* was *Illustrissimo* – which had flummoxed me for a while since the initial capital 'I' was so curly and florid it was almost a word in itself – and meant that the pupil's father was a member of the nobility. *S.A.S.* had me stumped me for weeks, until finally I cracked it – *Sua Altezza Serenissima*, the Grand Duke of Tuscany, and the most important patron in the region. Father Tosti sat with me, busy with his own writing, grumbling into his notes, never for an instant leaving me alone with his precious documents. I made endless lists, cataloguing the pupils by age, by class, by profession.

For the first three months, while I worked on the notebooks I would frequently look up at the shelves of dusty documents and wonder what they held. It was about the time that I learned not to address Father Tosti with the unforgivably informal 'tu', as I had unwittingly been doing until now, but with the more formal appellation for an elderly man of 'Lei', that he began to relax. My apprenticeship with the pupil lists and my proven enthusiasm encouraged him to allow me greater access. In all the time I worked in the Florence archive, I never met another researcher. I had a brief interview with the provincial, Father Tosti's superior, just to observe the formalities, but otherwise never saw anyone except the archivist himself.

I was allowed more documents. I read memoranda and letters between the fathers who taught in the order's schools, which, I learned, had been established specifically to teach poor boys. I sifted through bundles of crumbling papers wedged into cardboard boxes, crudely bound lists of school rules, correspondence with possible patrons, endless accounts of schools troubled by looming bankruptcy, and letters from the founder himself, disastrously covered a few years earlier in some kind of synthetic resin by a Japanese company promising eternal preservation, and now browning into oblivion with the crispiness of old Sellotape. These letters were treated as religious relics and minimal handling of them was allowed but, as the year passed, I was given more liberty to browse the shelves. Documents unopened since the great plagues of the early seventeenth century were fingered gingerly. The Florentine school had only been open for three months when it was hastily shut down over the summer while some 9,500 citizens, among them perhaps many pupils, died in great agony.[4] Although I reassured myself that the disease had been spread by vermin, not vellum, I nevertheless tried not to breathe too deeply. I washed my hands thoroughly after each session.

The Piarist schools are widely credited in Italian history books and Catholic encyclopedias with being the first free schools for poor children. They were established specifically to teach the vocational skills – good handwriting, accurate arithmetic – that would lead to jobs as clerks and book-keepers. Founded by a Spaniard in Rome in 1600, the schools spread at great speed throughout Catholic Europe, crossing the Alps in 1632, and opening at a rate of one every seven months. It seemed there was a crying need to educate impoverished children. But in 1646 the order was abruptly closed down by the pope.

Although the fathers were allowed to resume several decades later, the Vatican's unprecedented action was not satisfactorily explained in any of the existing books or documents I was being shown. When I asked Father Tosti why, he changed the subject, offered me another interesting stack of pedagogical material or social documentation, muttered something about heretical Galileanism and once – when I really pressed the subject – said something my Italian was not yet adequate to understand. It sounded like 'the worst sin' but it did not make sense at the time.

To discover the reason for the closure I would have to trace the history of the Scolopi, through the adventures of its founder and the vicissitudes of the order's expansion through Europe. I would spend months trawling through the dusty cupboards that served as archives in remote provincial schools and move to Rome to work in the order's main archive. I would also have to buy a longer skirt and a smart jacket to be allowed into the Vatican's Secret Archive, and ultimately into the heart of the Inquisition's own archive.

A year later I waited patiently while the Swiss guard checked my credentials, peering with knitted brow at the letter of reference. Wearing the winter uniform of long blue woollen socks, black ankle boots and a dashing blue cape, the guard pointed me towards a small doorway to the right of the Porta Sant'Anna where a crowd of people were begging for entry to the tightly guarded Vatican City. Most were elderly or sickly and were clutching prescriptions as they queued for permission to enter the first courtyard and access the Vatican pharmacy, where cheap drugs, supposedly not available in Italy, were on sale. A significant proportion of the crowd was made up of over-awed priests trying to enter for appointments with important church officials. I shouldered my way to the front of the queue and had my first triplicate form rubber-stamped. This allowed me access to the second courtyard, where two more guards, standing imposingly on either side of the gate at the arch of Pius XI, had only to lift their halberds slightly to the vertical to let me pass. Yet another guard then read my letter of reference, rubbed his square, clean-shaven chin worriedly and glanced up from the paper to me as though in an effort to decipher my intentions. Swiss guards have defended the papacy since 1506, the date when the militaristic Pope Julius II, fresh from taking the fortress of Mirandola with sword in hand and helmet over his papal tiara, had felt the need for a special bodyguard of mercenaries to preserve him from all enemies, whether within his own family or sent by foreign rulers. Nowadays only one hundred soldiers, trained in the Swiss army and of proven Catholic faith, are selected for the onerous task.

I passed the initial guards' muster and was permitted to cross a quiet courtyard, the Cortile della Belvedere, now a parking lot with an impressive reflecting fountain in the centre, and was shown to a waiting room ready to present my paperwork for the real interview. While awaiting my turn I inspected the merchandise displayed in glass cabinets and available for sale. On my most recent visit I was particularly taken with a selection of souvenir mouse-pads bearing famous signatures, including that of Galileo, selling at €7.50. As I went in for my interview it was hard not to be struck by the irony that this bastion of orthodoxy should be trying to make a profit from the signature of a man it had sentenced for heresy.

Once my credentials had been inspected, my letters of reference checked and filed away, I was cleared to enter the Vatican Secret Archive and the Apostolic Library. I was shown up an unpretentious staircase and into a large room where rows of academics in tweed jackets sat at tables alongside drably dressed nuns, and priests with dandruff dappling their shoulders. However hot it became, men were not permitted to remove their jackets. A large, strict Jesuit sat at the front of the room with Loyola's *Spiritual Exercises* propped ostentatiously open before him, while a subordinate brother sat alongside to do the work and collect the order forms. Every now and then the Jesuit left his book and strolled along the tables, checking that his charges were not desecrating the documents or removing priceless engravings from irreplaceable incunabula. It resembled nothing so much as a school examination hall.

The Vatican Secret Archives has a long and chequered history. In the fifteenth century the library had been the best stocked in Italy, but by the end of the century its role had been strictly delineated. Its function was no longer the pursuit of scholarship, but only the organization of documents and books for the business of the papacy. Gregory XIV decreed in 1591 that no scholar was to consult the documents without his express permission. This tranquil if restrictive existence was interrupted by Napoleon, but after Waterloo the Vatican once more closed its walls around its documents and throughout the nineteenth century allowed only selected outsiders, such as German editors of weighty historical tomes with impeccable Catholic credentials, to enter. Although the restrictions were eased in the twentieth century, as other national European state archives also opened their doors, the uninformative catalogue offered little guidance to the researcher.

The files are all numbered, but there is no index. This effectively requires the researcher to know the number before he or she can call anything up. And of course, if you already know the number from a secondary source, then someone else has already been through the file before you, so it is almost impossible to find anything original or hitherto undiscovered, except by sheer luck, or by spending many many years incarcerated within the archive. Each file that I requested from the sixteenth and seventeenth centuries consisted of a bundle of papers that stood about eight inches high when laid on the desk and comprised letters, documents, printed pamphlets and papal briefs – all hand-written, on crumbling paper, and laced loosely together. Most of it was turgid material dealing with bureaucratic intricacies. My mind often wandered away and I had to revive myself with a cup of excellent tax-free Vatican coffee in the tiny café. But occasionally the cleric who had sorted out the bundle must also have dozed off, or perhaps he failed to grasp the significance of a throw-away comment, and I would discover a tiny snippet of information. Sometimes it took a few lines before my brain would realize that here was something that did not quite fit the traditional interpretation and I would backtrack up the page to re-read the document carefully.

In 1998, years after I had completed my original doctorate, the Inquisition Archive was finally opened and limited access to special researchers was permitted. International pressure had been mounting to make material held by the Vatican of relevance to the Second World War available to historians, and in 1965 the secretary of state appointed three Jesuit fathers to sift and publish the relevant material. Over the next decades eleven annotated volumes appeared, but no independent historian, let alone a member of the public, has been allowed direct access to the primary documents, neither in the Vatican Secret Archive, nor in the Inquisition Archive. In the face of criticism from historians and polemicists, the Vatican set up a commission in 1999, but in October 2001 this initiative collapsed when the cardinal in charge, Walter Kasper, again stated that access would remain restricted to the years preceding 1923 'for technical reasons', and the commission was suspended. Gradually, more material is becoming available, perhaps as the Vatican realizes that what is imagined to be there is probably much worse than what is really there. At any rate, the Inquisition Archive was now open for business and I was curious to know if it held any material that would answer my questions about the suppression of the order.

Requests for admission must be addressed to Cardinal Joseph Ratzinger, prefect of the Congregation for the Doctrine of the Faith (the Inquisition changed its name to this innocuous-sounding Congregation in 1965 in an attempt to distance itself from its unsavoury past reputation). My letter, prepared in triplicate and hand-delivered with all the care of any ambassador to the Holy See presenting his credentials, announced me to be 'of great seriousness and commitment', made much of my limited achievements, and begged the cardinal, frequently referred to as the second most powerful man in Rome after the pope, to look benevolently on my application.

The archives are still held in the same palace, to the left of the colonnades of St Peter, which has housed the Holy Office of the Inquisition since 1566. Along with the Secret Vatican Archive, the Inquisition documentation was shipped to Paris in 1809 to form part of Napoleon's Central Archive of European Culture. Three thousand crates were sent via several convoys, mostly in the dead of winter. Two wagons fell into a torrent near Parma, eight cases splashed into a canal between Turin and Susa. After Napoleon's fall, and again after his second fall a hundred days later, the Vatican tried to organize the return of the documents. The cost of transporting everything back to Rome was exorbitant – the French Ministry of Interior refused to help ('We are not a spending ministry') – and Count Giulio Ginnasi, delegated to deal with it, was forced to make rapid decisions. He had been instructed to concentrate on the decrees of doctrine, all of which were to be returned, and otherwise told to get rid of the material 'as Your Excellency sees most expedient'. The count's solution was to sell the first batch of trials to the Parisian delicatessen shops, to be used for the equivalent of fish and chip wrappings. Hundreds more bulls belonging to the Dataria, another of the papal departments, were sold, but when the saved remnant reached Rome there was a great outcry that 'they had received the useless papers, and not those which were useful and necessary'. The papal commissioner hurried to Paris, reclaimed some of the Dataria's bulls, but sold 2,600 more volumes of inquisitorial trials as waste paper, though he had the sense to 'have them torn up into minute pieces first'. A total of 4,158 volumes – over half the archive – was destroyed. Seventy-seven volumes later turned up in Trinity College, Dublin; some have been found in Brussels. The rest – well-shuffled and partially destroyed – were returned to Rome and, apart from three brief military reoccupations of the palace during the rest of the nineteenth century, have been there ever since. Since 1940, two Jesuit archivists have been working through the documentation, and finally, in 1998, a small room in the palace was opened for researchers.[5] Pietro Redondi, a Galileo expert allowed in by privileged access a few years before the archive was made publicly available, wrote: 'This palace is an obligatory stop for anyone who wants to make an ideal pilgrimage to the key places of the history of ideas in modern Europe. Here petty and important informers, petty and important inquisitors, petty and important defendants have written many paragraphs, known and unknown, in that difficult history.'[6]

Even leaving to one side Europe's history of ideas, entering the palace knowing that this was the prison and headquarters of the Inquisition, and that many a poor soul must have been brought here chained and in terror, is a strange experience. Clutching my letter of reference and stumbling on the cobbles in my unaccustomed heels and skirt, I knew I had nothing to fear. What could Cardinal Ratzinger do to me, apart from bar me access to the archive, which would be irritating, but hardly life-threatening? Even so, I felt a chill as I entered the archway.

The Inquisition Archive reading room is small and holds only some twenty seats, eighteen of which are filled by priests. This is perhaps one of the reasons that access is so restricted for the non-religious. The smell of aftershave is over-powering. There are a couple of inadequate indexes, and researchers can order a fairly generous two documents every hour. Every sixty minutes a bell rings, a cleric shuffles in and silently picks up the ordering slips, and shuffles off. In the distance one can hear the fervent cheering emanating from the concrete Paul VI audience hall where the pope holds his weekly audience for the faithful. The noisy ecstasy of thousands of believers, many in folk costume, offers a striking contrast to the stultifying search for any remaining nuggets of information in the Inquisition that may have survived any censorship and the arbitrary cull of history. A certain sense of longing for the simpler route, the nostalgia for an easy way to enlightenment fills the room and at particularly loud cheers some researchers look wistfully at the small window onto the outside world, then sigh and drop their gaze once more to the documents.

Very slowly the story began to cohere, and the men who had written the letters and documents now stored in the Inquisition Archive, in the Vatican Secret Archive, and above all those in the various hidden libraries of the Piarist Order came to life and told their story.

'A patchwork city of strangers'

The founder of the Piarist Order, José de Calasanz, left Spain in 1592 when Cervantes was struggling with an early draft of his novel, *Don Quixote*. Calasanz was born in 1557 in a small village in Aragon, one of eight children of the local blacksmith. Hagiographers have since tried to prove that he was of noble origins, but the fact remains that his father Pedro Calasanz (or de Calasanz) was one of two blacksmiths of Peralta de la Sal, a village of olive trees and vineyards, renowned locally for its salt pans. In later life Calasanz was knowledgeable about mules and donkeys, presumably an inheritance from helping his father in the smithy. From the age of thirteen, young José wanted to become a priest, and even when his only surviving brother was killed in a scuffle with local bandits, he refused to renounce his vocation, although he remained in the neighbourhood until the death of both parents. An acquaintance later described him as being 'a tall man, of venerable presence, with a chestnut beard and a long pale face'.[1] Later portraits show a stern aquiline face with lean cheeks, and a strong physique that would enable him to climb on to roofs to fix heavy bells (and fall off – apparently pushed by a dark shadow – and survive) and to live to the exceptionally old age of ninety-one.

He pursued the customary path for a priest, studying canon and civil law and theology, and was ordained in 1575. He acquired a few sinecures as parish priest and visitor to various small villages, checking on the implementation of reforms introduced in the wake of the Council of Trent (1545–63), which were designed to help the Church fight back against the Protestant threat. Huguenot France was very close, and Calasanz's duties involved a mixture of travel, supervision and administration. For instance, as master of ceremonies at Urgel cathedral he was responsible for ensuring that in this church – as in all others throughout Spain – prayers and processions were held for the success of the great Armada against England 'to increase the Catholic faith, extirpate and punish the infidels and heretics'.[2]

Then came the major change in his life. For reasons that are unclear in the documents, in 1592 Calasanz suddenly decided to set out for Rome, the Eternal City and seat of the Vatican. Whether he went in search of promotion up the next rung of the ecclesiastical ladder or because an inner voice told him his destiny lay there, or possibly because his superior, Andrés Capilla, Bishop of Urgel, was obliged by the recent church reforms to send a proxy to report to the Vatican every four years, Calasanz set sail for Rome, probably travelling via the Balearics and the south of Sardinia, armed with a sheaf of letters of recommendation from his episcopal patrons.

At the end of the sixteenth century Rome was a city in crisis. Heavy taxation, floods, famines, epidemics and banditry had wreaked considerable damage on the metropolis and its surrounding countryside. A newsletter of October 1593 noted that, 'around Rome the bandits become every day more insolent and more numerous'. Ten years earlier Michel de Montaigne had travelled through Europe and visited the city: 'The approaches to Rome, almost everywhere, have for the most part a barren and uncultivated look, owing either to want of soil or what appears to me more likely, because this city has not many labourers and men who live by the work of their hands ...'[3] Since Montaigne's visit, a campaign against banditry headed by two renowned soldiers from Flanders had resulted in thousands of executions – the outlaws' heads displayed on prominent city landmarks – but so long as the harvests continued to fail, there was little choice for the hungry and desperate but to turn to robbery and intimidation, or to migrate to the city.[4]

As many as two in three of the population were not Roman citizens at all, but immigrants and passers-by. The city was more than just cosmopolitan – though the year Calasanz arrived, 1592, Cardinal Farnese noted that he could hear twenty-seven different languages spoken in the Jesuit refectory in Piazza Altieri – it was the centre of the world, with a great tolerance for foreigners. 'They give least heed to strangeness and differences of nationality,' wrote Montaigne, 'for by its nature it is a patchwork city of strangers; everybody there feels at home.'[5] It was not the capital, but it was, in Calasanz's own words, 'head of all the other cities'.[6]

It was also a tough and occasionally hungry city. Bread supplies only lasted for a few hours and queues formed each morning outside bakeries. The epidemics of the last few years had not affected only the poor. Four popes had been elected, enthroned and died in the past two years, and Calasanz arrived just in time for the tail end of the celebrations to elect Clement VIII, the rituals smoothly honed by too much recent practice. The conclaves and coronations had put further strain on the city's resources, and one of these short-lived popes had even requested that ambassadors should not be sent to Rome to compliment him on his accession in an effort to conserve the limited food supplies. At the best of times it was an unproductive place, and Montaigne could see no industry or farming and very little trade: 'It is a city all court and nobility. Everybody takes his share in the ecclesiastical idleness. There are no trading streets, or less than in a small town; it is nothing but palaces and gardens.'[7] The Venetian ambassador, Paolo Paruta, described court life in 1595 as being 'steeped in luxury and pleasure ... The city and court of Rome are presently at the height of their greatness and prosperity, as anyone living there may see through clamorous examples of such pomp and splendour ... the desire to live in great magnificence, with every convenience, is conjoined to the excessive wealth to do so.'[8] The city depended for its wealth to a great extent on the cardinals, the clerics at the top of the food chain. When new cardinals were created, the number of important people in Rome increased, trade improved, job opportunities opened up, alms flowed once more.[9]

It was en route for this great but troubled city that José de Calasanz, then aged thirty-six, disembarked, and joined the crowds of pilgrims, traders, travellers and refugees hastening along the Via Aurelia. There he would have been stopped and thoroughly searched by customs. Montaigne found that even the smallest articles of his apparel were well rummaged through, and his books were taken from him and kept for several months, but he probably came with much more luggage than Calasanz, who seems to have travelled very lightly.[10]

Calasanz headed for the Piazza di Spagna in the heart of the Spanish quarter in the town centre. Once there, priests from one of the two Spanish churches helped him to find lodgings with a young canon. After a few weeks, however, relations with his new room-mate had become tense after Calasanz, returning home, heard a young lady hushing the canon saying, 'Quiet, here comes the one who can't stand women.' The new arrival, after making his views on the canon's behaviour clear, decided to move out.[11] More congenial rooms were available at the palace of Cardinal Marc'Antonio Colonna in Piazza de' Santi Apostoli, and Calasanz transferred his belongings there. Twenty years earlier Cervantes had enlisted with an earlier Colonna and sailed to defeat the Turks at the battle of Lepanto.

Cardinal Colonna was something of a throwback to the Renaissance princes, with his love of culture and luxury, and perhaps even some illegitimate children.[12] He had twice been passed over for the papacy, but his main interests lay in the organization of the library of the Vatican, though he had some financial dealings in Spain, and his palace was a frequent port of call for travelling clerics. Among his duties, in committee with four other cardinals, lay the preparation of the Index of Prohibited Books, the next edition of which was due out in 1596. After a few months he appointed Calasanz his in-house theologian. The austere Spaniard seems to have coped with the sybaritic ways of the cardinal's palace as he stayed for nearly ten years. Calasanz took his credentials to court, lodged his petitions at the Vatican, and waited for the slow curial wheels to grind in his favour. Meanwhile, as time passed with no result, he slipped out each day to explore the biggest city he had ever seen and found himself drawn to the teeming slums.

The destitute immigrants and impoverished visitors that gravitated towards Rome imposed great strain on the city's infrastructure. Papal decrees and legislation against begging in the streets had little effect and the streets heaved with paupers, vagabonds and street children. Almost immediately after he arrived, Calasanz reported back to his Spanish friends, 'Rome is very expensive and supplies are sparse. It has become the most expensive town in Italy, and the common folk suffer greatly.'[13] Camillo Fanucci, a Roman writer, noted, 'In Rome you see nothing but beggars, and they are so numerous that it is impossible to walk down the street without their thronging around you.'[14] Rome was also a city under construction. New churches were being built, the new Vatican palace was completed in 1596, St Peter's cupola had just been finished after 800 workmen had laboured day and night, before finally in November 1593 – to the sound of the cannons of Castel Sant'Angelo and the church bells of Rome – raising into position the huge metallic sphere, which could hold sixteen people. Fountains and aqueducts had been installed throughout the city, work was underway on the Quirinal, on the Piazza Navona and on many other future landmarks. Classical remains were modified to enlist the support of Rome's imperial heritage as the revived centre of Christianity; a statue of the Apostle Peter was placed atop Trajan's column, obelisks were repositioned in strategically important piazzas such as St Peter's. An ongoing project to improve Rome's streets was underway, and in one year 121 streets were paved. The authorities also decided to have the roads cleaned weekly, and in 1599 untethered pigs were banned from running loose. A bewildered Benedictine abbot, trying to find his way around Rome in 1608 wrote: 'Here I am in Rome, and yet I cannot find the Rome I know: so great are the changes in the buildings, the streets, the piazzas, the fountains, the aqueducts and the obelisks ... that I cannot recognize nor find, so to speak, any trace of that old Rome which I left ten years ago.'[15]

Apart from writing the occasional letter in support of his request for a highly paid benefice back home with few duties, and lobbying various powerful personalities for their assistance to this end, Father Calasanz found himself at a loose end. Four or five sinecures slipped out of his reach and, by 1599, after five years of sight-seeing and diligent networking at court, he had achieved almost nothing. This was not unusual; the poet Alessandro Tassoni, who spent most of his life as secretary to cardinals and prelates, including one of the Colonna, warned would-be supplicants that 'the more affectionate and cordial the promises and proposals of the court of Rome seem to be, the more fraudulent and fallacious they are in fact'.[16] And so it turned out to be. Calasanz's applications for positions were mired in a morass of legal actions against rival claimants and others with more important and active patrons were invariably favoured.

The dissolute Cardinal Colonna died, but Calasanz stayed on in the palace along with a host of hangers-on, including a young painter later known as Caravaggio, who arrived in Rome in the same year as Calasanz and stayed in the Colonna palace until driven away by the menu. He complained it was all salad 'which served as appetizer, entrée and dessert'.[17] Calasanz never complained about the food, and never mentioned his fellow house-guest.

Nevertheless, perhaps the luxury began to offend the priest for he joined several confraternities that offered a combination of personal spirituality and active good deeds. Calasanz helped sufferers of 'putrid fever' in summer 1596, and lent assistance again when the Tiber flooded its banks at Christmas 1598, killing around 1,400 and destroying the bridge (whose fragments still sit in the Tiber) moments after the pope's important nephew Pietro Aldobrandini had crossed. Membership of these confraternities may have brought him into contact with other influential Roman clerics, such as Cardinal Roberto Bellarmino,

Cardinal Cesare Baronio and Filippo Neri, all important figures working to revive religious spirituality in Rome at the time. For instance, Calasanz devoted much of his time to the Confraternity of the Twelve Apostles, whose main aims were the worship of the Holy Sacrament and helping poor families with alms and concrete assistance. The organization prided itself on 'knowing where most neede [sic] is,'[18] and around 1596 Calasanz became a visitor for the confraternity. His duties included at least two weekly visits to the poor and sick within his allocated district of Rome, then meetings to report back on progress to the other members, as well as input on fundraising initiatives. The contrast between his rooms at the Palazzo Colonna and the impoverished surroundings of those he visited in the course of his duties must have been striking.

Another organization Calasanz joined around 1600, and which was to provide a deciding impetus for his future, was the Confraternity of the Christian Doctrine. This group aimed to teach catechism to children (boys and girls) on Sundays and holidays, usually in rooms adjoining the local church. Visitors to Rome were impressed that educated and respected gentlemen, including various bishops and cardinals, should be 'content to condescend to the capacities of infantes and babes' by spending their time teaching the rudiments of the Christian religion, and noted that though it might be tedious reading about such things, it was far less tedious than actually spending the time doing it.[19] In April and May 1597 Calasanz visited Trastevere, one of Rome's poorest quarters just over the Ponte Sisto, on behalf of the Confraternity of the Twelve Apostles, to get an updated list of sick and poor, and perhaps there he spotted a little school at the back of the church of Santa Dorotea.

Several churches provided these little parish schools but there was usually a small fee to pay. In the whole of the rest of Rome, with its population of just over 100,000,[20] there were only fourteen publicly provided teachers, one for each ward of the city. The rich could afford private education, and even orphans and those living in institutions had facilities provided. Religious orders such as the Jesuits offered only cat-echism classes, or secondary education for future clergymen and noble-men. But ordinary poor children had few opportunities. Even the highly overstretched fourteen free teachers were so poorly paid that they usually charged pupils a weekly fee, thereby automatically exclud-ing the very poorest. The families Calasanz visited in his charity work often had children who could not attend these local schools or the parish schools where even a nominal cost was out of their reach, and who had nothing to do but make mischief.[21]

Calasanz convinced the parish priest at Santa Dorotea, Antonio Brandini, to accept poor children for nothing, promising to cover the costs himself.[22] Reading, writing, arithmetic, grammar, Christian doc-trine and good manners were taught and pupils had only to provide a certificate of poverty from their parish priest to qualify for admission. It was a far cry from his earlier study of abstruse law and theology. Catholic sources date the first ever free public elementary school to this moment in autumn 1597.[23] Of course, such schools had existed before, but Calasanz's organization would grow bigger and spread further than others, thus ensuring him the title of 'founder of Europe's first free pub-lic, popular schools'.[24] As recently as 1948 the pope made Calasanz the patron saint of all Christian schools.

Soon Calasanz was teaching in the Trastevere school for a few hours a week. The flood of Christmas 1598, which covered great swathes of the city in a deep layer of stinking mud, swept away twelve of the Tiber's twenty mills and 550 cows on nearby meadows. Trastevere was badly affected, lying as it did so close to the river, and Calasanz real-ized that the meagre income he was still receiving from Spain was insufficient to guarantee the long-term survival of the little school. When the parish priest Brandini died in February 1600, two years after Calasanz had begun to teach there, the school was faced with closure. Meanwhile, Calasanz's hopes of ecclesiastical promotion had evaporat-ed. He had been awarded a useful, if small, benefice, but two other cler-ics had simultaneously been given the same post, and the matter proceeded to court. He assumed full responsibility for the school, but still lived at the Palazzo Colonna and trekked over the river Tiber each day.

After a lengthy and expensive court case Calasanz decided to renounce his claims to the disputed benefice. Instead he threw all his energies into his new job, which was fast becoming his life. The work was unremitting. After praying and preaching all day, Calasanz spent the evening training his fellow teachers and preparing the next day's lessons, before cleaning and tidying all the classrooms. 'Months passed,' wrote a colleague later, 'during which he did not undress or lie down in a bed to sleep, but worn out and overcome by fatigue and sleep, at most he would lay down his head on a table, and so for a brief space of time clear his head of that extreme fatigue and necessity to sleep.'[25]

After a time he saw the chance to rent rooms in the Campo de' Fiori on the other side of the river and establish a new base for his school. Campo de' Fiori was even then a major shopping area, selling everything from grain to crossbows, but it was also the place where the worst offenders against Catholic orthodoxy were punished. When the school opened its doors in March 1600, the ashes of Giordano Bruno, whose philosophical concepts were reviled as incoherent pantheism and who was burned in the centre of the square for heresy, were barely cold. Bruno, one of the most famous victims of the Inquisition, had been brought from the Tor di Nona prison, where, for six years, seven priests from different religious orders had tried in vain but 'with great affection and much doctrine' to lead him away from his 'thousands of errors and vanities'. These errors included support of Copernicus's heliocentric theory, denial of the Trinity, of transubstantiation and of the divine origin of Christianity, as well as his denunciation of Christianity as a degenerate form of religion. In the centre of the piazza, Bruno was stripped naked and tied to a stake, but continued to declaim against his accusers and to turn away from the crucifix held out to him. The spectacle over, the ashes swept away, Calasanz's school opened a few yards away only two weeks later. Within a few days 500 pupils were attending what was becoming known as the Pious School. Very few of Calasanz's letters have survived from this period and he makes no mention of this awkward event, although he and Bruno would have had many acquaintances in common. Gaspar Schoppe, for instance, whose special quick grammar system Calasanz would later commission for use in his schools, was present throughout most of Bruno's interrogations, and watched the burning.[26]

Calasanz had also finally moved out of the Colonna palace, where, since the death of his cardinal, he had been feeling increasingly surplus to requirements. More moves followed, nearer to Piazza Navona, considered the true centre of Rome, an area specializing in mattress-making, and paper and glove shops. Traders sold old books, artists exhibited their pictures, news sheets were on sale. In the adjacent Piazza Madama there was a flower and plant market on Wednesdays; on Thursdays and Fridays there was an animal market nearby where cattle, sheep and poultry were sold. The new school building provided 'greenery and a courtyard – airy and with good rooms' ,which meant Calasanz could take on more staff and pupils, and by 1602 there were 700 boys in the Rome school cared for by eighteen teachers, seven priests and eleven laymen.[27]

The school's fame began to spread. It was surprisingly well run, as a colleague later reminisced: 'He organized things so well, especially the class distribution, that where many thought there must be confusion because of the huge multitude of children, seeing everything so well run they were very impressed.'[28] The fourteen existing Rome teachers started to see the new school as a serious competitor and lodged an official complaint, as did the rector of the University of Rome, the Sapienza. Pope Clement was reported as saying, 'We are very happy that you have started the Pious Schools. We had planned to do something similar – but then we got distracted by the war in Hungary … we are very pleased, very pleased indeed. We would like to come and see.'[29] He was of course too busy but instead asked two famous cardinals, Silvio Antoniano and Cesare Baronio to drop by and lend their support, so firmly quashing any budding opposition from the local teachers.

Soon the Pope and the municipal authority both awarded the school small grants and though it was far from luxurious, the teachers all moved in together on site. As the numbers of pupils increased to nearly 1,200 – perhaps 20 per cent of Rome's entire population of boys – the teachers' lodgings became more and more restricted. According to Father Alessandro Bernardini, soon to become involved in the school:

All the best rooms were used for classes, and very few remained for the inhabitants. So the teachers had to live in the upper rooms of the house, and used wooden partitions to make separate cells, in which they lived in great discomfort, especially in summer time, with many people in a small area.[30]

The Pious Schools acquired the services of their own cardinal protector, first Ludovico Torres, later Benedetto Giustiniani, to represent their interests at the papal court – 'so necessary in Rome', as Calasanz pointed out.[31] Benedetto Giustiniani was an extremely wealthy cardinal and, with his brother, Vincenzo, lived in a sumptuous palace, which they filled with the best art of the day. Many of Caravaggio's most famous works adorned their walls. An English visitor, Robert Toste, wrote back to the Bishop of London in 1589 that he found the cardinal 'somewhat hard favoured and black, his beard being of the same colour. Of sight he is spur blind and is low in stature, having a kind of odd fashion that when he talks with any he turns his head and looks as it were over his shoulder.'[32] Calasanz was lucky to acquire the interest of a cardinal so well-placed and so well-intentioned and Giustiniani used his influence to good effect. The number of pupils continued to swell, and Calasanz managed to purchase a proper building, by the church of San Pantaleo, from Countess Vittoria Cenci.

The Cenci family's notorious matrimonial affairs were already a *cause célèbre* throughout Rome.[33] In September 1598 Count Francesco Cenci, a tough brute of a man, was found dead beneath the balcony of his castle of La Rocca in the Abruzzo, 100 kilometres from Rome. Bloody sheets, however, revealed that he had been murdered in his bed before being thrown over the edge, and members of his family were soon arrested. Though the count had apparently been sexually abusing his twenty-one-year old daughter Beatrice in front of his wife, Lucrezia, and had beaten both women and kept them imprisoned, this was not considered reason enough for mercy. On 10 September 1599 the beautiful young woman was beheaded along with her stepmother, just outside Castel Sant'Angelo on the banks of the Tiber. Her brother Giacomo was executed by having his flesh picked off with heated pincers and his head smashed with a hammer, before being quartered, while another brother, aged only fifteen, was forced to watch the destruction of his family before being taken to the galleys. Local public opinion (and later Shelley, Stendhal, Artaud and others) would tell of Beatrice's beauty and dignity at her execution, and the justifiable defence of her virtue against the incestuous intentions of her evil father. However, when a few years later her relative Vittoria Cenci decided to take a more conventional route and sort out her separation from her husband in court, she was offered the palace adjacent to the church of San Pantaleo as partial recompense for the dowry of 14,000 scudi, which her wastrel husband no longer possessed in ready cash. She accepted, and sold the building on to the Pious Schools in September 1612. With its attached church dedicated to the patron saint of doctors on the site where a church had stood since 1216, the Pious Schools established their headquarters.

By now the fathers were 'esteemed by the Holy Pope, by various cardinals and gentlemen of the court, and desired by the main cities both inside and outside Italy'.[34] When he met Calasanz in town accompanying a group of children, Pope Paul V even stopped his litter and chatted to him at great length. As a token of his esteem, he even conceded them a water supply for the interior playground courtyard – free and for ever (until 1979 when the local council imposed a charge) – from the old acqueduct, which ran to the Trevi Fountain.[35] In 1617 the group of fathers lobbied for and was awarded the status of a separate congregation, an entity with legal and religious rights in the papal city.[36]

With the election of Pope Gregory XV in February 1621, the congregation saw a radical change of fortune. Aged sixty-seven and in poor health, the new pope already knew of the Pious Schools from Bologna, where one of Calasanz's early collaborators had opened a similar institute. Indeed, he had stayed at the school in Narni for a few days when passing through the town.[37] Pope Gregory's private physician was Bernardino Castellani, a close friend of Father Calasanz and a great believer in the work of the order. He had recently insisted that Calasanz open a school in his own home town of Carcare in northern Italy. Even more to the point, Calasanz and the pope also shared the same barber, Messer Agostino. Father Calasanz realized he was now excellently placed to make progress. 'Messer Agostino will be close to him every day and can pass him our letters, and give him my best regards!' he crowed.[38] With barber and doctor whispering in his ear, Pope Gregory probably had no chance.

One of Gregory's most important innovations was the Congregation for the Propagation of the Faith, aimed at fostering missionary activities in non-Catholic areas, and it is quite likely that he saw the Pious Schools as a useful tool for conversion in Protestant Europe. Within nine months the congregation had been elevated to the rank of a full religious order – the Order of Clerics Regular of the Pious Schools of the Poor of the Mother of God. Scolopi or Piarists for short. Clerics regular were a relatively new creation, comprising communities of priests who were meant to serve in the outside world, rather than in old-fashioned monasteries where their time would usually be taken up only with choir service and prayer.[39] Father Calasanz, self-appointed father general, promised that the new organization would prove to be 'very worthy, very noble, very deserving, very handy, very useful, very necessary, very natural, very reasonable, very pleasant, and very glorious'. He promised that his members would 'live like angels in the world; in their senses without sensuality; in their flesh, with no carnal affection; from free men they will become subject; from sociable beings, solitary; they would keep themselves spiritual and heavenly'.[40] The movement had begun. Within a few years there would be Piarist schools throughout Italy and further afield in central Europe. Local dignitaries – bishops, princes, doctors, cardinals, counsellors – requested foundations and provided suitable buildings. Before long there were more than forty schools.

CHAPTER TWO

'Little beasts or untrained animals'

'It is so difficult dealing with so many children who are virtually little beasts or untrained animals,'[1] moaned Father Francesco Castelli, a close colleague of the founder. Pity the teacher of the first class, theoretically restricted to teaching a mere fifty boys, but often confronted by more than twice as many. In 1614, for instance, 104 boys started the autumn term in the reading class in Rome. The smell of squashed and unwashed schoolboys must have been overpowering.[2]

Ten days before term began in early November, the day after All Saints' Day, the fathers put up posters around town to invite new pupils to join the school. When they arrived, the boys were divided by ability, not age, into classes for reading, writing, arithmetic and various levels of Latin grammar. They were supposed to be aged between seven and fifteen, but some were too young to learn and Calasanz complained that 'many mothers are sending tiny children to school with an older sibling in order to be rid of the bother of having them at home; it follows that the little one does not learn, since he is not capable, nor does he let the big one concentrate'.[3]

Classes were held for two and a half hours in the morning and three in the afternoon. On the first day the children learned to make the sign of the cross. Then came the alphabet. Big paper letters were stuck to the walls and the teacher walked around, pointing to each one with a stick while the children called out the names. The bright ones were immediately obvious. 'You can see pretty quickly who has a good brain,' commented Father Calasanz.[4] After short syllables came short words. The teacher often had a lay brother to help him with this huge class, and these brothers were encouraged to practise their reading each night themselves so as to keep one step ahead of their pupils.[5]

Next came writing. Children nowadays learn to read and write at more or less the same time, but several sixteenth- and early seventeenth-century educationalists found writing an unnecessary luxury, particularly if pupils were expected to provide their own paper, ink and pens. To make matters worse, schools that taught writing faced the hostility of the calligraphers, writing masters and the guild of scriveners, who all feared an infringement on their lucrative market. Parents, however, considered this class one of the main attractions of a Piarist education and, in a period of increased demand for secretarial skills and with all materials provided for free, pupils flocked to learn.

The first writing teacher to work with Calasanz was Ventura Sarafellini, a calligrapher of such renown that in 1605 he created the inscription, 'Tu es Petrus' around the inner ring of the cupola of St Peter's, for which he was paid the handsome sum of 20 scudi (the monthly salary for a builder was 4 scudi). For a Roman calligrapher there could be no higher accolade.[6] Nevertheless he taught writing in the Pious Schools from 1604 for at least forty years. Calasanz considered it very important that the order be well provided with calligraphers and also told his teachers to practise themselves for half an hour after lunch each day and a longer period in the evening. Those who wrote to him were apt to have their handwriting shredded by return. Brother Andrea in Frascati, for instance, was criticized for the uneven size of his letters, although he earned faint praise for the satisfying straightness of his lines. Brother Giacomo's writing was much too big and he tried to do everything with the pen held at exactly the same angle.[7] Brother Ambrogi, who had been sent to teach in the German province in 1632, was completely flummoxed by the German style of writing, since the

Piarists usually taught chancellery script, and confessed with commendable honesty 'many of my pupils could write better before they came than they can now'.[8]

The reading and writing classes were so crowded that there was no room for desks, so each pupil had a board to balance on his knees on which to write. Paper, pens and ink were supplied by the Piarists. Only older pupils learned how to trim their own pens, since the thought of hundreds of small children flailing pen-knives in cramped classrooms was enough to make even a saint quail.

Modern schoolchildren (or rather their parents) take for granted that their teachers will teach them in the vernacular, that they will be taught to write and do sums, and that they will be equipped with useful skills, which should help them to get a job. All these elements were innovations when introduced consistently by the Pious Schools at a time when most schools were purely geared to a Latin education, a distinction that lingers in the terminology of 'grammar' schools.[9]

Once they could write, the boys learned arithmetic, or 'abbaco'. By the thirteenth century 'abbaco' had become synonymous with mercantile arithmetic and had little to do with higher levels of mathematics and philosophy (although some of the Piarist abbaco teachers were interested in these fields in their own right). Merchant centres such as Florence, Genoa and Venice were well supplied with abbaco teachers (for a fee), but the Jesuits would not touch it, even though new technology was making it an increasingly attractive subject, with the development of ballistics, hydraulics, watch-making and cartography. Again one of Calasanz's earliest collaborators was an expert in his field, 'a Florentine mathematician renowned throughout Rome',[10] author of a treatise on princely fortifications, and one on measuring without using instruments, Giovan Francesco Fiammelli, who would later return to his home town and facilitate the foundation of the Florentine school.

Piarist historians are justifiably proud of the introduction of the arithmetic class, a vocational initiative that helped pupils to get jobs or to run their own businesses, since 'the majority of pupils can now do their own accounts, without having to get someone in'. The class was always very popular.[11] Some of the examples of calculations provided by Father Alessandro Fantuzzi in his *Arimmetica pratica* are very challenging, at least for today's calculator-dependent children: 'Two people want to barter wax for pepper. The one with the wax values it at 133½ lire per hundred. The one with the pepper values it at at 1⅔ per pound. If they exchange 864½ pounds of wax, how many pounds of pepper does this involve?'[12] Pupils also learned how to calculate interest on loans, exchange rate mechanisms, and some geometry to measure land and volume. Calasanz considered abbaco along with writing to be the most important, because from there pupils were ready for the world. 'This science and its practice are very useful for the poor,' he wrote.[13] Armed with this knowledge they could find jobs 'in banks, in warehouses, in counting houses and in other trades'.[14]

And if they continued to the grammar classes other paths would open up for them. 'The poor need a bit of grammar, as lawyers, copyists, surgeons, shopkeepers and similar,' wrote Father Pietro Casani in 1645, when the order was fighting for its survival.[15] Grammar was necessary for a boy, so he could learn a decent and correct way of speaking and writing. Even if he remained in the lower professions, he could at least discuss his business clearly or write a respectable letter. Some could even become parish priests and play an important part in the Counter-Reformation. The communities who invited the Piarists in to run schools for them insisted they offer Latin grammar. Education without grammar was no education.

Calasanz was always on the hunt for a new method of teaching Latin and the Piarists experimented with various systems. Gaspar Schoppe, the erstwhile Protestant who had converted to Catholicism in 1597 and had sat in on Giordano Bruno's interrogations, promised a rate of 1,200 sentences in four months with his new system, but he offended the Jesuits with his open contempt for their more traditional methods. As a result of this diplomatic *faux pas*, the Inquisition was encouraged to hold up publication of his book. In the grammar classes, Cicero's *Epistulae ad familiares* were usually the first 'real' Latin texts, followed by Virgil's *Aeneid*. After three grammar classes, the most advanced proceeded to the humanities, mostly Horace and more epistolary honing, and then rhetoric, where they studied primarily Seneca and Martial.

However, there was opposition. Some thought the poor would get above their station if they acquired too much learning. Father Casani, writing to Cardinal Ginetti in 1644, backtracked hastily:

We don't just let anyone who asks, indiscriminately, into the grammar classes. First we examine them, and consider their temperament, intelligence and character quality, and the needs of the parents. And if perhaps we do make a mistake, we quickly recognize it, and remedy it, removing them from the grammar class, and sending them back to writing and arithmetic, and often they themselves want to go back, feeling themselves unsuited to do grammar, so no one need fear that the trades will be damaged by the Pious Schools.[16]

Writing in 1584, several years before Calasanz arrived in Rome, Silvio Antoniano, the great Catholic reformer and educationalist who visited the school in its early days, author of *Dell'educazione cristiana*, held that 'not all can or should study'. While the job of the noble classes was to maintain the public peace, uphold justice and provide the poor with money and stability, the poor could 'carry on their trades and exert the strength of their bodies to earn their living'. They were thus better placed to enjoy 'the best things of nature – sunlight, wholesome fresh air, life, health and vigour' and for these privileges 'the poor must be grateful and mindful, rendering love, observance and loyalty to [the rich], and showing great care and diligence in the cultivation of their fields'.[17] His views represented the social orthodoxy and desire for stability that perhaps epitomized the Catholic Counter-Reformation, in which the Piarists played a part. However, as the schools became better known and spread further, opposition to their mission began to grow.

By the late 1620s there were enough mutterings of discontent to spur Tommaso Campanella to put pen to paper in defence of the Pious Schools. Campanella was a controversial character whose fame today is based on his utopian work *The City of the Sun*, which offered a revolutionary plan for transforming society along egalitarian lines. A heretical Dominican friar who had been accused of fomenting rebellion in Calabria and had spent twenty-seven years in prison in Naples, including several in the underground ditch of Castel Sant'Elmo, Campanella's *Apologia* in support of the Piarist schools was greeted with muffled enthusiasm by Calasanz, who buried it away at the back of his cupboard where it remained undiscovered for some three hundred years. Written in 1616, the year of Shakespeare's death, it was only finally published in 1932, though it probably circulated in Rome in various manuscript copies. For Campanella, the Piarists were a useful implement to help introduce his utopia. Tradesmen and artisans would become more skilled and successful if they were more knowledgeable, noblemen 'with dull minds made blunter through neglect' would have to work harder to compete, there would be mobility between the classes, and everyone would be happier and more religious.[18] Calasanz must have been repelled by the political implications of this meritocratic message, and although he let Campanella, released five years earlier from the Inquisition jail, teach some young novices in Frascati in summer 1631, the following year – when he had perhaps read the *Apologia* properly – he still let him spend a summer break at the school, but kept him away from the students. A few years later, after irresponsibly foretelling the pope's death using astrological calculations (in direct contravention of a bull of 1631 outlawing such predictions), Campanella was forced into a speedy midnight flit to France, probably to Calasanz's great relief. The friendship, and the *Apologia,* were quietly forgotten.

For Calasanz, education was to be just enough to let the poor earn their living honestly and provide an opportunity to instil in them 'the fear of God'. He was keen for schooling to be obligatory – there are several mentions of the local police being used to round up truants, and any child who was hanging around at leisure was to be frightened into attending school, where they would soon learn 'the fear of God'. Father Berro recounted the tale of one young pupil who was considered very well taught. The Bishop of Lucca was visiting a garden, and the gardener, wishing to present him with a gift, went to pick some fruit.

When he climbed the tree, the branch suddenly broke, and the poor man fell down and was left hanging helplessly by one foot from another branch, head downwards, and in grave danger of serious injury. His little boy of eight or nine years old was at the foot of the tree and seeing he was unable to help his father in this dangerous situation, he started to say in a loud voice: 'Father repeat after me with all your heart: "I repent, oh Lord Jesus Christ of all my sins ..."' and continued thus with such emotion that the bishop and his court heard him and out of curiosity came to investigate. Seeing the poor gardener in such peril they liberated him, and were amazed at the piety and courage of the boy, and asked where he had learned such prayers. He answered: 'I go to the Pious Schools. My teacher told me to say this prayer when I find myself in some danger.' The prelate was very impressed.

Father Berro does not recount what the gardener thought.[19]

Religious instruction was an important, though not overwhelming, part of the curriculum. Before school there was an hour's Mass, with another fifteen minutes at the end of the day. Sunday mornings and holidays were taken up with religious education with a public sermon in the morning and Christian doctrine in the afternoon. Throughout the day continuous prayers were held in the adjoining church and small groups of ten pupils at a time came in to pray there. The practical instruction offered in the schools tempted the boys in, while the religious instruction instilled in them the fear of God and saved their souls. And if the economy was bettered and their standards of living improved, why then they would have more leisure to devote themselves to piety. Throughout, pupils were 'to keep themselves low and humble, so that they remember they are poor'.[20]

Most pupils would not have needed reminding. In the earliest years they came armed with certificates of poverty from their parish priests. This was soon dropped and all children were accepted. Apart from in a couple of noble academies such as the Nazarene College, which

Calasanz had been persuaded to run almost against his better judgement, all ranks were taught together, and the vast majority of children were from the poorer sections of society. The lists of pupils compiled at the beginning of the term revealed a wide selection of professions among the pupils' fathers, including cooks, grocers, woodcutters, stablemen, masons, oil-sellers, gardeners and silk-weavers, with a sprinkling of wealthier pupils, and a substantial proportion with no information provided, whose fathers perhaps did not work or who were no longer in contact with the family.

Calasanz was adamant that no payment was to be accepted. Vincenzo Berro, then a novice, worked as door-keeper or porter for the school for a while and was given strict instructions not to accept anything which might be construed as a payment.

Believe me [he later recounted] I'm really not exaggerating when I say that I had no small difficulty in convincing people gently that we could not accept what they brought, and several times they left quite upset. There was one poor mother in particular who brought us a bowl of ravioli at carnival time, and I thanked her and begged her to eat it with her own son because we didn't want her to go to this expenditure, and she really didn't need to bother, but she pleaded with me not only in words, but with floods of tears, and since Signor Gabrielle Squarciafichi [a local gentleman] was going out at that moment, he told me to accept it to make the woman happy, and that he would explain the matter to Our Reverend Father [Calasanz].

On another occasion a boy, Nicolò, brought in a lamb, all skinned and ready. Berro sent him away, but his father, who worked as a groom, soon returned and insisted on seeing Calasanz.

Our Reverend Father didn't want the little animal, so he thanked him for his kind gesture, saying, 'You are a poor man burdened with a family, and I don't want you to bear this expense. You needn't worry about Nicolò because he is well regarded, and if the Good Lord helps him to learn, we don't need such payments.' The groom insisted with great energy that we accept, but finally he was convinced by the courage and reasoning of Our Reverend Father, and went off, much impressed. And Our Father turned to me and the others and said, 'These poor people, they think that if they don't give us presents we won't take care of their children, and we have to disabuse them of this perception, and not cause them any expenditure, because they are poor, and they suffer much more than we do.'[21]

The pupils were instructed to kiss their parents' hands when they arrived home from school and obey them, but it is clear from other comments that the Piarists had little confidence in the parents' own abilities to educate and discipline their children. Indeed, they rather hoped that the children's participation in school life would draw the parents back or closer into the Church's fold.[22]

However, the children's behaviour often left something to be desired. Tommaso Garzoni, an insatiable collector of information on all aspects of sixteenth-century life, gave a vivid description of school naughtinesses, which included secretly eating chestnuts, using crickets, butterflies and frogs to disrupt the class, and drawing caricatures in grammar books. Judging by what the school rules forbade, the Piarist pupils had a tendency to bring in unauthorized reading material, to draw graffiti on 'benches, desks, walls, doors, windows and many other objects', to play cards and dice, and to bring money, food and even wine into class. They also came in with weapons, mainly daggers and swords, and even threatened to do some damage with metal-tipped pens. On the way home, if not accompanied, they stopped to watch street performers, to pop into taverns or to go swimming.[23]

To counter this tendency the fathers introduced a door-to-door school escort for the pupils.

In the same month of June [1615], the Pious Schools started an exercise, which though it was very tiring, was nevertheless a great charity and very useful for the pupils. Usually when they came out of school in the mornings and in the afternoons they did many things in the streets, not just the usual boyish stuff, but others of a bad nature. Moreover, vicious men, of which the world is full, were bold enough to tempt them and take them away to do hideous and unspeakable things. In order to remedy this, the fathers having received many complaints from various parties, it was resolved after much consideration, that the children be accompanied to their houses by our members morning and evening …'[24]

This is one of the earliest acknowledgements in the documents that undesirable things could happen between men and boys if an opportunity presented itself. Calasanz preferred not to emphasize the moral danger, warning his staff rather to watch out for traffic, 'for the dangers of carriages, wagons, horses, and others, of which there are many in the city'. An edict issued by the cardinal chamberlain a few years later forbade 'infants and children from driving carts, carriages and barouches through the streets of Rome', so the dangers from inexperienced drivers as well as sheer pressure of traffic must have been very real.[25]

All the pupils of the school were divided up into six squads, each one led by two of our members who accompanied them, ensuring that the boys walked along with modesty … Each squad was very large, some had over 200 boys, and they were so led that they went very modestly and decorously, with rosary in hand, so that seeing these processions going through Rome, the people were very pleased, and nobility, prelates and cardinals praised the work, considering it one of the main works in Rome.

The public relations value of accompanying the children was invaluable and many tourists to Rome commented on seeing obedient squads of little boys filing to and from school.[26]

Teachers were instructed to defend their charges from attack. 'If any pupils are insulted or attacked in the streets, the teacher should modestly and religiously defend them. However he should not quarrel or swear, or use uncouth language, let alone come to blows, unless it be with some boy who can be stopped with threats.'[27] In 1620 things got so bad in Frascati that the local council was forced to issue an order forbidding people from throwing stones, mud or anything else – even as a joke – at the Piarist pupils. Unsurprisingly, the teachers hated taking the boys. It wasted their time, tired them out and made them look ridiculous. In Florence, one particularly hostile headmaster claimed that there was such an inherent aversion in the Florentine character to going around in big groups that although he had tried, it had proved simply impossible to introduce, with pupils either sneaking out from class or sprinting away as soon as they left the school building.[28] In Florence, accompanying was abandoned.

Disobedience could be dealt with in several different ways. If the example of the good behaviour of the teachers and frequent prayer were not enough, the last resort lay in the application of corporal punishment, although 'confession always has a far greater effect'.[29] Each teacher was secretly permitted to give up to two smacks on the palm of the hand with a small stick, or five blows with a strap on the backside. Anything more serious had to be referred to the corrector, a father delegated to deal with discipline. All punishments were rigidly controlled in written instructions sent to each school. Pupils were never to be punished on their bare flesh, but through linen shorts – the school kept some handy just in case. 'Be careful not to cut the face, or the body with your hands, be still more cautious if you use a rod or stick or whatever other instrument, so that on the legs or wherever else no bruises should be left. Do not pull their hair so that it comes out by the roots, nor make blood come out of their noses, or their ears, which often happens easily if you hurt those parts.' Teachers were strictly forbidden to invent their own methods of punishment. If all this failed, the child was to be expelled. But sometimes the teachers must have got carried away. For instance, in June 1624, Calasanz wrote to the headmaster at Frascati about a pupil who had died shortly after being punished, exculpating him from blame on this occasion, but nevertheless warning him to be careful in future:

As for the disobedient pupil, you did well to punish him, but the punishment must always be carried out with piety and prudence so that the pupils them-selves know that they really deserve much worse. Trombetta's son can't have died from his beating because a few days later he was better, and already going out. However he then fell sick again through over-eating at a meal in his house, but by then the doctor had stopped visiting him since he was already safe and healthy again.

Judging by this account, the beating was severe enough to warrant sev-eral visits from the doctor and a stay indoors, and a week later the child died, though apparently (and unconvincingly) from an unrelated bout of over-indulgence.[30]

A few years later Calasanz again had occasion to write to the new headmaster at Frascati, but this time about the opposite problem, a lack of discipline. He had received a couple of letters from citizens reporting that Father Matteo's pupils were leaving school an hour earlier than the others, claiming that they were going to confession, but instead 'they go and play at throwing stones, causing scandal to the townsfolk, since it seems that Father Matteo often falls asleep in class'. Anyhow, he demanded, why were the boys not saying their confessions on the premises, or in the adjoining Piarist church? But another teacher, Brother Domenico, was making things even worse by going with some of the older boys to the vineyards to eat fruit, 'something utterly unworthy of us since laymen always notice imperfections in eating or talking'. The headmaster, Father Giovanni Garzia Castiglia, was clearly not keeping a firm hand on the reins of government. 'I will send you an order, signed by me,' commanded Father Calasanz, 'where I will prohibit anyone from eating outside the house, or even carrying fruit if it has been given to him unless all can enjoy it later.'[31]

Teaching was a position that offered many occasions for irritation and frustration and few opportunities for glory, even as headmaster or father provincial in charge of a whole region. 'It is true that at first sight the work might seem to some to be mean and insignificant,' wrote Father Alessandro Bernardini in 1614 when he was trying to encourage his group of priests to join with the Pious Schools in a short-lived union.[32] A few centuries earlier Petrarch had written:

Let those men teach boys who do nothing greater, whose qualities are a plodding diligence, a rather dull mind, a muddled intellect, ordinary talent, cold-bloodedness, a body tolerant of labour, and a mind contemptuous of glory, desirous of petty gains, and indifferent to boredom ... Neither grammar nor any of the seven liberal arts deserves the entire lifetime of a noble talent ... I ... pity those who wasted nearly all their lives in public school.'[33]

Even Calasanz had to admit that, 'the exercise of teaching children seems to our enemy world so lowly and vile', though he added, 'but with practice one can find the value in it'.[34] The overall perception of life as a teacher, however, was negative, although the occasional commentator was impressed with the sacrifices made by those who dedicated their lives to children.

For most members the value of the mission, educating the poor and opening their eyes to the 'fear of God', must have been sufficient. But if it offered little by way of recognition, working with children offered ample opportunity for those whose motives were not so pure.

'If I had 10,000 priests now'

The majority of the Piarist teachers were devout and religious. They had joined José de Calasanz to do good and to instruct the young. Some also simply wanted to belong to a religious community, where their practical needs would be taken care of, where someone would tell them what to do, organize dinner on the table each night, show them when to pray and how to take care of their souls. A church official, writing from Rome to the papal nuncio in Naples in 1626, complained that some only joined religious orders 'to escape the jurisdiction of the civil courts and not because they have an inclination to religious life'.[1] But the Piarist Order followed a particularly rigorous regimen, and it could not have been the first choice for someone seeking merely to escape onerous civil duties and the cares of life. Calasanz himself emphasized the spiritual significance of 'extreme poverty', even at the expense of mundane practicalities, such as having enough food or mending leaking classroom roofs. The order's *Constitutions* of 1622 contained a chapter 'On Poverty', which laid down how the Piarists were to be a mendicant order, living off voluntary donations, and owning and accepting nothing for themselves. Buildings and furniture necessary for the school, church and residence could not be donated, only loaned; everything else was to be left to Divine Providence. Sometimes Divine Providence fell short, as in the school in Narni in

December 1620, when Calasanz wrote that 'there are no clothes in this house to change into if one gets soaked, no undergarments, none of the necessary shirts, no drawers, no socks, no wood, no bread, and no money apart from 16 scudi per month. We are very miserable.' He himself had not changed his shirt for two or three months.[2] In another school, at Oregina in northern Italy, Father Pietro Casani painted a bleak picture of conditions in chilly February: 'You should try absolute poverty like we are experiencing it here. In such atrocious cold we have only four branches, just chopped from the tree, and with continual blowing on the fire we managed to use them up – you couldn't really say we burnt them. Last Friday, since we had no oil, we ate bread soup without.'[3]

Not only was the level of poverty extreme, but any small pleasures were rigorously excluded. When Calasanz discovered that a priest had a guitar and played secular songs on it 'in the Spanish and Sicilian style' he was irritated and ordered it removed. Staff and pupils were forbidden from playing draughts, or bowls, or any games in the classroom or in the courtyards. Any teacher disobeying repeatedly faced imprisonment. As for chess, 'your life is short, the hour uncertain and you would be better spending the time instead in preparations for your death, for if you do not do a short penance in this life, you will do a long one in the next'. When he heard that some of the teachers were swimming in the sea off the coast of Naples at Posilippo 'for recreation' he was appalled, not only by the indecency, but by the pure hedonism of the activity.[4]

Calasanz was renowned among his colleagues for the asceticism of his own way of life, and even his enemies could never accuse him of any form of extravagance or luxury. Father Berro recalled seeing him 'crawling on all fours from the oratory to the refectory begging that we all pray for him, and also stretched out on the floor at the door to the refectory, so that everyone had to walk over him. He ate under the table or standing up with one foot lifted in the air in order to suffer even while eating.' While such discomfort appears excessive to modern eyes, it seems to have paid off, for Father Berro noted that, 'After his death I know that the corridor where he had carried out those mortifications was adorned with celestial displays, and he passed along all resplendent, and one could not gaze upon him for it was too bright, and this was exactly on the anniversary of his birth.'[5]

Calasanz aroused great devotion among his adherents, but was not an easy man. Everything had to be done exactly as he wished: 'I insist on commanding all our members,' he wrote firmly in 1628 – although ironically the recipient of the letter was Stefano Cherubini, the father who would be least susceptible to his orders and whose disobedience would lead to complete disorder.[6] He had no hesitation in ordering punishments of fasting or even imprisonment for disobedient members, and the historians who summarized his character as 'a man who never laughs, who never even smiles (except at poverty)' were accurate.[7]

One of the main sources for the history of the order are the collected letters: those written by and to Calasanz and those exchanged between his colleagues. These documents reveal him to be a severe and direct disciplinarian, even a despot, with no time for any formalities or unnecessary courtesies. They do not begin with any flowery greetings, but rather with orders broken into little paragraphs, which often begin 'quanto' – 'as to the arithmetic class ...', 'as to the dormitory ...', 'as to the novices ...'. In the 4,869 letters of Calasanz there is not a trace of humour or lightness of touch. The couriers and postmen were given either money or small gilded pictures of the Madonna to encourage them to deliver the post promptly, so delayed correspondence rarely proved an excuse for disobedience.[8] Calasanz ordered his headmasters and provincials to write to him with great frequency, but the teachers were supposed to show their letters to their superiors for initialling before sending. Failure to do so would result in ten days' solitary withdrawal to their rooms, five of which would be spent fasting on bread and water.[9]

The meals, which Calasanz himself ate in such discomfort, were far from sumptuous. There were many fast days, and even proper meals rarely offered more than one ounce of meat, as Vincenzo Berro complained, 'for there were only ever two or three morsels, like little nuts', although the bread was not rationed.

The soups were usually cabbage leaves minced like those you feed to geese, picked in the garden – one leaf for each one of us – cutting off the stem with great solemnity, and once I remember that for more than 40 religious only four numbered beans were put to boil, so much so that we got one ladleful of boiled water (you couldn't call it broth) with some crumbs of bread each, but I only got the skin of a bean; and another time the same happened with lentils, and we were so used to that, that once along with the spinach the oven cloth went into the pot, having been left in the basin where the spinach was washed.[10]

Visible poverty, however, did serve a function. It enabled the Piarists to set a good example – every time a poorly-shod and ill-clad father accompanied his pupils home, the spiritual superiority of the order was publicly demonstrated. And the order was cheap to run, so less wealthy towns could afford the schools.

Some of the early fathers were rigorous almost to the point of sanctity in their outlook and their health suffered through the long hours and selfless devotion to their duties. Father Pietro Casani, Calasanz's right-hand man, spiritual, charming and generally respected, wrote a memo 'To Three Cardinals' – one of whom was Benedetto Giustiniani, later cardinal protector – in October 1615, describing the staffing levels needed to run the Roman school with its thousand pupils. In addition to the eight or ten priests who served the religious needs of the boys, teaching them Christian doctrine and taking confession, there had to be around fifty other staff members:

And because they work very hard, it is necessary that in addition to those who actually serve in the classes, there should be a certain number of others who are able to exchange with them when the overwhelming fatigue makes them ill, which happens often, otherwise they die. Also they need a break when they have worked three or four years in a row so that they can recover their physical and spiritual strength.'[11]

The young Glicerio Landriani is a perfect example of the physical breakdown that could result from too much religious severity. A wealthy nephew of the important Milanese Archbishop Federico Borromeo, Glicerio came to Rome to make his career, and fell under the influence of Calasanz in 1612, aged twenty-four. Two years earlier his great-uncle, Carlo Borromeo, had been canonized. Glicerio used his considerable fortune to contribute to the rent and eventually to help purchase the school premises. Meanwhile he studied, worked and prayed all the hours of the day. Occasionally he would go out on the street and pay a poor person to drag him along by a rope around his neck. 'He was so assiduous in his prayers that his knees were swollen and calloused ... He stayed behind every evening after common prayers, in the Oratory, spending many hours of the night praying ... I was always afraid he would become sick and gave him medicine,' wrote Father Casani. 'The austerity of his life would have been extreme, had it not been modified by obedience ... Sometimes he was concentrating so hard on the spiritual text being read aloud during the meal, that he sat with his mouth wide open, and the food remained there unchewed and unswallowed.'[12] And indeed, by the age of thirty, Glicerio could stand the way of life no longer and, worn out by penitence and prayer, expired. His mentor, Calasanz, heartened by his reputation for piety and the exemplary manner of his death, ordered that his heart be removed and placed in a special receptacle, which he kept by his desk in memory of one of the earliest and youngest Piarist fathers to meet his Maker. Within a few years of his death the order was petitioning the Pope for his beatification.

But not all new recruits were as saintly. The rapid expansion of the organization meant there was an urgent need for teachers and the headmasters could not always afford to be too selective when classes were desperate for staff. By the time Calasanz had finished writing the

Constitutions – using the rules and constitutions of many other ancient and modern orders – which were given papal approval in January 1622, the Roman province had already been created to encompass the schools in Frascati, Narni, Mentana, Moricone and Norcia, while schools were opened in Liguria (Carcare and Savona) and Tuscany (Fanano) to provide the first toe-hold in the north of Italy. The south soon followed and establishments were also opened in central Europe in Moravia in the early 1630s and in Warsaw under the protection of King Ladislaw IV in 1642. The lay brother in charge of the garden in Warsaw

introduced the vine, which had never grown there before, and cultivated it so diligently that there were beautiful ripe grapes. And Her Majesty the Queen [of Poland] tasted it and pronounced it the equal of those in France, and she ordered many thousands of vines to be brought from Hungary, and being well planted they produced beautiful fruit ... and she sent a barrel of wine to our fathers and we had generous donations and all because of two or three bunches of grapes.[13]

The long-lasting impact of the Piarist expansion to central Europe, however, affected more than the future drinking habits of the Poles. When disaster struck the order in the 1640s, the central European schools would remain as staunch outposts and their patrons as firm defenders of the order.

The Piarists were invited to the town of Nikolsburg (Mikulov) in southern Moravia by Cardinal Franz Dietrichstein, whose principal residence it was. Here they found themselves in a very different society from their Italian experiences. In theory, language problems were initially solved by resorting to Latin, although in fact when important visitors arrived to tour the school 'most of us hide, which is very prudent, *stultus si tacuerit, sapiens reputabitur'* (if a stupid man remains silent, he will be thought wise). Dietary differences caused some problems. Father Ambrogio Ambrogi was served 'salad dressed with a buttery sauce, or sometimes, when travelling, with molten lard, and I must confess I would rather have eaten hay. When we arrived [in Nikolsburg] for many days I ate almost nothing, and I was very troubled, thinking it would be impossible to get used to this kind of food. But now I eat like a bear, and whereas in Italy I ate very little, now I seem to do nothing else from morning to evening.' He blamed the air in Moravia for creating good appetites. The weather was also hard to get used to: 'It is 7 August and I am still waiting for summer, and every time it rains one has to put on one's coat. The other day Brother Giuseppe told the pupils about the Miracle of the Snow when it snowed on 5 August in Rome, and the children were not at all impressed because it does so quite often here.' By October snow lay over everything and the local inhabitants dressed appropriately:

Neither the men nor the women here are wearing hats any more, but a kind of Turkish turban made of fur, and they are dressed in fur from head to toe, even the mendicant friars; otherwise survival would be impossible. The pupils wear fur-lined jackets and all have a kind of tunic down to the knees, also fur-lined … Your Reverence will have to excuse us from wearing [sandals or sockless shoes] because there is so much mud that it is just amazing; whenever you leave the house, you sink in halfway up the leg. If the boys didn't all have boots they would lose their shoes every day. And when the streets are dry because of the north wind, then one's feet die of cold; this has happened to me twice and it is terribly painful, and whoever accompanies the children really feels it … You will have to change the coats too, for it will be unbearable in the cold, because people say we haven't seen anything yet, and already it is far colder than it ever is in Italy. The Danube freezes over so wagons and carriages can cross as though it were hard ground, even though the Tiber in Rome is a little stream compared to the Danube.[14]

Ambrogi was also amazed at the amount of drunkenness:

It will seem an exaggeration but it is the truth when I say that I cannot recall a day when I have not seen a drunkard. Sometimes I go out and all I meet is drunkards! This is such a normal occurrence that when we accompany the children home, they don't even turn their heads to marvel, even when we meet many at once. On the contrary, often they will see their own father reeling around, and without making a big fuss they just take him by the hand and lead him home. The worst thing is that if they meet you the drunkards want to have a deep conversation, but I don't even understand the language ... and it is no wonder [they get so drunk] because the glasses are terrifyingly huge. They hate water like the devil hates the cross ... I believe that is why you don't see many old people around here, because they drink so much.

He signed off his letter by asking the father general not to forget those he had sent 'to the end of the world' and it must indeed have felt like that for the predominantly Italian teachers.[15]

However, the work was appreciated by the local population and by Cardinal Dietrichstein, who wrote praising their debut to the Congregation for the Propagation of the Faith, and noting that they had recently confessed 2,000 souls and were teaching some 400 children in their classes.[16] Approaching conversion via the example of a strict way of life and teaching the children was a great success for 'those heretics who are here are simple idiotic people who are easily converted by the good example of our fathers, rather than by sermons or disputations'.[17] 'Everyone here loves our institution,' wrote another of the fathers happily. It was all very gratifying, particularly since Cardinal Barberini had predicted that the central European expansion would fail.[18]

So many schools opened so quickly and in such a diversity of towns and villages that the order had problems maintaining its standards. An anonymous report, known as the 'Memorial of the Inconveniences' was written by a member, possibly the influential Father Pietro Casani, and sent to the Congregation of Bishops and Regulars, an important committee. It pointed out that the schools were widely dispersed, from the mountains of Genoa to Calabria – let alone across the Alps – and often in tiny and unimportant hamlets with all the expense and problems that communication over this vast expanse involved. As a result, staff were often of poor quality and badly trained. The solutions were simple: no new schools should be opened for the time being; the smallest schools should be closed down; numbers of pupils should be restricted in the biggest schools in Rome, Naples and Genoa; Calasanz was to consult with his assistants before accepting any new foundations.[19] A few months later Casani wrote directly to Pope Urban VIII asking him to ensure that Calasanz consult with his assistants, one of whom was to be by his side in Rome to help him with all decisions at all times.[20] As a result, a papal ban on all new foundations was theoretically imposed. But the father general was unable to rein in his enthusiasm, and unable to share his authority, and the 'Memorial' had no effect. He simply said that even the small schools had large numbers of pupils, and that travel between the schools was cheap, and continued to ignore the advice of his assistants.[21] This inability to delegate or to hold back on expansion were among the major charges levelled against him by his critics in later years.

From Rome, Calasanz sent hundreds of letters of minute instructions, not only about the running of the schools, but covering every detail of the living and eating arrangements. To Father Pellegrino Tencani in chilly Norcia, for instance, he advised, 'Above all, ensure that the classes run well ... and make sure that if it is very cold, as I believe it is there, the brothers do not suffer, and if necessary get woollen underwear knitted and make sure they keep their feet clean and dry, because humidity can result in stomach aches.' The following week he wrote again, giving permission for the brothers to wear closed shoes, rather than sandals as the rule specified, so long as they were suitably impoverished-looking. However, if all failed and the teachers did get a stomach ache, he had an infallible cure:

I have used this remedy and it has worked in less than a month, otherwise I think they would never have been cured. Each morning I had them given a bread soup, grated quite finely, and little more than a loaf of bread and a couple of cooked apples, or a little egg, or a few figs, and in the evenings much less, so that their natural warmth, which had become enfeebled, could not only digest the meal, but also the evil humours, which otherwise medicine can never cure. It seems quite a tough remedy, but better to put up with it for a month or a little longer, than to spend the rest of your life with similar pains, and a risk of worse developing.[22]

Some ailments could not be cured by diet alone, and when Father Giovanni Garzia Castiglia, headmaster of Frascati, fell sick, Calasanz sent him a treasured possession guaranteed to make him better: 'In this sealed box I am sending you the remedy for your ailment which, in my opinion, is caused by too much work and disturbed nights caring for the sick. I warn you that the tiny fragment in this box is a piece of true unicorn horn, so take great care of it.'[23] Father Garzia recovered and continued to head the Frascati school until Father Calasanz required his investigative skills elsewhere a few months later in one of the key moments of the order's history.

But meanwhile requests for foundations outstripped availability of staff. Calasanz complained triumphantly, 'If I had 10,000 priests now in one month I could send them out to all those places which are desperately begging for us',[24] and the archives are full of letters from local figures of authority begging in vain for Pious Schools to be opened in their area. There was no time for any extensive training or selection procedure. In theory the teachers were supposed to be intelligent, well-spoken, vowed to poverty, chastity, obedience and the education of the poor. 'Only accept intelligent ones, and make sure they are not too short,' wrote Calasanz on an optimistic day.[25] They were to be perfect Christians – patient, humble, chaste, teaching by example rather than by words. No one guilty of homicide, tied by the chains of marriage, illegitimate, inclined to melancholy or with a physical defect could be considered. Tall candidates of even temperament and well-versed in grammar were especially prized. Lay brothers who played supporting but crucial roles with useful skills such as tailors, carpenters, cooks and cobblers were particularly welcome.[26] Even they could play a religious, though usually inferior, role. Father Berro told the tale of Brother

Giovanni Macario, a Genoese who had been a slave of the Turks for twenty-two years and joined the Piarists in 1617:

The Lord had given him the gift of tears, and such tenderness of heart, that he prayed and cried continuously, even while working in the kitchen, and many times during the day and night through excessive devotion he would leap and dance around shouting, 'The Passion of our Lord Jesus Christ is always in our hearts,' and whether he was in his room or in the kitchen, or elsewhere one would hear these excesses of love for God.

Once this brother was in the kitchen and very perplexed for he could not manage to divide up the portions of food for everyone, since being very poor we had very little (just one miserable cake he had made in a terra-cotta dish) and there were forty of us. He could not work out how to divide the cake equally for everyone, and drew the lines with the knife many times, but the portions did not come out fairly, and he became upset and at the same time praised holy poverty, requesting that our Lord help him to satisfy everyone. He raised the knife to start cutting the cake, hoping that God would help him. Suddenly he felt the knife being taken from his hands, and at the same time he heard someone say, 'What a dimwit you are that you can't manage it.' Turning, Brother Giovanni saw a Minorite friar, who sketched out the lines and then cut the cake, and gave him back the knife, saying, 'These are the correct portions, give them one each,' and left the kitchen. Brother Giovanni admired his work, and since he wanted to know who the friar was he ran after him, but could not find him, nor saw him ever again, so he was sure he was a celestial being, the angelic Saint Francis of Assissi, Father of Holy Poverty.

From that time onwards the lay brother in charge of the kitchen had to say a prayer at morning and evening meals in the refectory in memory of this miracle.[27]

In reality, some of the candidates were clearly unsuited to the job, through temperament, qualification or inclination. For example, in March 1626, a young priest, Paolo Rendina, wrote to Father Calasanz from Monte Flavio, a small village in the Appennines 50 kilometres from

Rome to ask advice about joining the order. He had done some work with the Piarists but was not yet a member:

For the last three years I've not been healthy. I have a great weakness of head and sight caused by study and other use of the brain … I cannot read continuously for half an hour without great difficulty, and it causes me such dizziness that I am obliged to interrupt and do something else, or rest and calm myself. At other times my limbs become languid, and my stomach fastidious. I am naturally susceptible to the cold, especially on my feet, and to melancholy. I imagine monstruous phantasms, and this is very bothersome to me. At the beginning of my illness I was afraid I was going mad … Many medicaments and cauterizations have done little or nothing to help me. … What would be better: to leave my homeland, or to persevere in the life I have begun? My doctor advises that I go and live where the air is heavier, and in particular he considers the air of Rome very healthy. I would like to give it a try.

Rendina went on to explain how he was useless to his family, and how just seeing 'the dissolution, gaming and triviality' in Monte Flavio were exhausting him. His mother was also unwell, which he attributed to spells cast on her. 'She says that at night lights appear to her, in other words there is a kind of splendour and then she is a little frightened at the end. She is frequently tormented by shooting pains in her body, which often remain in her stomach and head. Exorcisms and holy objects offer some relief, but after an interval all the pains return.' If he could come to Rome and join the order, initially accompanied by his mother, he felt all would be well. Father Calasanz, however, was not convinced. His answer was sent without hesitation and was brutally curt: 'As for the Order, I do not think it right for you. And you should not leave your mother while she still lives.'[28]

But more often than not Calasanz accepted those who wished to join the order. The young men were often only fifteen years old when they first entered the noviciate, so the development of their characters was not yet fixed. Two years as a novice with full training was supposed to be followed by another three years of service before full ordination. But in spite of many injunctions to take 'good ones or nothing', as Calasanz graphically wrote in a letter of December 1632, in practice the order was so desperate for staff that it took nearly everyone. Checking on six new novices for the school at Campi Salentina, Father Francesco Amalfa wrote, 'Half are unfit for our Order. Some suffer from dizzy spells, some cannot read, others have no skills whatsoever.' In Genoa, 'it is commonly believed, by both clergy and laity, that our Order is on the point of collapse through lack of educated men, and I must add that even those we have lack spirit.' And from central Europe one of the brightest Piarist teachers, Ambrogio Ambrogi, wrote sadly, 'Here it is said of us – and with good reason – that not one of us can put two lines to paper, either in prose or in verse.'[29]

The novices' training was rigorous and designed to make them obedient and humble, as well as academically suitable. Vincenzo Berro, whose *Notes on the Foundation* are an essential record of those early days, was born in Savona in northern Italy. He and his brother became Piarist novices in their teens. The brother, Pietro Paolo, would be tragically killed in Savona years later in a massive explosion that killed 2,000 and destroyed half the city.[30] As novices the brothers were brought to Rome by Calasanz in order to experience the Holy Year of 1625 and placed under the care of Father Melchiorre Alacchi. Alacchi was a very controversial character and though it was not his actions that would bring down the order, he would cause major problems and lay the foundations for later events. One of his favourite training methods to teach the novices humility and subservience was to send them to stand outside the important basilicas, where crowds attended for the jubilee, with a collecting box in their hands. Berro recalled:

We were to stand immobile like statues, without even chasing the flies away, which went in our eyes ... We were variously treated; some insulted us with rude comments, others put flowers, or fruit, or onion leaves, or artichokes, beans and such-like in our boxes. Others hit the steps or the walls behind us with sticks to make us turn around, or speak or lift our eyes. Others called us hypocrites, pains in the neck, bigots, and sometimes they made jokes to try and make us laugh: 'What, have you lost your tongue? Are they mute? Are they blind? Aren't they beautiful! Aren't they good! They must be dying of hunger, and of thirst!' And suchlike. But we stayed so still for everything that many not only shouted at those who mocked us, but chased away the flies, and kissed our clothes, and our feet, and one of us, out of pure devotion, was kissed on the forehead by a woman. Back at the house when the novice master heard that, not only did he make him clean that spot many times, but he also made him scrape it clean. He also did that to another novice, who was unsuspectingly kissed by his mother, and he had to use a pumice stone. The whole thing was done to show how much we must flee the conversation of secular people. This was no small mortification since apart from anything else, standing on your feet for four or five hours causes great weakness in summer, and in winter the north wind cuts into your legs. I remember that when I was called to go home I could not even move at first, since I was so frozen into position by the cold.[31]

Father Melchiorre, the novice master, was born in Naro in Sicily in 1591. Aged twenty-four he obtained a degree in law and worked in that field for a short period. When he was thirty years old he joined the Piarists and taught arithmetic and calligraphy, soon making a name for himself as an effective teacher, although he also acquired a reputation for unnecessary strictness. In spite of this criticism he was ordained to the priesthood and placed in charge of the novices. In later years Father Berro would be very critical of his severity:

No error could be made without its punishment, and if something got broken inadvertently, or for another reason, whatever it was, it had to be worn around the neck even in the public streets, until the father novice master ordered otherwise, so often you saw our members going through the city of Rome with broken ladles, jugs, cooking pots and suchlike, also pieces of brick, roofing-tile, piping, sticks or other bits of wood tied around their necks. Other times they sent us out with ... our heads half-tonsured or our beards half-shaved; so much so that we rarely went out without at least one of us having some punishment ... Once while taking hold of a rope I knocked an apple off a small tree in the loggia of San Pantaleo. I was ordered to place it around my neck until further orders even though I was on door-keeping duties, and accompanying the children to their homes morning and evening. And in the via della Scrofa near Sant'Ivone I dropped it under a stall selling herbs, and had to stretch out underneath it and managed to get hold of it, and tied it on again, and after three days our father ordered me to eat it.[32]

Father Melchiorre did not last long as novice master, and in October 1625 Calasanz provided him with a special licence to go wherever he pleased – 'to those places that seem most convenient and opportune within Italy and above all in the kingdom of Naples and Sicily' – and try to meet with cardinals, archbishops, princes and municipal authorities in an effort to set up new schools for the order. He was further permitted to admit whoever he wished into the order, an unprecedented freedom of action, and an uncharacteristic delegation of power by the customarily autocratic Calasanz.

The 250 kilometres between Rome and Naples were, according to John Raymond, an English visitor who travelled it a few years later, 'the most dangerous passage in Italy, because the wayes are so throng'd with banditos'.[33] The alternative was to travel by sea, which the fathers often did, but in the winter the storms could be ferocious, and in the summer 'sailing is terrible, because of the heat and the Turks' who regularly attacked merchant shipping. Only a year later the boat on which a certain Brother Benedetto and his companion were travelling would meet a Turkish brigantine just past Livorno. In the ensuing skirmish their own captain was killed, along with three of the Turks. Benedetto himself was wounded in the hand and barely escaped capture and the years of slavery that would have entailed.[34] On this occasion, however, accompanied by a dozen brothers, Father Melchiorre opted for the land passage and reached his destination safely.

Naples was the capital of Spain's Italian domains, which included all of southern Italy, Sicily and further territories in the north, most importantly Milan. Ruled by viceroys and supported by a large bureau-cracy and a massive military presence, Naples must have felt very different from the claustrophobic priestliness of Rome. When Father Melchiorre arrived he immediately managed to see the Marquis of Belmonte, Don Carlos Tapia, Regent of the Royal Chancellery and the most important man in government, after the viceroy himself. The mar-quis had met Calasanz a few years earlier in Rome to discuss the possi-bility of a Neapolitan foundation, and Father Melchiorre and his colleagues were even lodged by him while negotiations proceeded.

However, for reasons that are unclear, the Archbishop of Naples, Cardinal Decio Caraffa, was firmly opposed to the notion of founding Piarist schools in the area, and remained hostile even when the viceroy himself, the Duke of Alva, intervened. Giving up hope of a school in Naples, Father Melchiorre then set off for Palermo, but when suspicions of plague threatened his journey, he turned towards Messina instead. Once again, in spite of support from the secular authorities – the vicar general, Don Lucas Cochiglia, was very supportive and the senators offered a building and a grant – opposition surfaced from competing religious orders who may have felt their livelihood threatened by another organization seeking donations from a limited number of wealthy patrons. The senate and the archbishop were already at logger-heads over a novel attempt to eradicate sexual incontinence that the archbishop had introduced and that was causing great problems:

With indiscreet zeal and little prudence, Monsignor had devised a plan to eradicate abuses. He had a hole knocked through in the wall of his residence, for use as a postbox, with a little opening locked with a key, which he kept about his person. Here, secret information against concubinage could be post-ed; he promised good rewards to those who revealed the truth. But this led many through enmity, self-interest or jealousy to slander the most respected families and the nobility, while others paid prostitutes to report that they were the concubines of various respectable people. So great complaints, disorder and arguments resulted, and the archbishop was forced by an order from Rome to remove the postbox. And the Senate and the nobles and the city hated him.[35]

With the dual authorities of the town in such conflict, the senate failed to ensure that the Piarists' application to the religious authorities made any progress. Meanwhile the local members of the Society of Jesus felt threatened, and an ex-Jesuit who had joined the Piarists and then been defrocked for lack of humility started a rumour that Calasanz was a failed Jesuit, and had only started the newer order 'to make a monkey of the Jesuits'.[36] Once more, Father Melchiorre moved on and although he left a few teachers to try to keep the foundation going, it came to nothing and they were soon ejected. Meanwhile, on the way back to Rome, Father Melchiorre stopped at Naples once more, where he learned of the death of Cardinal Caraffa on 23 January 1626. With the main opponent out of the way, the Neapolitan school had another chance.

At the beginning of the seventeenth century Naples was more than three times the size of Rome and, after Paris, was the largest city in Europe with a population, according to one Piarist father, of around 450,000. As the great historian of the Mediterranean, Fernand Braudel, wrote:

Naples had no equivalent in Christendom ... The whole of southern Italy flocked to the city, both the rich, often very rich, and the hopelessly wretched poor ... Naples was excessive in every respect ... Order could never be maintained, and at night the only law was that of the strong and cunning. Certainly, even if one allows for the bragging of Spanish soldiers who were always ready to let their pens run away with them, it was the most astonishing, most fantastically picaresque city in the world. It was a more hard-working city than its very bad reputation gives it credit for, but that reputation was not undeserved.[37]

Salvator Rosa, the landscape painter who spent his teenage years as a Piarist novice before slipping off his habit, wrote in a moment of nostalgia years after he had left for good, 'The city of Naples is justly called a fragment of heaven that has fallen to earth.' Calasanz noticed that those who were born or brought up in the city tended to return there, so strong was its pull. Cervantes had called it 'the richest and most depraved city in the whole world'. It was also the busiest seaport in Italy and housed the massive soldiers' garrisons that helped to uphold Spanish power in the eastern Mediterranean. 'There are three times as many children in Naples as in Rome, and three or four of our schools wouldn't be sufficient,' wrote Calasanz. Crowded into the old town walls with buildings easily reaching six or seven storeys high, space was at a premium.[38]

With the archbishop gone, the way was clear for the Piarists and their services were in great demand. Father Melchiorre was immediately offered three sites and, encouraged by the regent and other advisers, chose the one in the poorest area, the Duchesca. It was somehow ironic that the building selected should house a huge brothel with an adjoining comedy theatre, and once the whores had been evicted and the theatre converted into a church, the building revealed its potential.

After renovations costing some 1,300 ducats were completed, Calasanz travelled down for the opening by litter from Rome in what would be his last major expedition – he was seventy years old and had hurt his foot. Within eight days of the opening on 5 November 1626, there were 400 pupils, after two weeks 500, at the end of the month 600. More teachers were summoned urgently from other towns to help out. 'We threw out more than six hundred whores who lived there ... and where previously God was offended, today more than six hundred children praise him,' he wrote triumphantly (although the area did remain prime prostitute territory as the edicts of 1687 and 1703 banning 'bad women' from the Duchesca area show).[39]

Father Melchiorre had achieved an outstanding success. The Neapolitan province, created in 1627, was a significant step for the order. Requests flooded in – 'at one point there were more than eighty places throughout the kingdom which with great enthusiasm insisted on having such a holy foundation'.[40] Another two schools were soon founded in the area, Campi Salentina, and a somewhat foolhardy attempt at Somma Vesuviana, which opened in November 1630 at the very summit of the volcano. Unfortunately, barely a year later, on 16 December 1631, the volcano swallowed up the town, the school and the Piarists among at least 3,000 other people in 'the worst volcanic disaster in the Mediterranean during the past 1,800 years' – in other words since the destruction of Pompeii. Ash blocked out the sun as far away as Naples itself and the viceroy sent 500 men to bury the dead. A series of earthquakes followed and smoke and ash continued to billow out from the ravine where the school had been for several weeks.[41]

A few months earlier a new school had opened in Cosenza but this too was to be destroyed in the earthquake of 1638, only a few years later. Calabria had been experiencing terrible tremors, which 'not only made the buildings fall down, but even in the countryside opened up terrifying ravines very suddenly, and fathers saw their children swallowed up before their eyes'.[42] The town of Cosenza had been free of problems, though inhabitants had sometimes heard what sounded like faraway claps of thunder, and much praying, penitence and processions had been organized. Suddenly, on the Saturday before Palm Sunday, a terrible earthquake struck. It lasted for several hours and by the time the earth stopped moving the castle, along with many churches and buildings, including those of the Piarists, stood no longer. Luckily the fathers had been warned to send the children outside, otherwise all would have been buried beneath the masonry. As it was, three small children were crushed as neighbouring buildings collapsed. The teachers escaped towards the sea and took ship for Naples; others left for the Sicilian school. The school in Cosenza was eradicated. An even more destructive catastrophe would affect the whole order soon after.

'A touch on his breeches'

In spite of the successful opening of the school in Naples, Father Calasanz was criticized for allowing Father Melchiorre Alacchi too much independence. Several of the schools he founded had opened without enough consideration of how they were to support themselves in the future. One of the main opponents of the Sicilian priest was Father Paulo Ottonelli, an ex-soldier with good court contacts and an atypical Scolopi background. As Count Ottonelli he had been married to the pious Isabella de Montecuccoli, Countess of Polinago, who had expired in 1608 after providing him with six children. His military training stood him in good stead one day when he saved Calasanz from attack by 'an unsuitable and obstinate man' who had been expelled from the order earlier that day:

Tempted by the devil, he waited one evening with a big cudgel behind the door of the stairs leading down from the Oratory of San Pantaleo, until our Father General and founder should go down to pray and then he would attack him. And it would have come to pass exactly as he planned, had not Captain Ottonelli – I mean Father Paolo of the Assumption – found himself just behind Our Father when he was passing by, and fended off the blow from the huge stick, which was already whistling evilly through the air.[1]

The quick reactions of his training as a soldier saved Calasanz from a potentially fatal blow. Aged fifty, the Count had joined the Piarists, dividing up his considerable wealth into six portions – one for each of his five sons, and one for himself, with which he endowed the school in Fanano, of which he was then nominated headmaster. His daughter, Chiara, had become a nun so inherited nothing. The sons, one of whom would later be ambassador to Spain, were extremely unhappy with this and complained to the pope that since the count had always acted 'with great charity and love, supporting them during their studies, and making every effort possible to provide them with all spiritual and temporal benefits' they now considered his actions to be 'contrary to good breeding and to what he owed them not only as Christian sons, but even if they had been pagans'. As a result, Ottonelli was served with an order stripping him of all his worldly goods on pain of excommunication. He immediately wrote to the pope, who was an old acquaintance of his – he had even chosen to be called Father Paolo in honour of the pontiff – to point out that

before taking the habit of the Order he had summoned the four sons who were with him in Rome and told them of the decision he had made to renounce the world … and that he wanted to divide up his wealth … and that he would take the best portion, since he deemed that portion worthy of Jesus Christ … [My sons] are ungrateful and impatient at the long life of their too-loving father, and desire to take control. Thus they have presented Your Holiness with a story very far from the truth. Since God will not permit such barbarous, monstrous impiety and ingratitude to remain unpunished, I beg you to maintain that justice which is the principal ornament of your pontificate. I beg you to order that this extravagant request of theirs be condemned to perpetual silence.[2]

It was and the Fanano school was successfully endowed.

Father Paolo had many influential contacts from his earlier career, including Cardinal Bellarmino, Filippo Neri, and the three most recent popes, and soon rose to the position of assistant general to Calasanz. So when he wrote a secret memo in August 1625 accusing Father

Melchiorre of arrogance and a lack of respect for the father general, and criticizing Calasanz's dependence on the Sicilian, and sent it to an influential committee of cardinals, it was taken very seriously:

The Father General lets himself be scandalously oppressed and bullied by the novice master in front of the very novices in the noviciate itself, and in front of the priests in San Pantaleo, and before laymen in both places. They say that the novice master, who is called Father Melchiorre the Sicilian, or the Calabrese, was expelled from the Capuchins, where he was a novice, and many are amazed that we have accepted him, though I don't know if that is true. It is, however, true that when he was a novice with us he never wanted to obey his superiors, and did many extravagant things, which he considered to be heroic deeds, like wanting to force a [picture of the] Madonna which was in his classroom to do miracles, by tipping out all the oil from the lamps which were kept lit there, or trying to heal all the sick people and other such things. But the lack of respect, in fact the complete absence of respect, which he shows towards the Father General, and his continued praising to the skies by the Father General amazes everyone.'[3]

Possibly Ottonelli was jealous of the huge influence Father Melchiorre seemed to have over the founder. It certainly seems strange that the usually authoritarian Calasanz should allow him such leeway.

Father Paolo died a few months later, having caught a malign fever from two gentlemen whom he had attended a few days earlier,[4] but others took up his complaints about Melchiorre. Much worse was to follow, but the father general was to continue entrusting his erratic protégé with responsibilities long after he should have dealt firmly with him.

After his major success in Naples, Father Melchiorre set off in early 1627 for Carcare with papers confirming his appointment as visitor general, an important position of influence. Accompanied by a small group of Piarists, he took ship from Rome to Livorno. Calasanz, perhaps sensing something amiss with the group, wrote to Father Melchiorre, warning him to keep a close eye on his travelling companions 'because these brothers do not have very good references'.[5] During the night, Brother Pier Agostino Abbate 'felt a touch on his breeches [*'il Fr. Pietro Agostino fù tocco nelle braghe*]'.[6] At the time it was not clear which – if any – of the three other brothers sleeping alongside had touched him. Father Melchiorre, meanwhile, was apparently sleeping above-deck in the helmsman's quarters. The next day Pier Agostino reported the event to Father Melchiorre. 'So why did you not call out?' asked the novice master. 'Because I did not wish to cause scandal for the others' came the reply. Father Melchiorre then interrogated one of the other brothers, Ambrogio Ambrogi, privately about the matter. This brother would later accuse Father Melchiorre not only of breaking the seal of confession, but also of carrying out the suspect touching itself, and of trying to pass the blame onto Brother Ambrogio himself. Ambrogio Ambrogi was not linked to any further sexual scandal, but ever since the incident on the boat became a bitter enemy of Father Melchiorre. Given Melchiorre's later reputation it is quite possible that Brother Ambrogio's version was accurate and that the novice master had indeed left his berth in the helmsman's quarters.

One of the accompanying brothers, Giuseppe di Messina, was instantly expelled – though it seems unclear why if Ambrogio and Melchiorre were later accused – while Brother Ambrogio remained silent for the moment, afraid of compromising himself further.[7] The accounts are contradictory, but whatever the truth of the matter, it seems clear that one novice had been fondled, another had been accused, yet another expelled, and yet the novice master himself fell under suspicion, not only from several of the novices, but also from his other colleagues and superiors. As the master in charge of the group, the ultimate responsibility for what had occurred and what would occur should have been his. Throughout his career scandal seemed to dog Father Melchiorre: on the one hand he was vociferously against any hint of sexual freedom between members of the order, and his later writings contained many vehement outbursts against men he suspected of indulging in illicit activities; on the other hand, he himself would be so frequently accused of overstepping the line, of making advances such as 'the touch on the breeches', that it is impossible to consider him completely innocent of having indulged in some way – certainly in his imagination, and most probably in reality. His later friendships with unreliable young men would indicate that his affection for them transcended the boundaries laid down in the *Rules* and *Constitutions* of the order.

Reassembling on dry land, presumably somewhat shaken by their experience at sea, the little group continued to travel around northern Italy. From Carcare, where they successfully negotiated for the foundation of a new school, Father Melchiorre and his novices travelled on towards Alba to meet with Bishop Ludovico Gonzaga and for the cleric Giovan Battista Poli to receive his first tonsure. But the next day, as the group was walking back, tragedy struck. Giovan Battista had been feeling unwell and was on horseback as they approached the River Monesiglio, its waters swollen by the recent rains. He had been laughing all the way, but calling out such things as, 'I'm dead, I feel dead,' when suddenly he gave his horse free rein and spurred it on so that it plunged into the river where horse and rider were instantly swept away. The accounts read as though he had decided on impulse to commit suicide. Father Melchiorre ripped off his cassock and leaped after him into the current. But the rescue attempt was in vain, and Father Melchiorre himself was nearly drowned, 'no longer able to right himself for the numbness in his arms and legs, and beginning to swell up with the water he was swallowing'. He was only saved by a branch held out to him from the river bank by the Milanese Brother Francesco. Three days later the body of the young cleric was retrieved some way downstream. The news travelled to Rome and thence to Narni where the local Piarists had to break it to Giovan Battista's mother. Father Melchiorre was banished back to the classroom, where Calasanz reported him to be 'very lonely, and needing the support of your prayers'. He was disappointed in his man: 'He did not behave on this trip from Carcare as I thought he would, God help him.'[8]

The flood waters had broken in more senses than one and the local Piarists gave in to an orgy of guilt and counter-accusation. Father Francesco Castelli, the provincial, travelled to Carcare for the funeral but soon found himself overwhelmed with new and unwelcome information.[9] Castelli was one of the earliest members of the order, an intelligent and cultured man who held a series of high offices, including provincial and assistant general. Although he disagreed with some of the more menial tasks of the order, such as accompanying pupils home after school, his loyalty, obedience and high moral values were never questioned – except by Father Melchiorre, who thereby aroused his bitter and voluble enmity. (Castelli would die suddenly many years later when a priestly colleague stabbed him in the forehead with a kitchen knife when he was trying to mediate in an argument in the refectory.)[10]

Using his position as novice master to full effect, it appeared that Father Melchiorre had asked each novice 'directly whether they knew anything bad or had ever done anything bad with this or that particular person'. He had even asked some, for instance, Brother Ambrogio, whether Father Castelli himself 'had ever tempted him or asked him to do evil things'. His aim, according to Castelli, was 'to find out whom he could trust and make use of to slake his unbridled and lascivious passions'. Castelli was incandescent with rage:

I really hope that when I arrive in Rome I do not find him there, because if God maintains these feelings in my head I will not be able to prevent myself from laying hands on him wherever I find him ... Villain, it was not enough for him to do what he did [referring presumably to 'the touch on the breeches'], but he hoped to cover up his lechery and desires by persecuting the innocent, bringing down worthy men, carrying out a special inquisition against them by means of the confession [referring to the subsequent explicit interrogations of Ambrogio, and of the novice who drowned].

In Carcare he made the young brothers carry out public disciplines naked from head to foot for no reason, and against all the rules of modesty and observance. And these are brothers who even have to sleep with their clothes on!

As well as these accusations of indecency, Father Melchiorre was also charged with breaking the seal of the confessional, a deeply serious offence. 'At Moricone, at Rome, and at Carcare and maybe elsewhere too, he revealed the particular sins of named individuals, not only in general but in detail, and to several people.'[11] Castelli recommended that Father Melchiorre be sent to jail or expelled: 'It is not enough for our order that the plague leaves, we must make sure that it does not return; it is not enough for the plague-stricken to hold their breath in their mouth, the source of infection must be closed in such a way that they can never open their mouths again.' According to Brother Ambrogio, Father Melchiorre had declared his intention, if expelled, of travelling from noviciate to noviciate in other orders until the death of Father Calasanz, at which point he hoped to return to ruin the Piarists. For Father Castelli, Melchiorre was a demon who must be exorcized immediately.

Father Melchiorre denied everything. 'Believe me,' he protested. 'Two old men [Alacchi was thirty-six years old] sleeping in one room cannot give rise to scandal ... As to the things that are written about me from Genoa, the witnesses, depositions, testimonies, believe me ... not within the Order nor even in secular life could any woman or person boast of having touched me, nor did I look at anyone and make myself think bad thoughts.' He offered to leave the order if Calasanz would put in a word for him with the general of another order and pay him some transfer money. He even claimed to be willing to join a stricter regime, but a few days later he said he would rather not change until he had sorted out the slur on his reputation, and offered to go through a proper trial: 'If the whole of Hell were against me, it would not worry me, having God on my side.'[12]

Everything came to a head at the chapter general in Rome in October 1627, the four-yearly meeting of all the heads of the various provinces, along with all the other important members of the order. As with most of these events, the details are shrouded in secrecy. It is hard to believe that the protests arose purely from a personality clash with one of the provincials or from jealousy of Calasanz's favour. All except Calasanz himself seem to have been unanimous in their hostility to Alacchi. The official records of the chapter general miss out the discussion that must have preceded the decision that

with respect to Father Melchiorre of All Saints, the provincial of Genoa in particular, and several others, will carry out new investigations and proceedings. The Father General, having sent him away on a long pilgrimage so that he does not disturb and infect the Order any more with the matters that have been brought up during the proceedings, will meanwhile – using the excuse of necessity, or any other more convenient pretext – obtain permission from the Holy Father [the Pope] that he leave the Order. Should he return without having done the pilgrimage of St James [of Compostela] we will proceed against him legally.[14]

By describing Alacchi as an infection that could pollute the whole order, the chapter general had very clearly given its opinion of his activities.

While this official declaration was menacing and clearly hostile, having as its aim the exact discovery of wrong-doing and the expulsion of Father Melchiorre, the actual pilgrimage licence, which Father Calasanz had already provided for him a few months earlier in July 1627, was neutral. It was to be a voyage 'greatly desired by the pilgrim'; there was no mention of the fact that he was teetering on the brink of prison, expulsion, disgrace or worse. Although it must have been clear that the chapter general would deal harshly with Alacchi, Calasanz drew up the licence in the most favourable possible terms, supporting him in the face of great hostility from the rest of his advisers.

As the rest of his colleagues gathered in Rome for the chapter general, Father Melchiorre set out from Rome on his pilgrimage with two companions. In Finale, in Liguria, one of the companions fell sick and died, and a few days later Father Melchiorre too caught the disease:

It lasted fifty-four days, and was caused by two grave tertian fevers caused by being in a strange place with poor lodgings, food and assistance, so that he nearly died. The doctor told him he must have a change of air, so assisted by two people, one on each side to prevent him falling, he got on a mule and travelled to Carcare, where the school refused to let him in. The headmaster, Father Giovan Battista Costantini di San Tecla, merely told him to go and fulfil his vow, so he had to book into a hostel, until Father Domenico Pizzardo della Nunziata was moved by pity, and took him home.[14]

Even Father Calasanz was disappointed with him by then. Writing in support of Father Costantini's actions, he instructed, 'Be careful and find out if they [Alacchi and his remaining colleague] are really ill, and if they are disturbing the school or intend to continue their voyage … If by any chance they decide to change their minds and stay, then I give you permission to use all your authority and if necessary ask the secular authorities to put them in prison even if it costs you a bit of money.'[15] However, after three or four days' convalescence, Father Melchiorre and his companion finally set sail for Spain.

While many of his colleagues felt that the errant father had got off lightly by being permitted to leave on pilgrimage, Calasanz must have felt relieved at having sent him far away from Italy's borders and from future opportunities for creating a scandal within the order. His curiosity about his novices' sexual fantasies, the accusations of impropriety with his juniors that followed him, and his inability to get on with his colleagues were distracting, and meant that Calasanz and the provincials had to spend time limiting the damage which was beginning to outweigh the benefits of Alacchi's achievements in creating new foundations. But not only was Father Melchiorre to return – and be welcomed with open arms by the father general – but a far worse scandal was about to break.

'Be very careful in your dealings with the pupils'

Stefano Cherubini entered the order in 1617 at the age of seventeen. His father, Laerzio, was originally from Umbria and had carved himself a distinguished career as a lawyer and legal historian at the Curia, holding many important public offices including conservator of Rome, where he was responsible for the city's public welfare and urban safety. He was closely connected with the Giustiniani brothers, one of whom was the Piarist's cardinal protector. His name became familiar to other lawyers in the field when he compiled and edited an important collection of papal bulls, which proved an invaluable reference tool for other lawyers. Cherubini senior was wealthy enough to commission Caravaggio, by then one of the leading painters in Rome, to paint a *Death of the Virgin* for Santa Maria della Scala in Trastevere, but conservative enough to reject it when it was delivered, on the grounds that the Virgin's feet were bare and dirty, her stomach swollen, and Caravaggio had used 'some dirty whore from Ortaccio', Rome's red-light district, as a model. The painting, the largest canvas he ever executed, became the talk of Rome, according to the Mantuan ambassador, and Laerzio Cherubini was keen to be rid of it, although as one of the men depicted chatting behind the dead Virgin, he would be for ever linked to the image. Luckily for him, Rubens recommended the Duke of Mantua to purchase it, and for 350 scudi – a large sum – it was safely removed from

Rome.[1] Meanwhile Cherubini senior continued with his glittering legal career. He also bought and sold property and dealt in loans with guaranteed interest from offices at the Curia. He was wealthy and devout and had already come across the Piarists, facilitating the foundation of the school in Frascati. His eldest son Flavio followed in his legal footsteps at the Curia, while four more sons, including Stefano, joined various religious orders. Highly connected, and with great legal experience and resources, the Cherubinis were probably among the worst families in Rome to offend.[2]

Church careers were often selected for children by their wealthy fathers. Xenio Toscani, a church official writing in 1626, barely a decade after Stefano had joined the Piarists, wrote:

Surrounded by their numerous sons and daughters, [parents] pick and choose among them as one would do with fish or apples, deciding without appeal that one must become a priest, another a nun, yet another a friar, and that this one should marry ... so as to save cash and to increase the pile of money or the properties intended for the remaining son, who, by marrying, will carry on the memory of your name and the reputation of the family.[3]

He could have been writing about the Cherubini family, for it was never clear why Stefano should of his own accord have chosen to join the Piarists, with their ascetic way of life, the grind of classroom teaching, the lack of potential for prestige and promotion. There are only two plausible explanations: either his father had insisted, or he particularly wished to work with young boys.

One of Stefano Cherubini's brothers, Fausto, also briefly joined the Piarists, but on seeing the way of life transferred to a different congregation. Their father Laerzio remained closely involved with the order, and a witness reported sitting in one day on a heated discussion between Father Calasanz and the lawyer about the lack of higher literary studies for the novices, which the latter clearly felt was a disadvantage. 'Signor Laerzio,' replied Calasanz, 'I would rather my priests had three grades of virtue and humility than ten levels of literature.' It was strange, then, that Cherubini should have encouraged his son, Stefano, to persevere with a calling for which he would prove so manifestly unsuited.

However, given his father's status and his own abilities, Stefano was rapidly promoted, becoming rector at the age of twenty-six in Narni, a small Umbrian town belonging to his father's friend, the cardinal protector Giustiniani, where the first Piarist school outside Rome had opened in 1618. In his early correspondence with Calasanz there are occasional gentle rebukes, foretastes of what was to come. But in 1626 Stefano's influential father died and it seems that a restraining hand had been removed. Calasanz must have received reports from visitors about Father Stefano's behaviour for, in May 1627, he wrote a long letter mildly asking Father Stefano to improve his observance of the rules of priestly behaviour as laid out in the *Constitutions* of the order. 'I hope that you will receive this advice with the same affection with which I send it,' he noted. Calasanz asked the headmaster not to stand at the door chatting to townsfolk, especially during prayer time. He had ordered bread from the local bakery, and this was delivered by women, who for some reason often brought it round in the middle of the night, a rich source of scandal and perhaps the clearest sign that all was not as it should be in the Narni school. The food served in the refectory was also far too sumptuous. Stefano, Calasanz had been told, ate 'more than necessary', and there were often four or five courses. According to the *Constitutions*, meals were supposed to be taken in silence, but there were no quiet areas in the whole school where silence was observed, not even the sacristy where the sacred vessels and vestments for services were kept and which was supposed to be approached with great reverence. Father Stefano's piety and discipline were not strict enough: 'In the main room of the school, football is permitted and sometimes the ball hits the picture of the Holy Madonna … In the choir the headmaster [Cherubini] sometimes sings at the organ in a falsetto, which is scandalous, not only because he can actually do that with his voice', but because the style of singing directly contradicted the *Constitutions*.

Worst of all, he went into town 'for recreation', a non-specific term, which could cover a multitude of sins, and even if it referred simply to visiting friends or strolling through the streets, was still not permitted under the rules of the order. Altogether these reports provide an image of a young man who was not taking his duties too seriously, or following the rules of poverty or obedience, but who was intent on enjoying his life in Narni.[4]

Though Father Stefano's answer has not survived, he must have protested against the Father General's critical comments very vigorously, because Calasanz's next letter a week later was much sterner: 'I would have been better pleased if you had made a simple excuse. You should be happy that I was told of this matter as I had requested ... It was not done out of spite, but because I requested it.'[5] The father general always asked visitors to the other schools to let him know what they saw and thought of the local staff. The next letter from Calasanz buried the reproof in the midst of the usual school matters: 'As for those boys who come to the piazza in front of the school especially to play football, I think you should inform the governor ... I recommend that you observe our rules and have another look at the warning I sent you in the last few days.'[6]

Father Stefano was not the only member who found the strict rules difficult to follow. Several members who came under his influence and were later transferred elsewhere began to cause problems in their new postings. One of the most notorious was Father Nicolò Maria Gavotti, for instance, who years later would indulge his appetite for luxury unreservedly at the expense of the order. Gavotti wrote a lengthy and almost incoherent letter to Calasanz in February 1629. After a lengthy rant against the father provincial, Francesco Castelli, whom he accused of eating different food from everyone else ('today the others were given a salad, while he had a fatty tuna, which I saw hidden under his serviette when I was passing through the refectory') he blamed all his troubles on his mother's behaviour:

Father, I confess my lack of humility, which is caused by some problems I had with my mother. During the one and a half years that I lived near her I didn't talk to her more than four times, and only went once to her house, when she was sick; this was because she did not want to take care of the house and my brothers properly, and also because she wanted to come every morning before daybreak to our church, because if she came later in the morning Father Antonio Rodriguez, her confessor, deprived her of communion, and she could go for two days without eating anything, and this would result in severe indigestion. Each year therefore she would fall mortally ill and be obliged to spend a great deal, [so] ... I developed a great hatred of her ... and one day I told her that from my point of view she might as well be dead and I didn't want to know anything about it ...

That everything that followed could be attributed to his mother's behaviour seems unlikely. Gavotti would later spend a fortune – though not his own – on his clothing and on donkey-loads of food, but for now he was suffering, and complaining to the father general:

I've been doing spiritual exercises in Genoa now for two weeks suffering from a terrible headache, and I also suffer from pains of flatulence; and some days the pains are so great ... but I am still forced to eat harmful foods like chestnuts, vegetables and other windy things, and when I sometimes leave these things on my plate the father provincial takes it badly and has me punished, calling me sensual ... I'm still dressed for summer and I don't dare say anything, and I have to wash not only our shirts but also those of the novices, as well as the plates and soup bowls, and I suffer greatly from the cold, especially on the feet, which causes me great pain, but I have decided not to mention it ... so maybe the Lord will have mercy and console me in another life, for I am ready to suffer everything for his love, especially knowing that I am innocent, while begging Your Reverence to let me wear socks, which would somewhat lighten my pain.

But I will just mention to you a consolation which the Lord provided last Saturday morning, 27 January. While I was praying, all troubled and afflicted, I heard a voice which said to me, 'Be of good faith, for the Father General wants you to come to Rome in spring,' which news I heard with incredible joy. I beg you to advise me whether this is true or not by consoling me with a letter, and I also beg you not to let the provincial know anything that I have written, because we were recently told that those who wrote to you directly would pay the price, so I beg you to write to me secretly by enclosing it with a letter to Marco Antonio Corcione, who will give it to me without arousing the suspicions of the provincial.[7]

Given that Father Calasanz was superior to the provincial, it does not seem to have occurred to Gavotti that his disobedience in writing directly to the general would be detected all the sooner, and that his preoccupation with food and the style of cloak to be worn over his habit was hardly likely to endear him to his sober superior. Calasanz reacted by sending Gavotti, not to Rome as the heavenly voice had predicted, but to Naples, where, by the end of the year, he had become 'individual companion'[8] to Cherubini. Particular friendships were not permitted within the order, but the term 'individual companion' suggests a level of intimacy well beyond the acceptable within the order. Whatever their precise relationship, Gavotti and Cherubini's behaviour had much in common and their friendship would endure until death.

Around that time Calasanz reproved Father Stefano again, this time for wearing unnecessarily luxurious and fashionable clothes. In the interim, however, he had promoted Stefano to take charge of the prestigious new foundation of La Duchesca in Naples, opened a few months earlier as a result of Father Melchiorre Alacchi's canvassing. The fathers were supposed to wear 'a black cassock down to the feet, with a single opening at the chest, closed with wooden buttons, and a coat to the ankles of the same coarse black cloth as horse blankets are made; with no socks and with closed sandals ... initially without shirts, but then on medical advice with very thick coarse shirts.'[9] Father Stefano, however, had his jacket cut quite differently, swooping low at the back, and rising indecently short at the front. A few months later he balked at the draughty sandals, and when Calasanz insisted, he requested permission to wear socks. The father general had let Cherubini have a certain amount of say over which staff he would receive at La Duchesca – such as Father Gavotti – and now Cherubini 'began to speak so absolutely of wanting this teacher or that, or that someone should come or leave, as though there were no general or provincial'.[10] He had clearly got above himself. The father provincial, Pietro Casani, was also based in Naples and there was tension between the pious but unworldly older man and his young, able but flawed headmaster. Calasanz often asked Father Stefano to sort out some organizational muddle which the provincial had created, or could not solve. In financial matters and fund-raising, too, the headmaster was outstanding. However, Calasanz was becoming increasingly concerned by Father Stefano's lack of observance, his penchant for 'recreation' and the example he was setting his pupils. He asked him to try to learn humility, suggesting he sweep out some of the classrooms as a start. Father Stefano, however, had no intention of acting as a cleaner.

The rules governing the teachers' behaviour were very clear:

Rule 20: Be very careful in your dealings with the pupils and with other children. Never touch them for any reason whatsoever, except in case of necessity. Do not make eye contact, nor indulge in any kind of familiarity.

Rule 21: Do not keep any of them back after the end of school, not even to sweep out the classrooms without the express permission of the superior.

Rule 22: Remember, even when alone in your own room, even at night, that blessed God can see you: so be modest.[11]

Father Stefano broke some of these rules, and he broke them with more than one pupil.

CHAPTER SIX

'The worst vice'

In the late 1990s Edward Stourton, himself a Catholic, wrote: 'In the Western Church – European and American – Catholicism is still about sex.'[1] He was referring primarily to the controversy stirred up by the advent of contraception and Aids, but by then sex had at least become a subject of conversation and debate. In seventeenth-century Italy, however, sexual desire and activity outside the marital bed were unacceptable. Subterfuge and suppression were the official response. The story of Leonardo Cerusi, a Neapolitan groom in the service of Cardinal Medici, demonstrates this attitude. During the freezing winter of 1582, Cerusi, ironically known as *Il Letterato* because he was illiterate, was distressed at the sight of abandoned children dying of cold and hunger in the streets. He rescued some of them and, in order to raise alms to feed them, became a street sweeper. Eventually Cardinal Federico Borromeo gave him a grant and Cerusi founded the *Fanciulli Spersi*, the Lost Children, providing education, bed and board for 150 children, until his death in 1595 (three years after Calasanz had arrived in Rome).

One day, Cerusi, walking through the streets, was suddenly overwhelmed with lust. Desperate that he could not control his physical passions, and noticing a nearby receptacle of boiling water he decided 'to overcome the heat of temptation by that of boiling water' and plunged the offending member into the pot. The result was that he 'seriously offended those parts of his body which refused to obey reason'. Unsurprisingly he was ill for several months thereafter.[2] These actions were described by his biographer with glowing praise, and that such a drastic solution could be described in laudatory terms underlines the depths of disgust for bodily functions – and especially sexual desire – that religious fervour could engender.

A colleague of Calasanz's in the early years of the century, Giovanni Leonardi, was particularly praised for his modesty: 'He never let anyone see even his foot or an arm naked,' wrote Father Pietro Casani several years later in response to a request for information about Leonardi's potential sanctity, 'and for every little thing, even though he was old, his face blushed a virginal red.'[3] These were considered to be positive characteristics in an applicant for beatification.

Calasanz, in common with many reformers, including Pope Clement VIII, had always been preoccupied by the temptations of the flesh. The enforced celibacy of the large priestly population contrasted with the enormous number of prostitutes in Rome. It has been estimated that prostitution was one of the largest commercial sectors in a city whose population was around two-thirds male. The very day after his election, and only three weeks before Calasanz's arrival in Rome in February 1592, Clement banned prostitutes from living in Borgo, a quarter situated right by the Vatican palace. Two weeks later came another edict insisting that all such ladies move into Ortaccio, a small area between Arco di Portogallo and Piazza del Popolo, where lodgings simply could not be found for them all within the ten-day grace period. Furthermore innkeepers were not allowed to rent rooms to lone women without special authorization, 'not even [to] wives, daughters, sisters, aunts, nieces, sisters-in-law or any other kind of relation'. Unfortunately for the puritanical pope, the supposed celibacy of a large proportion of Rome's inhabitants did not prevent business from flourishing, even though the occasional pimp lost his nose, and girls their ears in punishment. Even 'decent' women were forbidden to wear revealing clothing, which included shirt sleeves, loosely woven garments that might permit a glimpse of flesh or hint at the figure below, preciously worked slippers that drew attention to a well-turned ankle, or even dress their hair so that any locks fell forward.[4]

Calasanz himself was disgusted by the proximity of women and within two weeks of his arrival in Rome had been dubbed 'the one who can't stand women'.[5] He thought it best that his teachers did not even visit their mothers and sisters in case they had friends visiting or servants with them who might lead members into temptation, for 'the devil is more cunning than humans and prepares nets and traps from afar'.[6] In an effort to eradicate all such temptation, Pope Clement ordered many bare breasts and feet of painted saints and madonnas to be covered up, cloths were strategically placed or painted on immodest statues and pictures to cover previously flaunted genitalia and, in 1599, he banned nude swimming in the Tiber. He ordered priests and prostitutes to wear their recognizable uniforms at all times – in the case of prostitutes, a yellow sleeve hanging down to the ground – so that any priest misbehaving could be spotted instantly. These edicts attempted to pre-empt heterosexual contact and Calasanz clearly approved, since his own way of life and the rules of his order tried to prevent all bodily contact, even accidental, with anyone.

If heterosexual sex was considered bad in the eyes of the Roman religious hierarchy of the time, sodomy was worse. Initially defined as 'any emission of semen not directed exclusively toward the procreation of a legitimate child within matrimony', which would cover activities such as anal sex or simply recreational sex, sodomy gradually came to mean purely homosexual intercourse, although the term 'homosexual' was not used in English until the 1890s.[7] The first laws flatly outlawing homosexual relations were passed under the Emperor Justinian in the late sixth century, but nearly all legislation in the following centuries emanated from civic authorities, with the Church remaining aloof or unconcerned. The scale of transgressions can be judged by the punishments recommended in an eighth-century penitential of Pope Saint Gregory III: three years' penance for a priest who went hunting; a mere one year for sexual acts committed between males. Presumably because it was so common. One of the leading historians of the subject writes that during the early Middle Ages, 'in some areas the mere fact of having taken Orders seems to have rendered one liable to the suspicion of being a "sodomite"'.[8] However, the climate of relative tolerance changed and the Lateran Council of 1179 prescribed degradation or confinement in a monastery for clerics found guilty of unlawful sexual practices. Thomas Aquinas placed sodomy with masturbation and bestiality as one of the 'unnatural vices' and through the thirteenth and fourteenth centuries secular legislation became far more severe, usually involving castration, stoning or burning alive. The Church, however, still remained far more lenient than the state. According to sociologist David F. Greenberg, until the Counter-Reformation, 'urbane, sophisticated members of the Italian elite – both secular and ecclesiastical – considered [sodomy] a peccadillo'.[9] However, the atmosphere began to change. In Venice, for example, during the fifteenth century, civic authorities became increasingly concerned that, in the words of a modern Italian historian, 'a homosexual subculture was becoming a real threat'.[10] The Council of Ten began to pursue sexual offenders with increasing vigour, but frequently found themselves stymied by their inability to prosecute anybody who had taken the tonsure, which included even the lowest ranks of clerics. A letter written to the pope in 1408 complained that it was proving difficult to eliminate sodomy while clerics were initiating such activity. 'Case after case indicates that the Ten's fears of clerics as initiators of homosexual relationships had considerable basis,' wrote historian Guido Ruggiero. 'Clerics were perceived as a serious problem, seducing young men into homosexual relationships without serious fear of punishment.'[11]

Protestant propaganda played on the perceived popularity of sodomy within the ranks of the Catholic hierarchy, and reformers such as Luther noted that not only was sodomy the predominant Italian sin but, according to a recent historian, it was represented as 'a sexual behaviour characteristic of bishops, cardinals, and most of all, popes'.[12]

In 1432 Florence, concerned by its apparent prevalence, had even instituted 'an innovative judiciary magistracy solely to pursue and prosecute sodomy', the Office of the Night, although this was closed down in 1502 when it was realized that the existence of the Office itself was being perceived as an admission of the gravity of the situation. By then, however, the German verb 'to sodomize' had become established as 'florenzen' and Protestant writers were convinced of the primacy of Italy and the Catholic Church in the spread of the activity.[13]

But by the time Calasanz arrived in Rome the Protestant Reformation and the fight back by the Catholic Church after the Council of Trent had ensured a new rigour and a pronounced hardening of attitudes towards such behaviour. In January 1600 Filippo Galletti, one of the Medici agents in Rome, reported back to the Tuscan court that Friar Cipriano Boscolino, who had carried a cross in church processions respectably for many years, had been accused of sodomy. 'Without a trial and without a chance of defending himself, he was hanged and then burnt forthwith.' At least once a year someone, priest or layman, was executed in Rome by the secular authorities for this suspected crime.[14] Throughout Italy the penalties for 'unnatural activity' were draconian. In 1608, for instance, in Sicily, the chief hangman who had executed many homosexuals over the years, was himself executed for the same offence.[15] And those who had taken holy orders were expected to behave better than the rest of society in all respects. Calasanz himself wrote, 'It is better not to have been born than not to be a good priest, for sin in a priest is far worse than in a layman.'[16]

All opportunities for temptation were to be avoided. Teachers were never to go out alone and they were never to visit each other's bedrooms under pain of three days with no wine at dinner.[17] As the Piarist Order spread throughout Italy and then across the Alps to central Europe the schools fell under various rulers and legal jurisdictions. All of them were unanimous in their hostility to what Calasanz – and others – would call 'the worst vice'.[18] Catholic teaching to the present day considers the homosexual act to be an 'intrinsic moral evil' and even 'the inclination itself must be seen as an objective disorder', although if recent surveys cited on television claim that as many as 48 per cent of priests may be gay.[19]

Sexual sin in seventeenth-century Italy ranged from non-procreational sex within marriage via extra-marital heterosexual activity to homosexuality and sex with children. The sin lay less with the victim, than with the damage being done to the soul of the perpetrator, as a recent historian on the subject has noted, 'Unlike in antiquity, Christian theology's understanding of male superiority did not license penetration *per se*, whether women or boys were the object.'[20] For a priest, of course, all sexual activity was contrary to his vows to God. The concern was always for the sinner, the priest, never for the victim, however young; a reaction that still seems to have retained some echoes in the modern hierarchy's reaction to clerical scandals.

Teaching and the priesthood offered unprecedented opportunities for access to children and the combination of easy availability of young boys, celibacy and immunity from civic legal processes provided a tempting mixture. The best-known *Apologia* for schoolmasters falling for their pupils was published in Florence, probably in 1651. It recommended boys aged between nine and eighteen, 'although there is no fixed rule, since some retain their boyishness longer, and others fade early, just as some full, round little boys excite you from infancy on'.[21] Public opinion during the Renaissance held teachers to be 'notorious sodomites' and civic authorities, for instance in Venice, tried to restrict teaching to public halls and daylight hours in an effort to restrict opportunities for temptation.[22] Calasanz insisted that teachers were never to be alone in a classroom with a single pupil; his *Constitutions* and *Rules*, heavily influenced and indeed partially copied from the Jesuits' own legislation, show a clear awareness of the dangers. Our twenty-first century preoccupations with priestly sexual misdemeanours do not impose an alien and modern morality on an earlier period with a different scale of ethics. Far from being anachronistic, these concerns were of even greater importance in Calasanz's time, when society was far more aware of, and condemnatory of, sin and temptation than our own.[23]

Calasanz was clearly aware of the possibilities for temptation, and seems to have had particular concerns about the situation in Naples. On 9 September 1628 he wrote to Father Casani: 'For the last two or three months I've been worried, and this feeling has been growing rapidly, that the enemy will not have to try very hard to find different ways of destroying this Order; but I am most worried about the worst vice, which on its own would be enough to ruin our Order, since one can always find solutions to other problems.'[24] The enemy he worried about was presumably the devil. In the vocabulary of the legislation of the time, sodomy was commonly referred to as 'the sin against nature', 'the most infamous deed', or a similarly vague but condemnatory expression. 'The worst vice' – *'il vitio pessimo'* – can only refer to sodomy, or if pupils were involved, sex with children. Even the twentieth-century Piarist editor of the letter, who in general avoided any comment that was not purely hagiographic, commented in a footnote that Calasanz was 'trying to combat the deadly vice of impurity'. Just over a year later the father general's suspicions were confirmed.

The year 1629 had started ominously. Near Castel Sant'Angelo, the massive fortress on the Tiber originally built as a mausoleum by Emperor Hadrian and reinforced through the years as an impregnable bolt-hole for popes in danger, a deep ravine had suddenly opened up in the ground. 'A terrible and fetid stink emanates from the crack, and great noises can be heard deep down,' wrote Calasanz to Cherubini. 'Many people cannot believe it, but I'm only writing about what I know truthfully.'[25] Although spring should have been well advanced by March, the surrounding hills were still covered in snow, and it frequently hailed in Rome. Then a few days later a strange and ominous sight was seen in the sky. Again Calasanz described it in a letter to his close colleague in Naples:

Last Tuesday an extraordinary phenomenon appeared above Rome. It was a circle in the air, almost the size of the whole of Rome, greyish-blue in colour with four huge globes, brighter than the circle, and the centres of these four globes were rainbow-coloured. The spectacle lasted for an hour and nearly all the inhabitants of Rome saw it. Along with most of our members I went up to the top loggia to see it better, and around the sun there was another circle of the same colour but much smaller, which did not last as long as the main one. May the Lord make it a sign of his mercy and bless us.

Calasanz included the only illustration of his entire correspondence, along with 'a horrible prediction' from Germany.[26]

Later, the phenomenon in the skies above Rome must have seemed like an omen foretelling the events that were about to engulf the order.

After the unusually wintry spring of that year, the temperature rose to an equally abnormal summer. Throughout Rome, wrote Calasanz, 'the hospitals are full and people are dying in great numbers'. Hundreds more beds were placed in the cloisters of the Hospital of Santo Spirito and were immediately filled with people dying from the heat. Three cardinals also succumbed, and at the end of July Calasanz wrote to Father Stefano warning him not to take on any new novices at present because the change in clothing during the great heat would be enough to make them very ill. In an incongruous throwaway line he also advised the Neapolitan head, 'Be careful that in the presence of children nothing is said or done that is not appropriate.'[27]

As the summer passed and the temperature fell to a bearable level, torrential rains washed away what was left of the crops.[28] But the terrible year was not over yet. A letter arrived from one of the Neapolitan teachers begging to be transferred elsewhere, 'for here it is worse than when I was a soldier and engulfed in a great multitude of different vices and sins.'[29] Father Calasanz wrote back with soothing and spiritually uplifting advice.

Father Stefano Cherubini, son and brother of eminent papal lawyers, headmaster of the Neapolitan Pious School, accepted member of Neapolitan society, closely trusted colleague of the father general and recipient of the lengthiest and greatest number of letters from him, had been abusing his pupils in the order's largest school. Although it is not known when it had first started, the few comments in Calasanz's correspondence indicated that hints had begun to reach Rome, so perhaps it had been going on for some time. Why else would he suddenly voice his concerns about 'the worst vice' or warn about inappropriate speech before children?

'The devil persecuted the headmaster in Naples and with all his force and malice made him seek out impure friendships with schoolboys [*amicitia impura con scuolari*],' wrote Father Vincenzo Berro, Calasanz's last secretary and constant companion, some years later in his *Notes on the Foundation*. Initially, Father Casani, 'along with two other main priests of the house attempted to remedy the situation by paternal advice'.[30] The arrogant and well-connected Stefano Cherubini shrugged off the older fathers' concerns. Most of the letters dealing with this original complaint have been excised from the archive, either snatched by the Cherubini family in a partially successful attempt to cover up the scandal, or burnt in the big cleansing bonfire that sanitized the archives in 1659. Father Casani's original letter, for instance, is missing, along with Calasanz's reply.

The first contemporaneous document still existing is Father Casani's next letter, which he wrote secretly and posted under someone else's seal in order to avoid interception by Cherubini or his family. He tells how when Father Stefano received Calasanz's letter telling him that his activities had been discovered, he exploded into action. Rather than denying the accusation, or confessing, his immediate priority was to discover who had informed on him. 'Barely had I received, and read the letters from Your Reverence,' wrote Casani, 'than our friend [a coded reference to Cherubini] burst in on me all furious and breathing fire, and firstly he interrogated me as to whether I had written to Your Reverence about this business.' Casani had told the father general, but he himself had heard the rumour from a layman, Signor Salvatore Cesario, who was staying at the school, who in turn had heard it from a priest, probably not a Piarist. Neither the layman, nor the priest, obviously wished to be identified, but the participants' reactions – and later events – reveal that the rumour was not simply an insubstantiated piece of gossip. Father Casani thought Father Stefano was over-reacting only in order to create an impression of wounded innocence. When his physical threats subsided, 'he began to bluster about what he was going to do, and say, and write to Signor Flavio, and order him to clear up the truth, and that he was being wrongly persecuted, it was all calumny'. This threat to bring his brother and the whole weight of Rome's legal might down on the order if they exposed him meant that Calasanz would be facing a major crisis. Casani reluctantly advised his superior to ignore the whole matter. 'Since we have promised to keep Signor Salvatore and the priest secret, we cannot reveal them, so Your Reverence must show yourself to be calmed, and advise him that in future he must proceed with great caution and not give the slightest occasion to enemies of our religion to come out with such rumours.' An approaching wedding of a relation offered a good pretext to remove him as soon as possible, and Father Casani suggested that 'the upcoming break in the weather, and the state of the roads, along with the arrival of winter, and the arrival of rainy times' could be used to transfer Cherubini speedily.[31]

At the same time Calasanz received another letter from Casani, one written under duress, with Cherubini standing over his desk and effectively dictating every word. This one contained only protestations about the headmaster's purity and innocence.

Father Berro, who knew the protagonists but was writing years later, commented that 'the evil weighed very heavily [on Calasanz] both for the scandal and the offence to God, and seeing the obstinacy of the criminal he ordered that a trial be held with great care, and sent to call him to Rome with all the trappings of honour.'[32] Calasanz was forced to move carefully. Writing to the father general without permission, or failing to pray with sufficient humility could entail an instant penalty of ten days' incarceration on bread and water, but sexual misconduct with children was approached with less immediate punishment and with far more caution. Calasanz did not seem to fear making a false accusation, only to avoid arousing Cherubini's ire and public opprobrium. Father Berro, like many modern priests faced with evidence of paedophilia, mentioned the public scandal before the offence to God. Perhaps it was obvious to him, but nevertheless, the hierarchy of anxieties seems distorted. And as for any potential damage to the victims – this was never mentioned.

Cherubini did not rely only on Father Casani's letters to exculpate himself. His own letter started with cries of outrage that anyone should accuse him of such a thing: 'It pierced my heart so deeply that if blessed God had not helped me, I would have done something mad, or been locked up for ever.' It pained him that Calasanz, who had always shown him 'paternal affection', especially since the death of his own father three years earlier, should give any credence to such rumours. Obviously he was innocent and 'all thirty-six fathers and brothers in this house can bear witness to my actions, as can all the patrons and the Congregation members and many others'. Unfortunately for him, many could, but not with the evidence he anticipated.

Cherubini also threatened Calasanz, reminding him that his reputation and that of the order were inextricably linked, and warning him that both would be besmirched if the matter became public. 'I have no doubt that a trial could be brought before the Pope,' he wrote and hinted at the terrible consequences that could result if he brought his influence to bear in this matter.[33] But his overweening concern, outweighing all other considerations, was to track down the informer. 'It is essential that you tell me which false tale-bearer told you verbally or wrote to you with these calumnious accusations. If it was from a letter, please send it to me, so that I can find out the truth ... I will discover who it was, and I will have him punished in such a manner that he will remain an example to others!' No wonder Casani, Signor Cesario and the unknown priest were so reluctant to be discovered.

Father Stefano could not let it rest. A few weeks later, he was still bullying Calasanz to reveal the identity of the tale-bearer:

I can see no other remedy, other than that Your Reverence tell me who is the enemy, so that I can defend myself, and decide on the road to take, to discover his aims and intentions, so that I can ruin his plans. And in case Your Reverence does not wish to give the details to me, you could tell Flavio, my brother, so that if necessary he can deal with it in the correct way, so that we can remedy the situation without offending anyone.

He did have some suspicions, but these were wrong: 'I believe it's that priest who was annoyed with me because I refused to lend him 20 ducats,' he raged. His defiance was absolute: 'I will not stop living as I have done in the past, since anyone with whom I have had any dealings is greatly uplifted by the experience.'[34] At this stage it seems he still had no idea that the father provincial was deeply involved and far from supportive, whatever his protestations to Cherubini face to face.

These wild rantings made life very unpleasant in the Neapolitan school, with the headmaster prowling the corridors looking for his enemies, and in Rome where Father Stefano's threats to involve his brother and the papal court were clearly serious. The Cherubini family was powerful in its own right, and behind it, should more heavyweight backing be needed, lay the even more important Ludovisi family.

The previous Pope, Gregory XV, had been a Ludovisi and had left his family in possession of great wealth. While the Barberini Pope, an erstwhile ambassador from Rome to Paris, was generally considered to be pro-French, the current head of the Ludovisi clan, Cardinal Ludovico Ludovisi, who had been a papal nephew under the last regime, led the opposing Spanish faction. International European politics were reflected in the Vatican court, and the pro-Jesuit Ludovisi family could not be ignored, even if the current head of their family no longer sat on the papal throne.[35] Only a few years later the cardinal would be threatening to depose Pope Urban himself for heresy and at that point outright conflict would become impossible to avoid, leading eventually to the expulsion of the Ludovisi cardinal from Rome. But over an issue such as the sexual misbehaviour of a junior member of the Cherubini family, the Barberini Pope and nephews would not be prepared to face a fight against such powerful forces. Where religious practice and regulations, morality or the safety of children ran contrary to clerical careers or family prestige, the latter would win for many centuries yet.

So taking Father Casani's secret advice, the father general decided to let the matter die, and wrote to this effect to Cherubini: 'There is no one in the world today that wishes more than I that this rumour would disappear and that no one would speak of it any more, because I have at heart the honour of the Order and of the individual people in it more than anyone else … The Lord make everything disappear as I wish and pray to his divine Majesty.'[36]

The father general heeded Casani's warnings and trod warily. Father Stefano remained in Naples for another year, business seemed to go on as usual. However, secretive complaints must have begun to filter through to Rome once more for Calasanz again remonstrated with Father Cherubini 'with the true love and heart of your spiritual father'. He limited his criticisms to the headmaster's unacceptable failure to attend regulation prayer sessions and once again to the luxurious diet on offer in the refectory in Naples, but underlying these words of counsel neither man was likely to have forgotten Cherubini's more serious transgressions.[37]

Finally, after a traumatic year for the Neapolitan school, and at the suggestion of the father provincial, Calasanz wrote to Cherubini in understated terms: 'I have heard that where I would like total agreement and peace there is some perturbation amongst our members,' he began, and went on to make a tempting proposal. The recalcitrant headmaster would be transferred, but in order to achieve this with his agreement – as was of course essential in order to prevent retribution from his family – he would be offered a major promotion. The most recent biographer of Calasanz, Father Severino Giner Guerri, one of the first to acknowledge Cherubini's actions – although downplaying their importance in the history of the order – calls this 'a very handy solution in ecclesiastical circles: *promoveatur ut amoveatur*' (promotion for avoidance).[38] Father Stefano was to be kept away from tempting contact with young boys (in theory) by being made procurator or visitor general for the whole order. As such, he was to travel from school to school, commenting, inspecting and criticizing. It was exactly the same promotion as Father Melchiorre Alacchi had received after similar accusations with regard to novices were made against him a bare three years earlier. 'As you have helped the one house, now I'd like you to help all the other houses as visitor general,' wrote Calasanz to Father Stefano without any apparent trace of irony. 'Start with Norcia where you can stay for a fortnight or a month as you see convenient, then Narni, then Moricone, then Poli, then Frascati, and around spring you can come to Rome.'[39] Cherubini was reluctant to accept and Calasanz was bombarded with letters from important Neapolitans requesting that he be allowed to stay as headmaster. A terse response to Duke Lotario Conti noted, 'I have taken on board what you say about Father Stefano, and I am absolutely sure that this letter was procured by Father Stefano, along with many others I have received, to make me reconsider and let him stay in Naples, which he is leaving for his own good and that of the Order.'[40] To Signora Angelica Falcone, sister of the well-known but dissolute painter Aniello, Calasanz wrote that, contrary to rumour, 'While I am alive [Father Stefano] will never return to Naples.'[41] Over the next few weeks he inundated Cherubini with instructions for his first official visit, perhaps tempting him by showing him the power he would wield as a visitor general – in Norcia, for instance, Calasanz asked him to check each teacher's room, then interview each member of staff, including the novices, and carry out diplomatic visits to important local citizens who had voiced some complaint about the Pious Schools. 'Make sure that each house you leave is well set up in the observance of our rules,' he concluded.[42] Cherubini was reconciled to his promotion and wrote gleefully to Father Alacchi – his fellow in controversy – who was again awaiting a ship to carry him on pilgrimage: 'I need many prayers, for all the matters of the Order must now pass through my hands.'[43] Presumably Calasanz felt that the scandal had to be defused and Father Stefano placated and removed at all costs. The contemporary Catholic Church's practice of moving a suspected paedophile away from the original scene of the crime for fear of the ensuing scandal and the backlash clearly has long antecedents.

Meanwhile Calasanz, desperate to keep the matter secret and not involve the authorities, but aware that the rumours were continuing to bubble away,[44] initiated a detailed investigation, and sent Father Giovanni Garzia Castiglia, the mild and gentle headmaster of the Frascati school, to Naples 'to interrogate the boys and adolescents involved about Father Stefano degli Angeli, against whom many accusations of impurity and ill-renown have been made by the fathers of that house'.[45] The plan was to hush up the whole matter. 'I want you to know,' he wrote to Garzia, 'that Your Reverence's sole aim is to cover up [*cuprir*] this great shame in order that it does not come to the notice of our superiors, otherwise our organization, which has enjoyed a good reputation until now, would lose greatly.' He advised Garzia to tell the other teachers that concealment was the best solution for the good of the whole order and that they should obey their superiors by ceasing to mention Cherubini's activities, while at the same time telling

Cherubini's important lay supporters that the man had been promoted because the father general thought so highly of him.[46] It is a familiar strategy: hide the problem for fear of public scandal, and force those uneasy with this solution to go along with it by assuring them it is for the best. A shocking letter written by a man later sanctified by the pope for his contribution to the education of children, but one whose sentiments have been replicated by those in authority throughout the history of paedophilia in the Church. The patron saint of schools and education was actively covering up child abuse in his own schools.

A few days later, in case the point had not been taken, he wrote to Garzia once more: 'I want this business to be kept quiet, which will benefit both the party under investigation and our Order.' Calasanz continued that 'it seems best to me, that if we are allowed to be the judges of this case, we will not permit it to come into the hands of outsiders.'[47] A week later another letter followed, ordering Father Garzia to burn any incriminating paperwork for fear of it falling into the wrong hands.[48] Evidently Father Garzia missed some documents.

When Cherubini heard of Garzia's trip to Naples, he immediately wrote him an ostensibly friendly letter:

Be my defender and do not let yourself be persuaded by others until you have heard my reasons ... Some may be motivated by disorganized emotional reasoning, and not consider the evils that may ensue both for individuals and for the common good; enough, I know you understand my meaning ... Your Reverence knows where I stand on this, but if matters are not dealt with amongst ourselves with loving kindness, I doubt but that iron will be needed to sort them out.[49]

The velvet glove certainly covered a mailed fist.

Nevertheless, Father Garzia's report, apparently detailed and damning, was written over the next couple of months. On its completion he decided not to entrust it to the normal postal service. Instead he asked a friendly lawyer, Don Felice de Totis, who was journeying to Rome, to take the dossier with him, under strict instructions that it be handed to Father Calasanz in person. It is possible that Don Felice was unaware of the contents, but likely that he was a friend of the Cherubini family since he worked in the Apostolic Chamber as a prestigious papal notary, side-by-side with Stefano's brother, Flavio. He was friendly with Calasanz and had provided him with legal advice on how to get a permit to send Father Melchiorre Alacchi to the Indies and Japan, probably the furthest point in the world at that time and an appropriate distance from Rome for the troublesome father, although he would in fact never get that far. A few years later de Totis's men would be permitted by the cardinal chamberlain to carry arms while protecting a lucrative tax concession on wine, but he would later end up in prison for reasons which are unclear, begging Cardinal Barberini for release.[50]

On his arrival in Rome, bearing the precious burden, Don Felice went straight to the Piarist headquarters in Piazza de' Massimi. Unfortunately, Calasanz was momentarily hearing Mass in the adjacent church of San Pantaleo. In a hurry to get to his next appointment the lawyer handed the packet to a charming young priest, who assured him that he would place it directly into the hands of the father general. That priest was the son of his erstwhile colleague, Laerzio Cherubini, and the brother of his current colleague, Flavio, and it seems unlikely that Don Felice would have failed to recognize him.

It was a scene straight from a popular farce. No sooner had Don Felice left than Father Stefano, who was spending a few days in the Roman headquarters, presumably between trips around Italy as visitor general, ripped open the package he had just been handed. Now he had the names and statements of all those who had accused him. His rage and vengeance knew no bounds, and he ran immediately to summon his brother. Later that night there was a confrontation, and faced with threats of physical violence and legal action against all concerned, Calasanz caved in. Father Stefano was to receive a brief absolving him of all crimes, and all stain against his honour; in return he agreed to restrain his vengeance against the tale-bearers.[51] All the correspondence concerning the affair was to be removed from Calasanz's office and handed over to the Cherubini family 'where it was torn up or burnt,'[52] according to Father Berro's account, leaving a gap in the archive.

According to Father Berro's account, some of the Piarist fathers were so incensed at Cherubini's escape that they complained to Cardinal Antonio Barberini, the Pope's brother, 'that something so serious should be allowed to pass without punishment'. The cardinal, a Capuchin known as the most religious of the Barberini family, immediately summoned Calasanz. The father general knelt patiently before the cardinal to hear 'what was not so much a religious humiliation as a storm of invective',[53] before he managed to take the cardinal aside to a private room and explain to him that he had been ordered to look the other way by Cardinal Francesco Barberini himself, the pope's nephew, who in turn had been asked to act by the Ludovisi family. Cardinal Antonio immediately apologized and the matter was closed. It is clear from this account that the Barberini – and certainly Cardinals Antonio and Francesco – knew the truth of the matter. Influence triumphed over morality.

Father Stefano wrote triumphally to Father Giovanni Garzia Castiglia, who had carried out the investigation in Naples, attaching a copy of the 'absolution' he had received from the father general, and asking Father Garzia to show it to everyone, Piarist and layman, to prove his innocence.[54] Those who knew better must have ground their teeth in despair but, tied by obedience to the ancient father general, they swallowed their feelings and kept silent. For the time being.

'Prayer and penitence have been cast aside'

Father Melchiorre Alacchi's pilgrimage to Spain lasted just over a year, during which time Calasanz was preoccupied by Cherubini's activities in Naples. Having fallen out, typically, with his colleagues, Father Melchiorre returned alone and all too quickly to Italy. Although Calasanz was tolerant of the wayward Sicilian – many in the order would say too tolerant – the other fathers must have despaired at the swift return of another troublemaker.

No sooner had Father Melchiorre's feet touched the solid ground of Sardinia on the way back from Spain than he arranged a series of meetings with the municipal counsellors of Cagliari, the capital, and with the viceroy, the intricately named Don Jerónimo Pimentel y Zúñiga, Marquis of Bayona. But Father Pietro Casani's 'Memorial of the Inconveniences', which highlighted the problems that the lack of trained staff were beginning to cause, especially with regard to the quality of the teaching, had recently been received and digested in Rome. As a result, the pope banned the order from opening new foundations without specific permission in each case, and so the Sardinian negotiations came to naught.[1]

Father Melchiorre took ship for Sicily and went to visit his home village of Naro. Again he opened discussions for a Piarist foundation; again the father general had to remind him that there were no teachers available.[2] He seemed incapable of comprehending that further expansion was simply unacceptable for the time being. Father Melchiorre travelled on to Naples where the swirl of allegations and counter-threats surrounding the accused headmaster had just reached crisis point. He found the school reduced to squalor, so rapidly had the numbers of pupils and staff outgrown the facilities, and so distracted were the staff by the disputes between the headmaster Cherubini and the provincial Casani. Father Melchiorre threw himself into negotiations for the purchase of a neighbouring property and was soon criticized by the father general for outspending the budget. In the centre of the courtyard he arranged for a drinking fountain to be built, with ingenious piping to bring the water into the kitchen and refectory. This offended Father Calasanz, who declared he was unhappy with the ostentatious image the fountain would convey, and the provincial, who declared the waterworks trivial, superfluous and more appropriate for laymen, and had them ripped up. Father Melchiorre fired off a sour letter to Rome pointing out that any debts incurred came not from his building work, but extraordinarily from the excavations, which the father provincial had been carrying out under the new house, where he had apparently had 'grottos and caves' dug in a fruitless search for occult treasure.[3]

Father Melchiorre had left Italy on pilgrimage under threat of expulsion and disgrace, 'in order not to disturb and infect the Order any more', and the Genoese provincial had been charged in his absence with ongoing investigations into several unresolved and unsavoury incidents.[4] Although the investigation had failed to produce concrete evidence (possibly because more immediate events in Naples had taken priority), nevertheless, Father Melchiorre was not popular. To arrive back and start arranging impossible foundations, and commissioning building work that he had no right to be organizing, aggravated his colleagues. Having characteristically antagonized everyone except the father general, he requested permission to leave once more on pilgrimage, a desire strongly encouraged by all around him. As the weeks passed, even Calasanz became increasingly irritated, and almost every week came another frustrated outburst: 'With his pride and impetuosity, I am inclining towards giving him permission to go to Jerusalem and be fervent there. By being here and not behaving with due obedience, he is starting to create resentment of his past.' The events on the ship, Alacchi's behaviour on the way to Carcare, and the resulting death of the student and accusations of breaking confessional confidences had not been forgotten by some. 'Father Melchiorre will only be quiet when he is dead.' 'I wish the Lord would give him a bit of supernatural judgement – natural judgement has got him into this predicament.'[5]

On 29 November 1629, with great relief, Father Calasanz wrote out a licence permitting Father Melchiorre to travel to the Holy Land and the Eastern Indies for as long as possible – in fact, the longer the better. After a short sickness, Melchiorre embarked for Venice where he hoped to find a ship to take him eastwards. He stopped off for three weeks en route at Ancona, where naturally he was unable to prevent himself from entering into negotiations for a foundation. This one would in fact be approved by the local council in June 1630 and eventually opened three years later. Papal bans seemed to have no effect on Father Melchiorre.

He arrived in Venice in early March 1630. Twenty-five years earlier Venice had been placed under interdict by the Vatican. A canon of Vicenza, Scipione Saraceno, had been arrested for scornfully tearing down a public announcement bearing the seal of St Mark, Venice's patron saint, and for other offences against public decency, which had underlined his moral turpitude. Another Venetian clergyman, Abbot Brandolino of Nervesa, was accused of sorcery, incest and murder, and also apprehended. The newly appointed Pope Paul V took great offence that the Republic of Venice should infringe his jurisdiction over the clergy by imprisoning these two men. The Republic's senate had also recently passed a law limiting the right of laymen to donate lands to the Church, to which the pope had strongly objected, since it clearly had major financial implications for the Church's financial and landholding future. Negotiations failed and in April 1606 the pope had excommunicated the entire signoria and placed Venice under interdict. This was an extremely serious matter: no sacraments, no Masses, no baptisms, no marriages and no burials could be carried out. But instead of crumbling before the papal will as expected, Venice had given its clergy an ultimatum – ignore the pope and continue as usual, or leave Venetian territory. The Jesuits left. Other clergymen ignored the pope and continued with business as usual. Eventually, fearing that Venice might become Protestant, Rome had backed down and Venice claimed a great victory in defence of her independence. However, neither Venice nor Rome had enjoyed the fight, and the Republic remained suspicious of and alert to any hint of what it saw as papal interference. Gaspar Schoppe, author of Calasanz's special new Latin grammar method, was briefly arrested when passing through the territory, for possessing a copy of the controversial *Antiveneti* – a pamphlet that supported the pope in the conflict against Venice – by Tommaso Campanella (another friend of Calasanz). The Jesuits were kept out of Venice for fifty years after the interdict, and although the pope was permitted to send a nuncio, he was surrounded by spies, and even his gondolier submitted detailed reports of his activities every few days. When Galileo fell foul of Rome, his friends wrote from Venice to offer him sanctuary in a city where the papal writ had no force. And just to prove that it was in charge, Venice continued to imprison and even execute clergymen.

But by 1630 Venice was suffering economically. It was still a city with a great merchant tradition but had been excluded by England and Holland from lucrative markets in the Levant, while the Thirty Years War had destroyed much of Germany, which had been its main market. Constant conflict with the Turks and the outbreak of plague (which would see the population fall from 150,000 to 100,000) further isolated the city. The ruling Council of Ten became increasingly nervous of plots and conspiracies, and several innocent men whose actions seemed suspicious were hanged.

It was thus an insecure city in which Father Melchiorre Alacchi arrived in March 1630. He immediately visited the Bishop of Torcello, Monsignor Marco Zeni, who was impressed, as many important figures were initially, by the charming father, and appointed him as his confessor and clerical examiner. He was permitted to confess, preach and administer the sacraments throughout the diocese, including acting as confessor for a convent of enclosed nuns, while he prepared for his trip to the Holy Land.

But as Father Alacchi waited for his passage (although evidence is sparse that he was actually seeking one), bubonic plague broke out and all shipping ground to a halt. The contagion had entered northern Italy in September 1629 with the Hapsburg troops, who had marched down towards Mantua to participate in a quick war in support of one of the claimants to the disputed dukedom. A contemporary physician, Dr Tadino, noted, 'Most of these Germans are infected with plague because of their wantonness and their dirtiness', and commented on the 'unbearable odours due to the rotting straw whereon they sleep and die'. Doubtless the straw was full of fleas. Though Italian cities had well-organized committees and health magistrates, the German soldiers 'roamed without health passes' and inexorably the disease spread.[6] By October it had reached Milan where 60,000 died in six months. On 8 November the news reached Florence, and merchants and traffic coming in from the north were hastily banned. Father Francesco Castelli, the avowed enemy of the erratic Father Melchiorre Alacchi, was trying to get to Florence, but became trapped in Genoa initially by adverse winds, for several weeks. He complained bitterly about the breakdown in communications: 'I don't know if the plague in Susa and other places near Milan, where business has been completely ruined, is the reason for the late arrival of the post from Rome, because this morning, which is Saturday, I sent for the letters, and was told they had not yet arrived, which surprised me because the weather hasn't been that bad.' Eventually he managed to get through to Florence, 'all worn out and with his feet in rags', but only because he was able to rely on princely intercession from the ruler of Massa, who permitted him to pass in spite of the plague restrictions – thereby circumventing any attempts at a *cordon sanitaire*.[7]

In June 1630 the plague was discovered in the Papal States in Bologna, where nearly all the priests who tended the sick succumbed, leaving no one to administer the last rites.[8] It was drawing inexorably closer and closer to Rome. Calasanz's correspondence was badly affected, but he noted that 'the Spaniards are really suffering because they have no information at all because of the postal situation, and we are expecting all the Spanish cardinals to arrive in Rome but no one knows why.' Everyone was preparing for the inevitable by buying 'a kind of ball with holes all around it to put antidotes against the plague inside, while prayer and penitence have been cast aside'.[9] Though precautions delayed the spread of the disease, they proved to no avail in Tuscany; at the beginning of August a chicken merchant arrived at Trespiano, a few miles north of Florence on the road in from Bologna. He looked poorly and walked painfully, but he had gold coins, and a local resident offered him a bed. Within days, he and several residents of the house were dead, and although the bodies were removed and the possessions and bedding burned by the authorities, the contagion had already taken hold since other members of the family had moved away immediately the sickness had been diagnosed. Just down the road from the Piarist school in the centre of town a wool-maker fell sick. He had been farming out wool to the peasants in the countryside to spin and then selling it on at a great profit to Bologna.[10] From such small commercial temptations did the epidemic seize its foothold and then engulf Florence.

It was not known exactly what caused the plague – the microbe was not finally identified until 1894 – but it was thought to originate from poisonous miasmas and to be spread by physical contact or inhalation. Somehow it could clearly stick to skin, fur, letters or foodstuffs. Many believed, like Calasanz, 'that it must be the effect of some grave sin, so until the cause is removed, perhaps the effect will also remain',[11] and the inclination to cover all bases – spiritual and physical – in an attempt to find a remedy or a preventative is understandable. Pharmacists were ordered to stock up on important remedies, such as pearls and emeralds, which could be ground up into a curative powder, and also aloe, myrrh and saffron for mixing into anti-velenous creams. Vinegar, lime and sulphur were used for disinfection, but realistically it was acknowledged that the only true remedy was to get away fast, go far, and stay away for a long time. The rich often managed it – a contemporary chronicler of the Florentine epidemic estimated that only twenty-five wealthy people died, whereas thousands in the poorer quarters were afflicted.[12] The Piarist school in Florence, which had only just opened, was obliged to close its doors, and several of the fathers turned instead to nursing duties. In Carcare, near Genoa, Father Domenico Pizzardo and his colleague were already dead, infected while nursing the sick, and many houses and surrounding villages were abandoned as the population either died or fled and the harvest was abandoned for lack of manpower or will to bring it in.[13]

A week after Florence heard of the appearance of the plague in Milan, Rome reacted with a flurry of edicts ordering the suspension of trade with infected towns and the establishment of a top-ranking committee on health, headed by Cardinal Francesco Barberini, nephew of the pope, with real and immediate power, to meet twice-weekly and do all possible to avoid the infection. Pesthouses were opened outside the walls to keep the diseased secure, lists of infected cities were posted daily, goods and letters were treated with sulphurous smoke and vinegar baths before being permitted through, strict watch was kept at the gates with no exceptions made, at night a rope was stretched across the river to keep out water-borne traffic, and a hail of edicts was issued to keep potentially infectious refuse such as ashes, manure, pigs, dead cats and dogs, and rotting fruit off the streets. By the summer of 1630 schools were closed, meetings banned, prisons emptied. There was great tension throughout the city; Calasanz described the situation in December 1630:

We are in great fear that the plague may enter, for on the frontiers with Tuscany are many who are suffering from hunger and wish to enter the Papal States and since they are not permitted, they say, 'We are dying of hunger, so we may as well murder you,' and others say they refuse to leave, so we are afraid that through various means the infection will enter, although for the time being the city is free.

Prices, however, soared, as all imports were affected and people stockpiled grain and wine in order to avoid contact with others if the worst came to the worst. 'Everything that comes via Venice has more than doubled in price … and some things cannot be found at all.'[14] With the rise in prices came a fall in revenue as people cut back on their alms-giving and harvests remained unpicked. Calasanz began to worry that even if or when the post did make it through the health restrictions, he would not have enough money to pay for its receipt.[15] Throughout Italy each state closed its gates and harbours, mounted 'a most exquisite guard'[16] on its borders, especially against the roaming bands of deserters or disbanded soldiers on their way back home, and retreated behind its city walls to hunker down and try to escape the terrible epidemic.

Father Alacchi in Venice, however, continued to make preparations and specific demands of the father general:

Dearest Father, I wrote that you should send me a clock, which I promised someone in Sicily, but I've spent the money here. If you love me, send it to me. I also need a letter of recommendation, with an apostolic brief, and your official permission, authenticated with a Roman seal. My description [for the passport to travel to Jerusalem] is as follows: 'The priest Melchiorre is around thirty-nine years old with a small scar on his forehead, with brown hair and beard, of medium stature.' Do not send me bucolic companions, and send me a holy apostolic blessing.[17]

He had also been demanding a special letter from Cardinal Barberini, which would provide a free trip as far as Syria, but since the papal family was annoyed with the Piarists over some trivial building permission near to the noviciate, Calasanz was trying to keep a low profile. It was enough that Alacchi received an official permit to travel. He continued to fret over his travel plans, and asked Calasanz for special permission to remove his habit when travelling in the east, 'in the land of the infidels', for fear of being attacked. But all this preparation was for nothing anyway, as the harbour remained closed to shipping and all travel plans were put on hold. Travel to the Holy Land or the eastern Indies was clearly impossible.

As the plague spread through the city, Father Melchiorre got himself a ladder, and visited the sick, putting his ladder up to their windows to give confession from on high. And since he could not travel onwards, he began to spend his time trying to establish a Piarist school in Venice. The expulsion of the Jesuits and the closure of their school had left a clear niche in the market, and although the Republic had been happy to see the back of the Society, their departure had created a vacuum. The Spanish ambassador wrote that he found the Venetian nobility to be nine-tenths illiterate. The English ambassador Sir Dudley Carleton noted that the town was very bureaucratic: 'They have an infinitie of officers. The lest thing hath his superintendent. For example, there is one appointed to oversee the sellers of mellons and pepponi, etc.' But the general skills of literacy and numeracy were being neglected. The townsfolk used to send their sons 'upon gallies into the Levant to accustume them to navigation and to trade. They now send them to travaile, and to learne more of the gentleman than the merchant.'[18] Father Melchiorre saw his chance. He wrote to the father general asking him if he could have permission to re-edit the *Constitutions* to allow him to publicize the order's work. Father Calasanz refused point-blank, annoyed at the suggestion of an infringement of his prerogative or any reworking of his carefully written manual, and moreover told the wayward father very clearly not to try to open a school. The pope had banned it, they had no teachers and it was not worth starting what they could not continue honourably.[19]

A few months earlier, however, he had been less categoric, and had even offered some encouragement, making contact with the Venetian ambassador in Rome and agreeing to send two Venetian Piarists, Father Giovanni Mussesti ('an excellent man, but not very literate') and his son Pietro ('aged twenty, but of excellent intelligence and behaviour ... and skilled in prose and verse'[20]), to help with any possible future teaching. Unfortunately the Venetian ambassador then fell out with Taddeo Barberini, one of the papal nephews and prefect of Rome. The ambassador's carriage met Taddeo's in a narrow street and refused to give way, causing a terrible diplomatic incident, even though an apology was immediately proffered. The matter was resolved a few weeks later when the Barberini had the coachman decapitated in a night-time attack, but although honour had been restored, it was not a propitious time for relations between the Barberini regime and the Republic.[21] On such trivial incidents of baroque road rage could international policy depend.

After the diplomatic dust had settled, Calasanz decided to send the Mussestis, and though initially delayed by the terrible mud on the roads, they eventually set off in April 1632. The aspirations of the Empire, headed by Spain, always made Venice nervous, so in order to assuage any anti-Spanish accusations against the order, Calasanz pointed out that 'the teachers would all be Italian and some Venetians', and apart from Calasanz himself 'there is only one Spaniard, and he is in Moravia, so once I am dead there will be no trace of Spaniards in our Order.'[22] But the Venetian authorities were not convinced and the death of the Doge Nicolò Contarini from plague set negotiations back. Padre Melchiorre also had a moment of deadly panic when he discovered an abscess on his neck, but a few days later it split open and he felt much better, so perhaps it was not the dreaded contagion.

In September 1632 the irrepressible Father Melchiorre rented a house and built himself a tree-house in a pear tree in the courtyard where he spent most days 'withdrawn where it was cool, and sometimes even slept there'. Calasanz was very dubious: 'I don't know if the invention of the little room in the tree will be praised by everyone because one should avoid appearing different in order not to give occasion for people to gossip ... Not everyone will take it in good part.'[23] The treehouse, however, not only helped to keep the plague at a distance, but also provided a convenient viewpoint to survey the surroundings. He started to offer private lessons in return for payment, in direct contradiction to Calasanz's orders.[24] He soon took over the adjoining buildings and hired more staff to supplement the Mussestis. Two of these men immediately began to cause great scandal. According to one report they conspired together to put either glass or poison into Father Melchiorre's food. One of them, Brother Antonio Marotta, aged twenty-seven, took a wooden ladder and climbed up into Father Alacchi's main room (not in the tree) while he was away saying Mass, and stole reams of new cloth, a new hat and the alms money. Calasanz retorted that Father Melchiorre should be grateful it was not worse, given his poor choice of staff, and begged him to send away the other brother, Biagio Salamino, before he too caused some scandal.[25]

But the gossip had already spread even as far as Rome. Father Melchiorre 'shouted too much at the members of his household, and treated them like galley slaves'. Brother Biagio remained attached to the household and walked the streets of Venice dressed in an immodestly short version of a Piarist habit and occasionally annoyed people – especially young girls – in the streets. He ate and drank freely with laymen, he went out whenever he felt like it, and he socialized with women more than with men. Father Melchiorre's extraordinary reaction was to ordain him, acting directly in the face of oft-repeated opposition from Calasanz, contrary to all common sense, and even though the clearly dubious Biagio had not spent the requisite time as a novice. Perhaps Father Melchiorre was besotted, for what other reason could there be for this promotion? When a gentleman, Giovanni Contarini, stayed a night in the house opposite Alacchi's, 'he was very scandalized to hear Father Biagio being flagellated [*mortificato*] by a layman, in a loud voice, so that he and many others were scandalized at the terrible language used with a religious priest and in your [Alacchi's] presence, and he lost the good opinion he had had of our Order. It cannot but displease me that among our members such shouting and noises should be heard,' wrote Calasanz, horrified that yet more scandal had attached to Father Melchiorre. 'If only you had not given these two vagabonds and scandalmongers the habit, we would still be well regarded in Venice and perhaps our Order would have been approved, which now by their madness and scandal is rejected. Do not accept *anyone* else unless I approve.'[26] At this point Alacchi finally sent Biagio away, but he still could not keep himself out of trouble.

On the feast of St Nicholas he held a party for his pupils, which Calasanz was afraid might be wrongly construed, although other schools in Venice did the same. Melchiorre did try to improve himself, and had two huge nails fixed in the wall, between which he could stand in a Christ-like position for hours trying to overcome the temptations of the devil, and shouting to Satan to 'go to hell, and leave me alone'.[27] Meanwhile, apparently unconcerned by public opinion and the fact that his classes were completely illegal, he opened his private oratory to the public, thereby creating an unlicensed place of worship, and added a bell to the roof of the tree-house to broadcast the fact and to notify the children of school times and the faithful of prayer sessions. For the neighbouring Theatine Order, the installation of the bell marked the end of their patience. The senate was notified, came to inspect the buildings and was appalled to realize how far things had gone without a vestige of official permission.

Calasanz was fed up with him: 'You should behave as though you might die soon, and not build so many castles in the air, as the expression goes, but accept being alone rather than with bad companions. You have proved that this year at the cost of your reputation.'[28] Calasanz had several schools crying out for new staff, especially in central Europe, and should have been concentrating on their needs, rather than trying to persuade a reluctant Venetian Republic to allow access. Although he was scathing of Alacchi's future plans for expansion, he nevertheless still seemed to be drawn along by the wayward father's enthusiasms, and contrary to all evidence, to believe in his progress:

I very much doubt that in Venice, where there is such a shortage of land, you could find the kind of garden or orchard that you describe to me with all these fruiting trees and so many flowering arbours at such a reasonable price to rent. However if you do find one, it should be well maintained, and in that case I would write to Naples for a priest and a lay brother who knows about gardening, and about woodwork, and also about sewing, shoe-making and masonry. We could send them via Ancona, and if things were going well we could send more.[29]

And while he was planning the layout of the future gardens of the putative school in Venice, Calasanz also passed on a message from Brother Marc'Antonio, the gardener in Poli, who 'has frequently asked me to write that you should send him some cauliflower seeds, since he has heard that the ones from Venice are excellent, and that when planted in Poli they grow extraordinarily huge, so include a folded paper with some seeds in your next letter'.[30]

But this was all gardening on clouds. The orchard, the arbour and the cauliflower seeds fell through the vapour. Not only was Father Melchiorre running an increasingly busy and completely unlicensed establishment in the heart of their city, but as a Sicilian – under Spanish jurisdiction, and a member of an organization founded by a Spaniard – he was also suspected of spying for Venice's enemies from his tree house. Rome and Venice were also in dispute over border fortresses between Ferrara and Venice, and the Republic was on high alert.[31] Suddenly it all became too much for the authorities. His arrogance, his strange living arrangements, his immoral colleagues, his unorthodox confessions of enclosed nuns and his blatant lack of respect for the Republic's jurisdictions and laws were discussed by the senate; as a result Alacchi was given a generous four days to leave the Republic. As Venetians, the Mussesti father and son were exempted from the ban and Cardinal Cornaro even tried to encourage them to stay and continue running the school, but a disgruntled Father Melchiorre withdrew them and fled the territory on 1 May 1633. 'I'll take them all away with me, since you don't care that during the plague I placed my life at the service of your Republic. I won't have anything to do with those who persecute me.'[32] And thus ended the attempt to open a school in Venice.

'This is really going to be a troublesome affair'

In the midst of the traumatic events in Naples and Venice, and the fractious dealings with Fathers Cherubini and Alacchi, Calasanz's attention was also drawn to the next major foundation. This would be an establishment with a different kind of ethos. With schools already established in Rome and Naples, Florence was the next obvious target. In the months just before the plague paralysed Italy, Father Arcangelo Galletti, travelling back to Rome, stopped at Florence and stayed the night at Giovan Francesco Fiammelli's house. Fiammelli was an old colleague of Calasanz's – he had taught arithmetic in the early days in Trastevere, where he had been mentioned as 'a Florentine mathematician renowned throughout Rome', before returning to his native Florence and setting up his own school in the Via de'Cimatori.[1] Fiammelli was now seventy-five years old and, in his own words, 'decrepit and weary of such hard work',[2] and as he chatted to Father Arcangelo, the temptation to hand over his school to his old friend and retire in peace grew at the back of his mind.

The Archbishop of Florence was positive, but the adviser to the Medici Grand Duke Ferdinand II was not enthusiastic, apparently fearing that too many educated poor boys might eventually result in a dearth of servants and artisans. According to tradition, however, the young duke overcame his objections, saying he preferred to be 'a prince of men, rather than of animals', although in reality he was still so dominated by the two regents, the intensely pious grand duchesses, his mother and grandmother, that he probably made no independent decisions at that period. Father Arcangelo found everyone amazingly helpful. 'These Florentines are unimaginably nice, affable and courteous,' he reported to Calasanz. 'If you ask them for a bit of sole for your shoes, they not only give you the whole sole, but offer to send it round to your house; if you ask them the way somewhere, they take you right to the door. They look at us like people from another world, but they want priests of good example and with modest eyes.'[3] On 20 March 1630 permission duly arrived from the secretary of state for a trial run of five years for a Florentine school. Father Francesco Castelli, fresh from his battles over Father Alacchi and future provincial of Tuscany, pointed out the particular advantages for the duke: by allowing the Piarists to open a school he would at one stroke, very simply – and incidentally, very cheaply – increase the loyalty of his subjects and please God.[4] Faced with such overwhelming arguments, the school duly opened on Wednesday, 22 May 1630, only to be closed a few months later as the plague restrictions hit Florence and the full force of the health magistracy's regulations began to make themselves felt.

According to a contemporary diary, between August 1630 and September 1631, while the plague was at its height, 9,500 people died in the city alone.[5] With no teaching possible, the Piarist fathers turned their attention to nursing and morgue duties. Father Arcangelo in particular, 'robust and with a good complexion', enhanced the reputation of the order by exposing himself to great danger, even going so far as to carry the bodies of those who had died of the plague on his own shoulders. One writer calculated that of 191 priests who served during the plague, 112 died. If these figures are accurate, the Piarist fathers were extremely lucky not to lose any members of staff.[6] Father Arcangelo must have acquired some sort of rare immunity.

As the contagion ebbed away, the Florentine school opened again a year and a half later, just in time for the new academic year in

November, and soon grew to 500 pupils and twelve fathers. The Piarists enjoyed great support from the Medici court and the Florentine nobility. One of the teachers at the school in particular would soon make an important name for himself. Famiano Michelini, born in 1604 and known as Brother Francesco di San Giuseppe, was initially assigned to the writing and abacus classes. He had been studying mathematics in Genoa and came to Florence armed with a letter of reference addressed to Galileo Galilei from the physicist Giovan Battista Baliani, which described him as 'a virtuous and studious young man, who seems in my opinion to be above average in mathematics'. Within three weeks of his arrival in Florence, before the school had even opened, Michelini had presented his letter to the scientist and had also made the acquaintance of various other courtiers, including Archbishop Marzimedici, who also dabbled in mathematics. By the time the school was forced to close for the duration of the plague, Michelini had already laid the foundations for a private mathematics study group for adults to run parallel to his normal school duties. When the school re-opened after the epidemic, his classes recommenced and were clearly very popular, his pupils including the grand duke's brothers, Cardinal Gian Carlo and Prince Leopoldo.[7]

The Florentine school began to develop an identity very different from the other Piarist schools. The courtly and scientific links, initially established by Michelini, were supported by Calasanz and during the next few years he sent other young Piarists who expressed a particular interest in the scientific work being carried out in Florence to join Michelini. The school grew into what one historian (one of the very few non-Piarist scholars even to mention the Piarists) calls 'the most exciting – and the most thoroughly Galilean – religious community in the city, as well as in the whole Church'.[8] Meanwhile, the Medici court also had its own demands. In 1638, responding to considerable pressure and contrary to their original brief, the Piarists agreed to open a special nobleman's class where some thirty aristocratic boys could be taught separately from the rest.

Galileo had been appointed chief mathematician and philosopher to the Medici court in 1610, mainly on the basis of his work with the telescope. In 1612 his *Discourse on Floating Bodies* had discussed an ancient idea that heat was composed of fire atoms. This atomism was to develop in the following years and a decade later his work on comets, *The Assayer*, would offer 'a corpuscular theory of all the elements of nature and of all perceptible phenomena'.[9] In 1613 he published the *History and Mathematical Demonstrations concerning Sunspots* in which he first came into direct conflict with Jesuit teachings, denouncing Aristotelian physics in favour of 'the book of nature' as if 'nature had not written this great book of the world to be read by others besides Aristotle'.[10] A Florentine Dominican, Father Lorini, denounced Galileo for heliocentrism, a view not upheld by biblical authority. The Holy Office 'judged the heliocentric doctrine to be philosophically foolish and absurd, formally heretical, and the doctrine of the earth's movement to be erroneous *de fide*, inasmuch as the first contradicts the Scriptures and the second does not conform to them'.[11] Copernicus's work, *De revolutionibus*, which had inspired Galileo, was placed on the Index of Prohibited Books, and historians argue about whether Cardinal Bellarmino, inquisitor at the trial of Giordano Bruno, simply informed Galileo of this (as a certificate from the cardinal shows), or formally warned him (as a record produced at Galileo's later trial in 1633 proves).

When Maffeo Barberini was appointed pope and took the name Urban VIII in 1623, Galileo hastily redrafted the dedication of *The Assayer*, which was just about to go to press, and added a new title page prominently sprinkled with Barberini bees. An attack against the Jesuit Father Orazio Grassi's work and on 'the obstinate worshippers of antiquity', as a friend of Galileo's noted, the book was eagerly awaited.[12] The new pontiff seemed delighted and even had it read out to him during meals. Perhaps it had not yet sunk in that *The Assayer* contained a stylish rejection of Aristotelian philosophy, a philosophy that had become 'inextricably connected with the Catholic religion and the reigning mentality',[13] and drew a clear distinction between the favoured practical experimental method and pure received wisdom, proven only by Aristotle and by the past cohorts of writers who had repeated his conclusions. Meanwhile, emboldened by this initial approval, Galileo visited Rome and was warmly received, meeting with Urban six times in as many weeks, and departing with promises of pensions and gifts and the warm feeling evoked by a pope calling one 'beloved son'. It was during these meetings that Galileo worked towards permission for his next book, which would re-open the Copernican debate.

While in England William Harvey published his description of the circulation of the blood, and plague entered northern Italy and began to permeate slowly southwards, Galileo worked on this new book, *The Dialogue on the Two Chief World Systems: Ptolemaic and Copernican*. The writing may have been easy, but the six years of negotiating, diplomatic backtracking and correcting had seemed long. The text had been examined and censored and approved, but never by the Society of Jesus, always by the more friendly Dominicans. The difficulties of postage during the plague restrictions meant that the final checking of the manuscript was entrusted to the Florentine Inquisition, and the *Dialogue* was finally published in February 1632; judging by the initial sales it was an enormous and immediate success. Several of Galileo's Jesuit opponents, however, were mortally offended and while Urban did not have time to read the book himself, it was presented to him by his advisers as a glorification of Copernican astronomy, with Urban himself in the unflattering role of Simplicius unsuccessfully defending orthodoxy against the cleverer characters. 'This is really going to be a troublesome affair,' wrote the Tuscan ambassador presciently.[14]

The Barberini pope meanwhile was under international pressure. On 8 March 1632 Cardinal Borgia, the Spanish ambassador, supported by Cardinal Ludovisi – one of the main Cherubini family supporters – and in front of the other assembled cardinals, read out a strong criticism of Urban's perceived lack of support for the military efforts in the war in central Europe against Protestantism, where the Catholic forces had recently been doing very badly. The pope, he said, was favouring France where he had served as nuncio for many years and acting too leniently against the heretics in what was to become known as the Thirty Years War. Perhaps, he hinted, a council should be convened to assess the pope's will and ability to defend Christendom. A scuffle ensued as the pope's nephew and brother tried to restrain the ambassador and hustle him from the room before he completed his speech – during the scuffle, Cardinal Pio's glasses were smashed and Cardinal Spinola ripped up his hat in anger. Urban, affronted but terrified of the secular powers ranged against him, withdrew to his summer residence of Castel Gandolfo. His dislike of Spain and the Spanish knew no bounds. His poison-tasters were put on full alert, all visitors were thoroughly searched, military manoeuvres in Naples were watched with trepidation, the movements of the fleet of the Grand Duke of Tuscany were under suspicion. Unfortunately for Galileo, it was not the time to be writing books about potentially heretical subjects from within a possibly enemy territory. The Tuscan ambassador noted that, 'While we were discussing these delicate subjects of the Holy Office, His Holiness exploded into great anger, and suddenly he told me that even our Galileo had dared enter where he should not have, into the most serious and dangerous subjects which could be stirred up at this time.'[15] The order came to stop all sales of the *Dialogue* immediately, and Galileo was summoned to Rome in January 1633 to explain himself before the Inquisition.

After a stressful wait of several months, interspersed with tense sessions with the cardinal inquisitors, on 22 June 1633, Galileo, dressed in penitential white, abjured his beliefs: 'I have been judged vehemently suspected of heresy, that is, of having held and believed that the Sun is the centre of the world and immovable, and that the Earth is not the centre and moves ... I abjure with a sincere heart and unfeigned faith, I curse and detest the said errors and heresies, and generally all and every error and sect contrary to the Holy Catholic Church.' He swore never to speak or write of such things again.[16] And although he would have been foolish to have muttered too audibly, '*Eppur si muove*' ('But it *does* move') as the Inquisition officers led him back to captivity, he must have believed it still. The *Dialogue* appeared on the next edition of the Index of Prohibited Books and was only quietly dropped from it in 1822.

Galileo's incarceration was soon softened and he was passed from the Inquisition's jail to the care of the Tuscan ambassador in Rome and thence to the gentle custody of the Archbishop of Siena. Within a few weeks of his arrival there he began work on a treatise on motion, *Two New Sciences*, which he had been mulling over for several years, and which seemed at first glance to offer a relatively uncontroversial subject for analysis. Meanwhile the Tuscan ambassador laboured unremittingly to convince the pope to permit Galileo to return home to Florence. When reports began to reach Urban that Galileo was living in unacceptable luxury in Siena and being treated with great respect by the archbishop, he finally agreed in December 1633 that the old scientist could return home, so long as he remained under house arrest, as Galileo put it, 'in my own house, that little villa a mile from Florence, with strict injunctions that I was not to entertain friends, nor to allow the assembling of many at a time'.[17]

It is not known whether Father Calasanz ever met Galileo. They had a mutual acquaintance, Tommaso Campanella, author of *The City of the Sun*, the *Apologia* on behalf of the Pious Schools,[18] and many other works – the majority of suspect orthodoxy. Campanella had met Galileo in the 1590s and written an *Apologia* on his behalf in 1616 when the scientist had had his first brushes with Copernican theories. During the late 1620s, after his release from Spanish incarceration, Campanella lived at the Dominican convent of Santa Maria sopra Minerva where Calasanz was a frequent visitor, and where Galileo's final meeting with the Inquisition and his abjuration were held. Calasanz had invited Campanella to teach some of his novices at the Frascati school for a couple of weeks during the summers of 1631 and 1632, and several were particularly interested in mathematics. Two of them, Angelo Morelli and Carlo Conti, were soon sent to Florence to join the group of like-minded teachers surrounding Michelini at the Medici court. From Frascati, Campanella wrote to Galileo offering his services as a defender before the Inquisition, an offer based presumably on his extensive experience, and also tried to encourage Calasanz to intervene in the scientist's favour.[19] In the words of one historian, 'Galileo could not have hit upon a more ill-starred and compromising champion' to run his defence; the earlier publication of Campanella's *Apologia pro Galileo* had done him no service, probably damaging his reputation wherever it had been read.[20] Campanella's own credit was now falling at the Vatican and his undiplomatic – and illegal – astrological forecast of the pope's death sealed his downfall. In October 1634, after sending his regards to Galileo via Father Michelini, Campanella packed his bags and disappeared from Rome in a pre-emptive night-time escape from certain imprisonment in a papal dungeon to Paris, where he lived the remainder of his life under the protection of the French court.[21]

Within two months of Galileo's return to Florence, Michelini was summoned by Calasanz to Rome for other duties. If the father general hoped to remove Michelini from the temptation of becoming too close to the condemned scientist, it proved a failure. As soon as he arrived in Rome, Michelini visited Galileo's close friend and associate, the Benedictine Father Benedetto Castelli (no relation of the Piarist provincial Francesco Castelli), who was a specialist in hydraulics and professor of mathematics at Pisa. He had tutored the Medici princes, before being summoned to Rome to tutor the papal nephew, Taddeo Barberini, and to organize hydraulic projects in Ferrara and Bologna. His special patron was Cardinal Francesco Barberini, but Galileo's trial had thrown him into disgrace by association so he was keeping a low profile. Nevertheless he seemed to act as a sort of admissions tutor, sending Galileo promising young scientists for the unofficial school, which began to gather around Florence.[22] Michelini brought Castelli a letter from Galileo and from then on visited him every day while he was in Rome. The Benedictine was very impressed with the young father, and wrote to Galileo:

Father Francesco, more worthy of the title 'reverend' than many others, has been with me and comes often, and continually speaks of you so much to our taste that words fail me. Suffice it to let you know that the precious conversation of this good father has been the only consolation and relief for my melancholy. I have been stupefied by his knowledge, amazed at the subtlety of his intellect, very content with the sincere love he bears you, and enthralled at his generosity.

A firm friendship based on scientific enquiry grew up between the two men. Michelini also wrote directly to Galileo, and there is no hint in his letters that he is writing to someone condemned by the clerical authorities to live on the edge. He wrote of his 'immense desire to serve', of 'the great love I bear you', of 'a person so eminent of intellect, doctrine, urbanity and philosophy'. He was clearly completely devoted to Galileo's teachings, despite any papal interdict.[23]

Meanwhile, the Florentine court was putting pressure on Father Calasanz for Michelini to return. Cardinal Gian Carlo de' Medici, the duke's brother and not someone to be lightly ignored, wrote: 'The benefit Father Francesco di San Giuseppe brings to this city is such that since you have taken him away, a handful of gentlemen have begged me to intervene with you, that you not deprive them of such a person, and send him back ... I beg you to gratify this handful of spiritual and good people who have asked me to write, and believe that their satisfaction will also be mine.'[24]

The requests were acknowledged, for in May Father Castelli wrote to Galileo:

I have so enjoyed and appreciated the conversations with Father Francesco in Rome in these few days, that I am sad at his departure. I shall however console myself when I think that you will be able to enjoy the sweetness and gentleness of this good father ... who seems to be exactly cut out in the true

measure of your school, of sublime intellect and very modest in his preten-
sions, conditions which must ensure his amiability for those noblemen.[25]

It seems that Father Michelini had travelled to Rome with a hidden
agenda. A letter he wrote to Galileo in October, shortly before returning to Tuscany, reveals that he had hoped to recruit several young men
to create the nucleus of a scientific academy based in Florence, an
unusually risky undertaking, given the conditions of Galileo's house
arrest in Arcetri. Unfortunately, as he wrote to the great scientist, 'Our
Father General can only spare me two young men for our group, since
we don't have space and food for more in Florence. I'm sorry not to be
able to bring six or eight really clever ones. The Father General says
we should run this group in Rome, but I'm more motivated by being
close to you than by anything else.'[26] He asked Galileo not to forget the
Piarists when talking to the grand duke, perhaps hoping that the duke
might supply a building near to Galileo suitable for the new academy.
Calasanz, although unable to provide many students for the new study
group, nevertheless supported the idea and Michelini signed off his letter by saying, 'Our Father General is most grateful for the favour which
you show to me and our other fathers', a clear indication that he must
have had the blessing of Calasanz. The order's historians have certainly seen it in that light, with one of the main twentieth-century Piarist
fathers writing, 'for us Scolopi this is like a certificate of nobility, so
clearly does it show the intimacy of the relations between the great man
and our Institute'.[27] The two young students, Carlo Conti and Angelo
Morelli, who had been taught by Campanella in Frascati, were to prove
important members of the 'Galilean group' Michelini was starting to
build up in Florence. Calasanz wrote to Morelli soon after his arrival in
Florence, encouraging him to do well in his mathematics, 'for one can
see that this subject is popular'.[28]

It is one of the most attractive features of Calasanz's personality that
he permitted and even encouraged such contacts between his members
and Galileo. It is inconceivable that he did not know what Galileo's

writings were proposing, given their mutual acquaintances, the nature of Roman society and the publicity his ideas had received. He must also have been familiar with the opinion of the church authorities. Yet he chose, discreetly, to cast his lot with the scientist. This choice underlines the other, even more important, progressive decision Calasanz had made: to teach the poor. Access to education for all classes was far from universally popular, and this decision, along with his support for Galileo, stands in sharp contrast to his more conventionally conservative religious beliefs.

Father Benedetto Castelli wrote longingly to Michelini in February 1635, clearly wishing that he too were part of the Florentine group: 'I am delighted above all that you have the consolation of the gentle, joyful and most wise conversation of Signor Galileo, and I would so love to find myself there with you.'[29] At the end of the year, Michelini was back in Rome looking for more clever students for his 'academy'. Castelli again reported his progress to Galileo: 'I really find him so dedicated and appreciative of your merit, that you could not ask for more. And he is burning with enthusiasm, for the benefit of his religious Order, to start these studies properly, and I think he will be very successful, mainly because he does not want crowds [of students] but above all ensures that they are very intelligent.'[30] Michelini, like Calasanz, must have been politically naive, if scientifically enthusiastic, if he considered that association with Galileo and the creation of a study group based around him would be of benefit to the Piarists in the important world of Vatican politics. Nevertheless, Florence became the centre for the most dynamic of the Piarist houses. Michelini selected carefully. Clemente Settimi was serious and studious, and would soon become Galileo's personal secretary. Ambrogio Ambrogi – after his unpleasant confrontation with Father Melchiorre on the fateful overnight boat trip, with the accusations of indecent groping and breaking of the confessional – had studied in Naples, Rome and Genoa with some of the foremost mathematicians of the time. Angelo Morelli was reserved and timid, but was dubbed 'the good friend and secret master of Michelini', explaining tricky principles to him the night before so that he could amaze the princes the following day.[31] Salvatore Grise was a pupil of Benedetto Castelli's, who had already shown himself gifted in geometry and mathematics. He would be sent on buying trips to Venice to bring back lenses and books, and would act as a trustworthy postman for letters between his teacher and other famous scientists such as Giovan Alfonso Borelli.[32] Carlo Conti's real interest lay in poetry, but he too formed part of the initial group, before concentrating on his literary endeavours. Lastly, Domenico Rosa was a painter like his better known brother Salvatore (who was also later invited to Florence by Gian Carlo de' Medici), and whose own pictures, in the words of one of the Piarist superiors, 'may well be praised by those who understand about art'.[33]

Galileo, meanwhile, was beginning to chafe at his imprisonment in Arcetri. In summer 1637 he lost the sight of his right eye and a few months later the other. As he wrote to Elia Diodati, a lawyer friend in Paris:

Alas, a month ago your dear old friend and servant Galileo became completely blind. Now imagine in what state of affliction I find myself, while I think that this sky, this world and this universe which I with my marvellous observations and clear demonstrations enlarged a hundred, nay a thousand, times beyond what had been commonly seen by wise men of all the past centuries, now for me it is so diminished and restricted that it is no greater than that occupied by my own person.[34]

The Florentine inquisitor, Father Muzzarelli, visited Galileo in February 1638 'when I was not expected', accompanied by a doctor, in order to be able to report back accurately to Cardinal Barberini on his condition. He wrote that the old scientist was now

totally blind, and though he himself hopes for a recovery, his physician considers that his age renders the disease incurable. Besides the blindness, he suffers terribly from hernia, has continual pains all over his body, and suffers, as he himself declares (and those of his household confirm it), to such a degree from sleeplessness, that he never sleeps a whole hour together in the twenty-four. Moreover, he is so prostrate, that he looks more like a corpse than a living person.

Arcetri was inconvenient for doctors to visit, being a good half-hour walk up the hills to the south-west of Florence, and 'people do not visit him as much as formerly, for since his health has been so broken he does nothing as a rule but complain, and relate his symptoms to those around him'. Under the circumstances, Cardinal Barberini gave Muzzarelli permission to let Galileo move into Florence temporarily, but still not to receive visitors or to go out except to hear Mass. But the inquisitor promised to remain vigilant: 'Notwithstanding, I shall watch narrowly to see that his Holiness's commands are carried out.'[35]

In spite of Galileo's supposed isolation and the inquisitor's vigilance, his last manuscript was smuggled out, and published in Holland in 1638 (the year the Florentine Piarists opened their Nobleman's School) as *Two New Sciences*. A 'treatise on projectiles', and the laws of resistance, dynamics and motion, in Galileo's words, 'pertaining to Mechanics and Local Motions ... with an Appendix on the centre of gravity in various Solids', it has been described as his greatest book and 'the first modern scientific textbook'.[36] Given that the Piarist fathers had been visiting and corresponding regularly over the past few years and, given his poor state of health, it is not unreasonable to assume they helped him with any practical experiments, and may well be considered to have played a significant role in the development of this last book.

Father Michelini, meanwhile, had become so successful with his courtly teaching that he was scarcely with Galileo any more. In December 1637 he had been sent to Rome, where he wrote devotedly to Galileo:

The reverence which I bear for you is sculpted into my heart and is so great, that it has never permitted me to put on paper two words to show with some outward sign the great affection which I bear you. What happens to me is what happened to a Venetian gentleman, who was honoured by the Signoria with some dignity or other, and having prepared the most elaborate speeches of thanks, he was so abashed by the occasion, that he could scarcely utter a single word. I find myself now in that situation, and in fact it is an appropriate comparison, since the richness and great majesty of your knowledge in comparison to mine is in the same proportion as the infinite is to the finite. I just wanted to mention this, so that you fully understand the reasons for my silence. And now, kissing your hands, I beg you to excuse my failings, and to honour me with some command while I am in Rome which will be until Christmas.[37]

But in February 1638, just as Galileo descended into complete blindness, Michelini left for Pisa, where he initially stayed by recommendation of Galileo as a guest of Dino Peri, a lecturer in mathematics at the university. However, as Peri wrote to Galileo soon after, the Medici princes Gian Carlo and Leopoldo 'have developed an urge to try algebra' and provided Michelini with board and lodgings.[38] Once he had begun to instruct the princes, though he still kept in written correspondence with Galileo, Michelini usually travelled around with the court, especially with Prince Leopoldo, who moved between Pisa, Livorno, Siena and Florence.[39] Galileo was not best pleased and complained to the faithful Father Castelli in Rome: 'Good Father Francesco has become all courtly and is always with these most serene princes, teaching them mathematics and in particular algebra, so I rarely have a chance to speak to him.'[40] Michelini tried to console Galileo by recommending him to Father Ambrogio Ambrogi, whom he described as

my oldest and dearest friend in the Order, a person with the best manners and an excellent intellect, studious and keen to serve you at every occasion; and deeds will talk louder than my words. He will supplement my absences and negligence, and you will feel as though you have another Father Francesco [Michelini] with you as far as devotion and respect towards you are concerned; but as far as diligence and other qualities he is in fact far superior to me.[41]

Galileo seemed pleased with him and described him as 'a very praise-worthy person'[42] in a letter to Father Castelli. As well as the princes, Michelini was teaching an increasing number of clerics and gentlemen. Although still attached to the Florentine school and theoretically sub-servient to the headmaster's orders, it seemed politically more impor-tant that Father Francesco serve the court than the children of Florence, for whom he can no longer have spared much time. The generous patronage the Medici brothers provided in return must have convinced the father general, had he had any doubts.

Michelini remained in contact with Galileo and corresponded with him about his research on motion. He sent him gifts, for instance, of Montepulciano wine and two pairs of cotton socks, although the socks proved not to Galileo's exact specifications, so two weeks later Michelini replaced them with woollen socks, which Galileo found more to his liking.[43] The best gift Michelini sent was his young colleague, Father Clemente Settimi, who brought the six bottles of Montepulciano wine and stepped into Michelini's shoes as one of Galileo's faithful amanuenses.

Father Clemente had been one of the young men whom Michelini had recruited to Florence in 1634, and he had taken over many of Father Francesco's duties in the school. Soon, however, he was virtually excused classroom duties as Galileo's needs took precedence. For instance, on 7 January 1639, Galileo wrote to his physicist friend Baliani:

I was brought your very welcome letter yesterday by Father Clemente di San Carlo of the Pious Schools, friend of Father Francesco, along with your book on motion, and since it is my bad luck to be completely blind for the last two years, and I cannot even see the sun, let alone much smaller objects, and deprived of such light as writing and geometric figures, today I asked the above-mentioned Father Clemente to come and stay with me for many hours, during which time together we read your book.[44]

Being read to was better than nothing, but it took that much longer and was very frustrating for the great scientist who, although physically decrepit, was still blazingly mentally agile. Galileo described his irritation in a letter dictated to Prince Leopoldo, and quite possibly written by Father Clemente:

I am obliged to have recourse to other hands and other pens than mine since my sad loss of sight. This, of course, occasions great loss of time; particularly now that my memory is impaired by advanced age; so that in placing my thoughts on paper, many and many a time I am forced to have the foregoing sentences read to me before I can tell what ought to follow: else I should repeat the same thing over and over. Your Highness must take my word for it, that between using one's own eyes and hands and those of others there is as great a difference as in playing chess with one's eyes open or blindfold.[45]

Soon, however, Father Clemente became so necessary to Galileo's comfort that a visitor to Arcetri as distinguished as Evangelista Torricelli, the inventor of the barometer and the first to create a sustained vacuum and discover changes in atmospheric pressure, wrote to Galileo commenting on Father Clemente as 'a person of great kindness and also of extraordinary knowledge',[46] and the Tuscan ambassador in Rome, Francesco Niccolini, was sent to discuss the matter with Calasanz. Father Clemente had been visiting Arcetri so often and for such long periods, that Niccolini requested permission for Father Clemente to be allowed to stay overnight – strictly against the rules of the order. Fathers Michelini and Settimi were allowed a quite extraordinary degree of freedom, given Calasanz's normal strictness, or even rigidity, in observance. In a letter often cited by the order as an example of the father general's scientific openness and sympathy to Galileo's ideas, Calasanz did give permission to Father Clemente, and added, 'God willing, he will know how to draw the greatest benefit from that.'[47] This simple phrase threw Father Leodegario Picanyol, the order's archivist in the 1950s and author of the main work on the relationship between Galileo and the Piarists, into a paroxysm of hagiography, gushing about

that memorable letter in which the Sainted founder of the Pious Schools wrote those marvellously revealing words, which in their lapidary simplicity and their clearly Galilean sentiment, rendered immortal the name of Saint Joseph Calasanz, not only in the history of science, but also in the annals of the Church, as being the first among the heroes of sanctity to intuit the merit and the grandeur of Galileo.[48]

A few months later a young student of Father Clemente's from the Florence school, Vincenzo Viviani, aged sixteen, moved in with Galileo to help him full-time with his correspondence. Viviani was to remain Galileo's assistant until his death and to become custodian of his documents and to a certain extent his memory, writing an important early biography of the scientist, as well as several of his own mathematical works.

The Piarist contribution to Galilean science is not negligible. However, not all members of the order would be so sympathetic to the advance of science.

In November 1639 a new member of staff arrived in Florence, a young father named Mario Sozzi. When he saw what was going on he found himself so outraged by his discoveries that he saw no alternative but to call in the Inquisition. His actions were to prove disastrous for the order.

'How can the Holy Spirit be in such a house?'

While the school in Florence had been establishing itself, Father Melchiorre Alacchi's efforts to attempt the same thing in Venice had met in failure. As soon as he received his four-day banning order, he hurriedly fled to Ancona, further south, down the Adriatic coast, where he met up with Father Stefano Cherubini. Father Stefano, fallen into disrepute in Naples and therefore promoted to procurator, was spending his time visiting various schools, sorting out knotty legal and building problems, and organizing the finances of the Nazarene College, a new elite school that the Piarists opened in 1630.[1] Occasionally he needed a little reminder, such as when Calasanz wrote to him that 'classes should never be held in the father's residence, nor should pupils ever be brought there, avoiding evil, and opportunities for evil, and even cutting off any suspicion of evil, for we are all liable to exterior censure, so let this serve as a caution'.[2] Both Alacchi and Cherubini were forbidden by Father Calasanz from accepting children at Ancona, and Father Melchiorre passed a few weeks complaining loudly about his treatment at the hands of the Venetians, until ordered to be silent by the father general.[3] He then travelled to Sicily once more, where this time he had considerable success in ignoring the papal ban on new foundations, and opened schools in Palermo and Messina. The Viceroy of the Two Sicilies himself, the Duke of Alcalá, supported the foundation in

Palermo and paid for an excellent site in the centre of town that caused great uproar amongst the existing religious orders. 'All the furies of hell were let loose to prevent the possible new foundation, and you cannot imagine the opposition that broke out,' wrote Father Filippo Scoma in an eighteenth-century history of the Sicilian foundations:

Many religious Orders, some openly, others secretly, worked with the principal officers of the city, under the pretext that in Palermo there were already many religious Orders and it was not good to introduce another one, and such a poor one. They incited the school teachers to resent the new foundation and to rise up, and they said many malicious and calumnious things about Father Melchiorre, issuing death threats, and promising to have him chased out of town, and out of the kingdom. Even the cardinal archbishop summoned him and shouted at him loudly, crying that he had told him not to come, that there was no need of the Pious Schools in Palermo since the city already had many schools and teachers.[4]

Nevertheless royal authority prevailed and the school opened to great fanfare with a Mass attended by the viceroy, his court and even the hostile cardinal archbishop, a great tribute (according to Father Scoma) to Father Melchiorre's skills of persuasion. The viceroy's wife herself even supplied the linen for the sacristy and the church. A few months later the number of pupils had grown to such an extent that part of the neighbour's house came under proprietorial scrutiny. The owner, Donna Caterina Sabja, was not keen to sell, but was given no choice and forced to accept a reasonable price by the authorities and the courts. When the day came to take possession, however, Donna Caterina could not bear to leave.

She placed herself before the entrance with a musket in her hand, not letting anyone enter, and some of her servants threw stones to keep us away. Brother Antonio entered by force, but the lady threw a stone at his chest. Her son, who also wanted to defend the house, stood there with a sword in his hand, and the fathers were obliged to take up arms; but because he resisted the forces of justice, her son was arrested and put in prison. Finally the house was taken, but to capture the owner it was necessary to break down half the house, losing beams and doors. The lady was then frightened and decided to leave, but out of pique she ruined all the doors, the wooden staircases, the locks and the windows. Father Melchiorre immediately razed to the ground the part where she was to live, and made it a garden, with a fountain; so that in three weeks the garden was covered in grass as though it had never been a house.[5]

Messina was a republic in its own right, rich and lawless, and Father Melchiorre had been blocked a few years earlier in his attempts to found a school by Jesuit-influenced senators who had voted against it. Now he negotiated for the Piarists to be awarded the royal spring water concession, meaning they could resell the water, thereby making a handsome profit, enough to rent a building on the main road with a reasonable garden. Secretly one night, in order to avoid tipping off the other religious orders in town, the Piarists crept in and set up their chapel. Although they had permission from the archbishop, the neighbouring Carmelites, Franciscans and Theatines were aghast when they discovered the *fait accompli* the next morning, but by then it was too late: the building was prepared and the school soon up and running, and Father Melchiorre had notched up another successful foundation. Within two weeks it was realized that the school buildings were too small for the 1,200 pupils who were streaming through the doors and the foundations were begun for a larger building. By 1634, however, Alacchi had once again fallen out with the staff sent to run the schools in Messina and Palermo, although the Duke of Alcalà wrote in his defence that he personally knew of no scandal and thought Father Alacchi a person of 'intelligence, activity and diligence'. Calasanz wearily commented, 'If only Father Melchiorre could control himself, and if he could manage not to shout so much, he would be a great man.' Other comments in the correspondence hint that Father Melchiorre was a man who believed that bullying and cursing would succeed where gentler methods failed. One superior commented that he giggled like a a young boy on occasion.[6] At any rate, he lost the respect of his colleagues: for instance, in Messina, one of the lay brothers, Carlo Cesario di San Domenico, had been locked in his room in chains by the headmaster, for unspecified 'grave crimes'. When Father Melchiorre tried to override his authority and set him free, none of the other members of the household would admit to holding the key, each claiming the other had it and sending Melchiorre scurrying from one to the other in vain. He complained that 'everyone is rebelling against me', that Calasanz was not supporting him against his staff, that they all had evil hearts. He left town once more in a petulant sulk, but even the trip back to Rome proved eventful. His ship was chased by two Turkish brigantines and only rescued by Florentine galleys after a few tense days fleeing capture.[7]

Calasanz's continuing trust in Alacchi is extraordinary, despite the hostility and criticism he aroused wherever he went, and given the father general's own awareness of this and his almost constant irritation with Alacchi. Only his intermittent successes, in the face of these disadvantages and of the papal ban, can have persuaded Calasanz, against his better judgement, to continue supporting him.

Calasanz responded to Alacchi's latest expulsion by electing him visitor for Sicily and sending him back, possibly in the – surely vain – hope that the increased authority of his new position would have some effect.[8] In his letter to Alacchi, Calasanz added some advice: 'In order to sort things out one may have to pretend, and even to swallow a bitter mouthful, for the common good is more important than the individual. You must try to be more human with everyone and not fly into a rage so quickly, nor speak so loudly that even the neighbours can hear.'[9] But trouble continued to dog Father Melchiorre. Five members of staff were summoned by the local Inquisition and held without the charges being revealed. 'Usually this tribunal does not call anyone without sufficient indication,' wrote Calasanz, who was naturally worried. 'And since I think this tribunal is run like the Spanish [Inquisition] it may be a reserved [or restricted] case, the disgusting vice [*il vitio sgratiato*], which down there [Sicily] is not considered very important, but it would be terrible if it were to be discovered amongst our members. Meanwhile keep the matter secret ... .'[10]

'The disgusting vice' once again was sodomy, and accusations of it had been levelled at Father Melchiorre and those who associated with him before. The fathers remained in custody while Calasanz tried desperately to understand the situation. Melchiorre's letters were not helpful, and indeed were written with such emotion and such stream-of-consciousness rapidity that the father general complained that he had to read them two or three times before they made sense.[11]

Then came a remarkable outburst from Sicily. According to Father Melchiorre, all the staff in Palermo – except himself – were completely unsuitable. He went through the list of reasons:

Father Gennaro della Natività: A man carnal in various ways.

Father Giovan Battista di Santo Domenico: Seditious disturber of the peace.

Father Adriano della Visitatione: Disobedient even when reproved.

Brother Carlo di Messina: I have seen him kissing children. And he is publicly famous amongst both laymen and religious for carnal activity with both sexes. Undisciplined and unworthy of our habit. Perpetual prison – at the very least – is required.

Brother Eustachio dello Spirito Santo: Carnal with women and disobedient even when told. Undisciplined and unobservant of the *Constitutions*, unworthy of being a religious.

Brother Alessandro di Santo Ludovico: Suspected of sins of the flesh.

Brother Giovan Battista di Santa Maria Maddalena: For the short time he has been here, undisciplined, disturber of the peace and quiet of the house.

Brother Gasparo della Assumptione di Norcia: I am told that he has been with children, unobservant of the *Constitutions*, glib of tongue, although appears to be improving.

Brother Giovanni di Santo Antonio di Gorzegna: A soldier who willingly gets into fights.

Brother Giuseppe del Santissimo: Not very obedient and quite seditious.

Brother Angelo Morelli of Lucca: Badly behaved mathematician [who was later transferred to Florence] with no respect for his superiors and loose of tongue.

Brother Antonio, the porter: A good man.

Brother Giacomo di Santo Donato: A good brother.

Brothers Carlo di San Francesco and Francesco di San Pietro e Paulo: Both good brothers.

And he finished this impassioned enumeration with a cry from the heart: 'How can the Holy Spirit be in such a house?'[12]

If we are to believe Father Melchiorre, the school in Palermo was a fermenting pit of lust, sodomy and child-sex. Several of the staff who can be traced, such as Angelo Morelli and Brother Gasparo, went on to have respectable careers, but others continue to reappear in the correspondence for various disciplinary matters. Brother Carlo di Messina, for instance, went on shortly thereafter to steal a substantial amount of money from Calasanz himself.[13] Brother Eustachio used his outstanding calligraphic skills – he could write beautifully with both hands and was in great demand for his services – to forge a letter from the viceroy's daughter, singing his praises and damning his superior. But was Father Melchiorre's outburst a true reflection of what was happening in the Palermitan house, or was it the product of an unbalanced mind that seemed to find sexual misconduct everywhere? How could the father general ignore such a calamitous state of affairs if he really believed Alacchi's report? And if he did not, why did he continue to trust and promote him? Incomprehensibly, Calasanz reacted to Melchiorre's alarming message by simply sending some tranquil aphorisms in his next letter to calm him down. Father Melchiorre's own reputation and the opposition he managed to arouse wherever he went would seem to indicate that several of these charges had their origins in his fevered imagination, rather than in any reality.

The fathers held by the Inquisition were released, mostly without charge, although one was defrocked for unspecified causes and Calasanz scolded Alacchi for accepting 'people who go wandering around the world and appear to be wise' in the first place.[14] But that was as far as Calasanz's reprimand went. In the same year – 1637 – Calasanz appointed him consultor general and procurator general,[15] in addition to his other titles, sending him to visit the schools in northern Italy in preparation for the chapter general, the order's major four-yearly meeting.

The chapter general opened on 15 October 1637 to an unstoppable spate of accusations against Father Melchiorre, including the scandalous old allegations of breaking the confessional and of the negligent education of novices, and newer ones, including unarguable claims that he had founded houses without licence, and that he was too ambitious for the good of the order. It is probable that much of what was said, including some of the more serious allegations against Father Melchiorre, was not written down in the official record of the assembly. Presided over by two bishops, the chapter general's very first official action was to sack the Calabrian trouble-maker. He was banished from Rome and declared unfit to hold any office until at least the next meeting, which was supposed to be in 1641.[16] Ignoring this ruling, the following month Calasanz amazingly appointed him procurator general for Sardinia and Spain.[17] There was a strange weakness in the father general that he could not see that Alacchi was simply more trouble than he was worth; that though enthusiastic and energetic, he was incapable of getting along with people, or of running a school once it had been set up. His talents lay in the initial charm that convinced princes and municipal councils to support his schemes. But his unreliability and his wildly fluctuating tempers, linked with more serious allegations, including the continual rumours of sexual misconduct, clearly showed that Calasanz was most unwise to lend him his continued and unconditional support.

Melchiorre set out five days later, via Sardinia and Barcelona, and was soon soliciting the Bishop of Urgel to open a school in Guissona in Catalonia, with Calasanz's full encouragement.[18] The father general, however, delayed sending any staff for the potential foundation, claiming that there were too many corsairs at sea and too many assassins to risk the land route.[19] Meanwhile, as usual for Father Melchiorre, he fell out with his companion – a young cleric called Alberto Sansoni – who soon abandoned him. With the arrest of his patron, the Bishop of Urgel, for conspiracy against King Philip IV, his Spanish mission drew to a close.

A few years later, in September 1641, he wrote sadly to Father Calasanz, 'The Lord has made me unfit for manual work ... and has sent me a cancer of the breast which is growing so that I spend the greater part of each day in bed with the pain.' The doctors in nearby Barcelona offered no hope, so Father Melchiorre was treating himself: 'I use no other medicine, other than washing it with urine and then I bathe strips of cloth with barley water and rosy apples [to cover it], and so I spend my time, until the Lord wishes to gather me to him. I have had a ditch dug in which to bury myself, and the stone with its inscription prepared.' He found the Catalans unsympathetic, being, in his opinion, 'apt to rob and lie, so I would rather die alone than entrust myself to them'. However, help was at hand. 'I was in such affliction that the Lord decided to console me by sending me help and not letting me die alone like a dog. Two Sicilian soldiers arrived, and being fed up of war, have asked to be ordained; I immediately accepted them.'[20] It was a pitiful letter, full of pathos, perhaps designed to make the father general feel guilty at sending him so far from Italy. But, lying hundreds of miles across the Mediterranean, with a shooting pain in his breast and an arm so painful he could no longer lift it, with nausea catching at his throat, Alacchi could not resist issuing a final warning to his old mentor against those whom he had seen in his work as an official visitor, denying the existence of God, and above all 'relaxing into the temptation of carnal vice'. Once more, he provided Calasanz with a list of evil-doers: in first position was his erstwhile friend Father Stefano Cherubini, who seems to have fallen from his favour although the documents do not provide any further information as to the reasons. Then came Ambrogio Ambrogi, whom he had hated since the onboard groping incident; Agostino Pucci; Francesco Baldi; Carlo Cesario, who had already spent time in chains for his 'grave crimes'; and the calligrapher Eustachio Ravaggio. When Calasanz received this letter he ignored the warnings, but immediately sent permission for Father Melchiorre to come home.[21]

A few days later, with the two new Sicilian soldier-priests, presumably hastily ordained by a friendly local bishop, Alacchi declared the creation of the foundation of Guissona, then locked the doors and took a ship bound for Italy. He brought with him the keys to the school, which would be found and inventoried in Calasanz's room after his death.

By the time he returned to Italy Melchiorre was a very sick man, and the cancer in his chest had brought him very close to death. As he entered the gates of Rome on horseback, being too weak to walk, his horse was unluckily frightened by a shot from a nearby arquebus and, unable to control it because of the pain in his arm, Father Melchiorre was thrown to the ground and broke his thigh bone. He lingered through the winter and in spring Calasanz sent the dying man down to Sicily, 'where in the future he can do more being ill, than he ever did in the past being healthy'.[22] Perhaps Calasanz hoped that he could make some amends, if only by dying in a stoically virtuous and exemplary fashion. After so much unwise tolerance over the years, such a lack of pity at the end seems brutal. Alacchi's stretcher was loaded onto a boat and he set sail for Palermo where he arrived just in time for Father Vincenzo Berro to read the last rites for his old novice master.[23] Father Melchiorre died on 4 July 1642.

'See that this business does not become public'

Father Vincenzo Berro is remembered today within the order as the author of the *Notes on the Foundation*, 1,526 densely written manuscript pages (now 'plastificated' into a single volume by laminating each manuscript page and binding the result together), which he probably wrote between 1662 and 1665. Born in 1603 and joining the Piarists in his teens, Father Vincenzo's whole life was the order, and as Calasanz's last attendant he was ideally placed to observe the crisis that would engulf them all in the 1640s. Vincenzo Berro was a shy man and a great believer in the rigid observance of the *Rules*, and his historical information is generally very accurate, although it displays an understandable tendency to give priority to tales of the miraculous and prophetic signs of future sainthood. After a tough noviciate under Father Melchiorre's supervision,[1] followed by a few years teaching at the elite Nazarene College, Vincenzo was sent to the bleak upland village of San Salvatore Maggiore where the Piarists had been forced to open a school for Cardinal Francesco Barberini's tenants, from which they were relieved to be expelled a few years later when the cardinal received some unfavourable reports from a disenchanted father.

After a period in Naples and a return to Rome for the chapter general of 1637, Vincenzo was again sent back to Naples where he disgraced himself in a smuggling scandal. In order to alleviate the financial burden of running the school, the fathers had been awarded a special concession of tax-free flour. In 1636 the king had ordered the viceroy to 'take everything possible from this kingdom', and the viceroy himself, the Duke of Medina, had remarked that 'the city is making a larger contribution than has ever been made before'[2] to the coffers of the Spanish king, as he cranked the taxes ever upwards. A tax relief concession on flour constituted a considerable donation to the financial well-being of the school. However, Father Berro, then headmaster, had a better notion how to exploit the advantage this offered. He sent one of the lay brothers, Antonio Lolli (henceforth always known as Brother Antonio della Farina – of the Flour) to the local grocer, Giuseppe Matteo, to ask him whether he would like to buy a quantity of tax-free flour. According to Brother Antonio's report, the grocer said no twice, but his wife intervened on his behalf, saying, 'Bring it anyhow. Even though he says no, he does want it really.' Matteo apparently then enquired whether the deal involved any danger, but was told that as the Piarists had been given the flour as a charitable donation all was well. He decided that if there were any query, he would simply reply that it was being brought round to him so that he could make it into bread for the schools. Father Berro always intended to use the profits for the benefit of the school, not for his personal enrichment. He was not the only one to think of this criminal loophole; in 1647 Naples would erupt in a famous and violent revolt, led by the fisherman, Masaniello, whose own wife had been imprisoned for flour smuggling, the very same crime.[3] Father Berro was very aware that what he was doing was illegal, though it had been done before; not only did he try to keep it secret from the father provincial, but he arranged for some ten containers to be secretly transported one hour after sunset by four Piarists with two donkeys, which were not the actions of a man at ease with his tax obligations. 'Father Nicolò Maria Gavotti and others told him not to do it, since there were rigorous laws against it, which had been publicized,' but Vincenzo persisted, distrusting Gavotti, and knowing it had been done before. What he did not realize was that he should have bribed the police before his donkeys set out.[4] He had reason to distrust Gavotti, erstwhile 'individual companion' to Father Stefano Cherubini and a man who, in the words of the father provincial, 'has no equal when it comes to plotting and trickery'.[5] So Gavotti's warning to Father Berro went unheeded.

The next morning, Thursday, the authorities reacted. The donkey transport had been spotted trotting suspiciously through the streets in the dark; the grocer 'was accused by spies and thrown into jail, and on Friday morning he was sentenced to prison'.[6] His claim to be simply receiving the flour to be made into bread for the Piarists presumably looked very thin, given the secretive night-time delivery. The fathers' tax-free status was suspended, and a great deal of goodwill evaporated instantly. Calasanz was furious and accepted Berro's resignation of his headship with alacrity, pointing out that 'you knew the prohibition of the flour had been renewed and you did exactly the opposite, so that we have now been deprived of the privilege of the franchise and the house's relationship with a great benefactor has been spoiled'.[7] As usual, Calasanz's immediate reaction was that all this must be kept secret, but it was soon clear that this was impossible. The poor grocer languished in prison, although to be fair Calasanz ordered that no efforts should be spared to ensure his release. Father Giuseppe Fedele, provincial of Naples, ran around the vice-regal court: 'First we spoke to the viceroy's confessor, then to the Duke of Sermoneta, who sent his secretary to the regent Casanatta; but because nothing was done, we spoke to the vice-reine, who took the memorial and passed it on to her husband the viceroy. However, nothing was done, because without money these things are not achieved ... There is no hour nor moment that we are not trying to negotiate his freedom.'[8] But it soon became clear that although the pleas for clemency had been accepted, the grocer was to spend some six weeks in jail to provide an example to others not to flout the law. No sooner was he released than he and his daughter demanded substantial amounts of compensation, which the order was unable or unwilling to pay. After several months of haggling, in late 1638 they finally agreed to a settlement of 500 Masses, and Calasanz organized that these be divided amongst the schools so that Naples was not solely burdened with such a time-consuming amount of compensatory prayer.[9]

It was at this delicate moment, with Father Berro suspended from the headship and Father Fedele, the provincial, busy smoothing matters over at court and irritated with his colleague for flouting his authority, that another controversial incident took place. Brother Ignazio Guarnotto di Giesù, aged thirty-three, who taught the third grammar class, was reported to be misbehaving. Father Fedele reported back to Calasanz:

Not only is he a useless teacher [*inhabile*], but he is also tainted with sensuality [*molto macchiato di sensualità*], because:
1. The pupils were touching one another [*si toccavano l'uno l'altro*], and he became aware of it, but pretended not to notice and said nothing;
2. One pupil confessed to Father Giovan Luca di Rosa that not only did he permit a boy to touch another in class, but the teacher told him to let himself be touched;
3. He told a pupil to go and call another one because he wanted to give him several kisses [*voleva dare quattro baci*].

These things have been reported by the boys to Father Giovan Luca and to Brother Marco Manzella and to the parents of these children, and some parents have hinted by small comments that they know something about this, because they have asked to take their children out of school. I am writing to you in brief to request permission to send Brother Ignazio to Genoa, because there are some here who will defend him, as they defend the other vices in these schools, especially since this deals with children.[10]

It seems some members of the household were not that keen for action to be taken since the problem 'only' involved children. Presumably Genoa was chosen since it was geographically the furthest house in Italy from Naples. Calasanz, however, immediately ordered Fedele to lock up the errant brother, away from the rest of the house, while he tried to sort out a solution: 'Make sure it is a secure place to keep him locked away from everyone, which such a punishment deserves, and Your Reverence should pay particular attention to this, and keep me informed.' But Father Fedele thought that incarceration was too harsh, and that Brother Ignazio should rather be transferred elsewhere. Father Vincenzo Berro was disgusted by Fedele's proposal. 'He said we should jail brother Ignazio immediately,' Fedele wrote to Calasanz, 'which was not my opinion, because I knew it all by hearsay only and did not have enough proof.'[11] The provincial accused Father Berro of acting too hastily because he was so upset about Stefano Cherubini's activities in Naples a few years earlier. The evidence of a father, a brother, several children and their parents was not sufficient to arouse the father general to more decisive action. Brother Ignazio was duly transferred to Genoa, where he was ordained two years later and continued to teach as before.[12] As the order spun into turmoil in the mid-1640s, Ignazio, now promoted to Father Guarnotto, became a strong ally of his like-minded colleague Cherubini, supporting him faithfully in his bid to take over the order and perhaps enabling him to continue encouraging his pupils to touch one another.[13]

Father Berro was outraged by the solution to Ignazio's misconduct, and found himself in increasing conflict with the father provincial, but having lost his headship over the flour smuggling, was in no position to protest. Fedele protected himself further from daily criticism by moving Father Berro to Messina. Berro continued to chafe against his father provincial, and Calasanz was forced once more to admonish him: 'As Your Reverence must be obeyed by others, so you must obey the provincial, and if the two of you are adversaries the community cannot function well, and it would be good if you could agree, otherwise I will impose a remedy.'[14]

With Father Berro safely transferred to Sicily, the next sexual scandal could be dealt with by Father Fedele more discreetly. In July 1639 the father general received an irritating letter from a certain Signor Pacifico Tranzo. 'I have had a letter from the father of a pupil complaining that his son has been provoked to evil by Brother Stefano di San Giuseppe Battista,' he wrote to Fedele. As always, Calasanz's first priority was the cover-up. 'One should first assure oneself of the truth with all secrecy, which in such cases should be dissimulated and covered up, so it does not appear true even if it is true.' He then cast doubt on the reliability of Brother Giuseppe who had confirmed the story, though he spoilt the effect by admitting that Brother Stefano had done something similar previously in the school in Cosenza before it had been closed down due to earthquake damage. As a result of Brother Stefano's actions, Signor Tranzo's son had been thrown out of school and told to attend the Jesuit establishment. Even as Calasanz was writing to Fedele, another letter arrived from Tranzo senior. Although the father general sniffed at his epistolary style – 'it seems the letter comes rather from a schoolboy than from a grown man' – the message was clear and unequivocal: 'He tells me again what happened in the toilets at the school.' There can be little doubt about the nature of the activity. What other kind of 'provocation to evil' takes place in school toilets? Pacifico Tranzo was also clear about the solution. His son should not be thrown out of school; on the contrary, there was a younger son who should also be admitted, and Brother Stefano should be stopped. Clearly, his son's education should not suffer, and the perpetrators should be dealt with. He ended with a clear threat that if he did not receive full satisfaction he would take the matter up with the Church authorities and make a huge scandal. Father Calasanz immediately instructed Fedele to admit the younger child and to ensure that he was taught with particular attention, in order to pacify the father. Once more he adjured the provincial at all costs to keep the matter hidden: 'See that this business does not become public, but is covered up as far as possible, and write to tell me how you have dealt with it ... Your Reverence must behave with great prudence and cover up everything as far as possible from the public, even if in private we find the failings to be real.'[15] In a footnote, the editor of the correspondence, archivist Father Leodegario Picanyol, writing in the 1950s, noted astonishingly that this letter shows Calasanz 'full of truly saintly zeal'. Brother Stefano was doubtless moved to yet another school where it would be naive to think he did not continue to frequent the boys' toilets. Fedele was presumably successful in hushing up the scandal and pacifying Signor Tranzo, for the matter disappears from the correspondence. Without the incensed Father Berro to mollify, Fedele could devote his attention to disciplining another recalcitrant brother, Andrea Leonardi, whose tastes ran rather to theft and female company, perhaps equally shocking to the celibate father general.[16]

Where carnal passions were concerned, the father provincial himself was not completely above suspicion, which perhaps accounts for his leniency towards sexual offenders on his staff. The following year a disgruntled Father Gasparo Sangermano dell'Annunziazione sent a complaint to Calasanz, pointing out that he had mentioned the problem to Fedele directly but since he had failed to act upon the advice, he now felt obliged to write to the highest authority: 'The father provincial himself, not once but many times, told me to look at the beautiful boy students who were allowed to stay over lunch at school, and he condemned their staying and said he knows the problems that can come of it. And I replied to him that he should remedy it and prohibit it, because it is his responsibility. He did nothing about it, and then he is annoyed that I inform Your Reverence.'[17] Father Gasparo was clearly venting a grudge, but it sounds as though he was quoting his colleague admiring 'the beautiful boy students'. Calasanz does not seem to have followed up the complaint, but Father Fedele's appreciation of the temptations and his reluctance to remove them may account for his sympathy for colleagues who succumbed.

Father Berro, meanwhile, exiled to Sicily, was asked by Calasanz to keep a special eye 'on the purity of our members, for I understand that it is usually lacking in those areas'.[18] The father general seemed several times to hint that sexual purity was a particular problem for Sicilian members, but the most notorious offenders within the order would not be southern Italians.

Father Berro never had any problem with Calasanz's authority but with his immediate superiors matters often ran less smoothly. In 1641 he again ran into problems with his hot-headed decisions. The Society of Jesus hoped to open a college for nobles in Messina; they had received papal permission, and had rented a palace from the Prince of Roccafiorita, in front of the Monastery of Montevergine. All was ready for the opening on 11 February. But the night before, at around 7 o'clock in the evening, the head of the Theatines, an order that bore a great grudge against the Jesuits, together with many Fransciscans, Dominicans, Carmelites, Augustinians, Basilians, Fatebenefratelli and Piarists, along with a huge mob, broke down the door of the palace, and surged into the rooms, destroying everything in their wake. The Jesuits often aroused antagonism, partly for regional or purely local reasons, and partly in reaction to their political and intellectual success, but it rarely spilled over into outright violence. Many of the rioting clerics stayed on guard at the palace during that night and the following day, in spite of efforts by the senate and other officials who tried in vain to mediate. The Society of Jesus gave up on their attempt to open a college and withdrew for the time being, but the following year rented the palazzo of Marchese Pintodattolo and organized a new opening for 2 February 1642. Once again armed clerics invaded the palace, headed this time by the Dominicans. Father Vincenzo was among the attacking crowd. At this point the Jesuits abandoned their project of a college for nobles in Messina completely, but there was considerable ill feeling against the Piarists because of Berro's behaviour. Calasanz was furious. As soon as he heard about it he wrote:

I understand that the Senate of this city resents your actions in showing yourself opposed to the decision of the Jesuit Fathers who are favoured by the said Senate. Your Reverence will in public renounce your deeds and give your consent to the said resolution, so that in some way we may placate the just irritation the illustrious Senate has shown towards us, and understand that our Order is in that city to show its piety and not to fight against anyone.[19]

1. Portrait of Calasanz, aged 87. An authentic portrait, dated 1644.

North ←———

2. Map of Rome by Giovanni Maggi, 1625. Maggi ran out of money and died in 1618, a few years before this huge twelve-sheet perspectival map could be engraved and printed in time for the Jubilee year.

A. Towards Castel Sant'Angelo, the Vatican.
B. Piazza Navona.
C. Palazzo Pamphilij.
D. Piazza de' Massimi, headquarters of the Piarist Order and San Pantaleo, the Piarists' mother church.
E. Santa Maria sopra Minerva. Campanella's Dominican convent, where Galileo was interrogated by the Inquisition.

12. Calasanz's desk. A simple wooden desk where Calasanz wrote most of his thousands of letters. At the side is a stand with a seal, and underneath is a footwarmer. The room also includes Calasanz's bed.

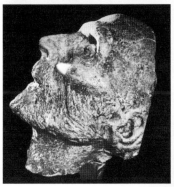

13. Death mask of Calasanz.

14. Relics of Calasanz. A gilded reliquary containing the saint's heart, liver, spleen and cranium.

15. (left) Last communion of Calasanz by Francisco de Goya, 1819. Surrounded by his pupils, Calasanz, already close to death, takes his last communion in this famous image by Goya, an ex-pupil of the Scolopi. Commissioned by the Piarist fathers of San Antón in Madrid to decorate one of the altars in their church, the image was used on a Nicaraguan stamp in 1999 to celebrate fifty years of Piarist presence in the country.

16. (right) Statue of Calasanz, 1755, by Innocenzio Spinazzi, in St Peter's Rome. Calasanz was beatified in 1748 and sanctified in 1767. In 1948 he was declared Celestial Patron before God of all popular Christian schools in the world, by Pope Pius XII.

Calasanz also wrote a grovelling apology to the senate. Vincenzo Berro was recalled to Rome.

He was soon sent back to Naples as a simple teacher, which is where he heard Father Melchiorre's last confession, and where he remained until he was expelled from the kingdom during the order's great upheaval of 1646. At that point Berro returned to Calasanz's side and remained there until the old man's death. After the two embarrassing events in Naples and Messina, Father Berro seems to have calmed down, and his behaviour from then on is exemplary. His eyewitness account, the *Notes on the Foundation*, provides – apart from the letters, which are generally written with a less coherent narrative – a rare contemporary source.

But at the time of the chapter general in 1637, which expelled Father Melchiorre, Berro's writing fame lay many years in the future. One of his least favourite colleagues, Father Stefano Cherubini, appeared at the assembly in Rome, flaunting his new appointment as procurator or visitor general. He had spent time in various schools, enjoying his high status within the order. His taste for luxury remained, and he scandalized the more observant fathers by travelling 'in a carriage, on horseback or in a litter', all forbidden according to the *Constitutions*, and by express decree of the chapter general. The most luxurious mode of travel usually permitted to a Piarist was a mule, and even that was only by special permission.[20] Father Stefano had been left to work with some degree of independence, although he had occasionally complained about 'working from morning until night without any recognition, while others take the credit'. He found it preferable to stay in Cesena where he established a comfortable regime for himself, and the correspondence between Cherubini and Calasanz continued at its previous amiable and conversational level. For instance, Calasanz wrote to him about the thunderbolt that fell on Campo Marzio killing a few bystanders; he told him how the murder rate increased in the city when the temperature rose; and how 400 Turks had attacked the island of Ischia and taken 700 prisoners including the Duke of Naples and his family; and he asked him to get hold of a few thousand goose quill writing pens for the schools.[21] There is no indication of any cooling in the relationship. Indeed, Calasanz became dependent on Cherubini's administrative and financial skills for regular monthly sums of around 100 scudi to keep the pupils of the Nazarene College fed and clothed, and the Rome school free of debt. He was clearly very astute in business matters, both financially numerate and speedy in his decision-making. Calasanz reassured the Archbishop of Chieti, when they were discussing a tricky inheritance the order had been left, that Father Stefano would be able to sort out in a very few days what others had not managed even to understand in several weeks.[22] When in March 1639 the Barberini sisters moved to Rome from Florence and took a liking to the Piarist noviciate at Monte Cavallo on the Quirinal for their nunnery, it fell to Cherubini to sort out emergency quarters for the order's novices. It was of course impossible to say no to the papal family, so within two weeks Father Stefano had organized a six-month lease on a new location. 'I'm so busy I could do with ten legs, ten arms and a hundred heads,' he wrote at the time.[23] The property in Cesena, where Cherubini spent most of his time in these years, produced quantities of grain, oil, animals and wine, which by judicious harvesting and sales kept the most pressing debt-collectors away from Calasanz's office.[24] The father general also continued to cultivate Stefano's important brother. When Flavio was having a new garden wall built around his property in Frascati in the hills around Rome, for instance, Calasanz wrote to the headmaster of the school there, asking him to go round twice a day to check on the workmen, so keen was he to ingratiate himself with the influential apostolic lawyer.[25]

After the outcry resulting from his discovery, and the subsequent arguments between his family and the order, Stefano Cherubini had gone directly to Pope Urban – via his brother presumably – and been awarded a pontifical brief confirming his appointment as procurator, and specifically placing him above the provincials themselves in status. This became particularly visible at the chapter general of 1637 where the seating arrangements were determined by the hierarchical position, and the members of the order had their noses publicly rubbed in Father Stefano's victory. There was an outcry when they saw how Cherubini had been rewarded for his behaviour by having his prestige and his position enhanced; as Father Berro understatedly commented, 'this rather displeased the whole Chapter'. Moreover the *Rules* absolutely forbade any procurement of honours or dignities and Father Stefano had clearly done just that. A motion was hastily passed that no one could go over the father general's head to the pope without the specific permission of the father general himself. But when it turned out that Father Calasanz had in fact solicited the brief on his behalf, the wind was taken out of the protestors' sails. Nevertheless the chapter general insisted that Father Stefano resign, and that it reappoint him to his position, a somewhat Pyrrhic victory one would have thought, although he did agree to sit below the father provincials. Then the meeting turned its attention to administrative matters.

Throughout the sessions, Father Mario Sozzi acted as one of the secretaries. He first appeared in an official capacity here, putting his name to one of the anti-Alacchi memos, along with a dozen other fathers. Along with Melchiorre Alacchi and Stefano Cherubini, Mario Sozzi is one of the most controversial of the Piarist fathers. He, even more than the other two, has been vilified by his colleagues and historians. Father Berro would write later that 'the calamities which befell us, all had their foundation in the cunning machinations of this man'. According to him, even Sozzi's mother was alienated by his actions, claiming he was no son of hers and must have been exchanged by the wet nurse, but this must be *ex post facto* rationalization. Born in Chiusi, Sozzi entered the Piarist noviciate in Naples in May 1630, aged twenty-two. He claimed to be of noble origin 'and in fact he did mention and even visit some people of quality whom he claimed were his relations, but I went with him in Rome to see some of these gentlemen,' wrote Berro, 'and it didn't seem to me that they treated him as such.'[26] At the age of twelve he received his tonsure along with a small benefice from the pope and his brother Claudio later allocated him the income from a farm, which brought him in a small annuity. By special papal permission, probably through his relative Cardinal Cenini, he took minor orders, and began work as an assistant to a blind lawyer, guiding him to court and reading out his documents. During this time he made the acquaintance of the respected senior Piarist, Father Pietro Casani, and soon decided to join the order. Calasanz and the cardinal organized it so that Sozzi was excused his two-year noviciate, 'since like a wolf he pretended to be very devout, and sold himself as a man of great humility, although he was the exact reverse of the medal,' as Berro later wrote bitterly about Sozzi's rapid progress through the ranks. He was ordained a deacon on 6 May 1630 and a priest three days later. Then began his duties proper with the order. He was sent from school to school – to Florence, back to Naples, Palermo, Rome, Poli, Frascati and then back to Rome again – which perhaps indicates that no house was particularly keen to retain his services. He had 'little literature, not having studied any of the sciences, and not even a mediocre foundation in Latin', according to one colleague.[27] Reports of his activities are not positive. During a short stay in Florence, the superior noted that he 'could not put much confidence in Father Mario, who is more impassioned than you could believe'.[28] A year later he is one of the 'restless and proud' priests who have requested a transfer to a different order, to whom Calasanz initially said good riddance, although the transfer eventually came to nothing.[29] In 1634 he was studying to retake his confession examinations, which would seem to indicate that he was not of the highest intelligence.[30] Then followed a major argument with Alacchi in Palermo – but it is hard to evaluate the significance of this, as everyone fell out with Alacchi. In Poli he seems to have taken the side of a local parish priest in a mysterious controversy against his own brother priests. He also caused problems when he told the Duchess of Poli that the headmaster, Father Diomede, hated everything about Poli, especially the wine, which of course offended the duchess, who was the major local patron.[31] The headmaster in turn noted that Sozzi was 'very greedy for property and gluttonous, and nobody knew how he managed to get hold of things and money, and when he had nothing to chew on, he would always be chewing paper', a strange kind of behaviour, which appears odd to the point of obsession. He kept devotional items and ribbons and suchlike worth a considerable sum of money in his room, claiming to have permission from his superiors, but it was noted that he had many more items than would ever have been permitted. Berro claimed that he retold events to the father general 'as he pleased',[32] but, in spite of this rather strange behaviour, Calasanz was satisfied enough to nominate him to the responsible position of secretary to the chapter general of 1637.

After the assembly, when Sozzi voted against Father Alacchi, and otherwise performed his duties unremarkably, the provincials returned to their far-flung schools. Father Mario Sozzi was appointed by Calasanz to go to Florence, where he would work as confessor in the Piarist church of Santa Maria de' Ricci, adjacent to the school and primarily catering for the pupils.[33] No one could have foretold the dramatic consequences of this appointment.

CHAPTER ELEVEN

'Touching the shameless parts
is not a sin'

By the late 1630s the school in Florence was well established with excellent contacts at court, a large and stable student base, solid financial
backing and the close friendship of the eminent, though theoretically
disgraced, Galileo. The community consisted of clever young men,
mostly aged around thirty, apart from the headmaster, Father Giovan
Domenico Romani, who, as an older man, was supposed to provide a
source of authority. The staff included Francesco Michelini's carefully
selected group of intellectual stars – the mathematicians Clemente
Settimi, Angelo Morelli, Ambrogio Ambrogi and Salvatore Grise, the
more literary Giovan Francesco Apa and Carlo Conti, the painter
Domenico Rosa. The new arrival, Father Mario Sozzi, found himself
outclassed intellectually, and totally out of sympathy with the scientifically enlightened and relatively relaxed society of the Florence school.
Lacking even a fragment of a sense of humour, he soon found himself
at odds with the rest of his colleagues, and even though Father
Clemente in particular often invited him to come and study with the
others, Father Mario kept his distance. During the carnival in February
1640 Calasanz was told that the Florentine school 'had been rather
lax and shown a bad example',[1] and by March Father Romani was trying to get rid of Sozzi. The request was turned down, for Father
Mario was one of the few priests in Florence enthusiastic to hear

confessions publicly in the church, rather than teach, and Calasanz had no replacement.[2]

Meanwhile, the Florentine school had been selected for a special honour. A young Jewish boy had converted to Christianity and the Grand Duke of Tuscany asked the Piarists to take him in and instruct him in the elements of his new religion. It was suddenly very important that the house be seen to be a model of Christian propriety. 'You must take great care to make him devout,' wrote the father general. 'Teach him with charity how to confess himself and how to take the Holy Sacrament with profit, so that he realizes he is amongst reformed religious and if you find anyone mentioning anything to him that is not about devotional matters, Your Reverence must punish him well.'[3] However, this was perhaps not the right place for him. Three weeks later Calasanz was warning the Florentine teachers not to mess around with mocking nicknames, even in the recreation period, under pain of eating their meals sitting under the table for three days in a row. He asked Father Romani to entrust the young convert to the special care of someone particularly pious. Romani chose Father Mario Sozzi.[4]

It was at this point in time that a plum fell into Father Mario's hands and the convert was forgotten in the excitement of his discovery. A young girl from the local orphanage came to the Piarist church of Santa Maria de' Ricci and asked Father Mario to confess her. What she told him must have made the stubble on the young priest's tonsure stand up in horror and excitement. The girl lived in an Institute for Poor Girls, run on supposedly religious guidelines with daily Mass and a guaranteed pious education, by Faustina Mainardi, a wealthy Florentine widow 'with a reputation as a lady of great prudence and bounty'. Her spiritual mentor was a respectable-seeming canon, Pandolfo Ricasoli, 'a most noble Florentine also held in great esteem as an excellent priest for reason of his doctrine, prudence and virtuous deeds, and much sought after as a man of singular quality'.[5] However, it transpired from the girl's confession that the canon and Signora Mainardi had been renting out their wards for sex to local noblemen for some time. Initially the girls had been persuaded by Ricasoli's spurious theological explanation that 'even touching the shameless parts is not a sin because the natural passage is not broken', and, reassured on that point, the girls 'had many friendships with young men and satisfied their every desire, within the terms of those conditions'.[6] In fact, a few years earlier, the inquisitor in Florence, a Franciscan, had heard rumours about this select brothel for the wealthy – or more particularly about this 'pernicious heresy' – and had attempted to investigate. Canon Ricasoli, a relation of the ruling Medici, had managed to get that inquisitor moved elsewhere before he came too close to the truth, but with the girl's confession to Father Mario the fat was in the fire, especially after he persuaded her to repeat the tale out of the confessional while he took notes and drew up an official accusation.[7] Armed with this document, Father Sozzi rushed to the nearest office of the Inquisition. Ironically, Ricasoli would be primarily accused of 'stinking heresy' for his cunning explanation of permissive fondling, whilst his negligence towards the young orphans entrusted to his care came a very distant second.

The new inquisitor general in Florence, Giovan Francesco Muzzarelli, who incidentally was also responsible for supervising the conditions of Galileo's captivity, was delighted with the exciting evidence of misconduct he had been handed, and in Father Mario he realized he had a convincing witness for the eventual court case.

Over the course of the next few months, the two men became close friends, the relationship lubricated by gifts from Father Mario of several flasks of a particularly good wine from his farm in Montepulciano. As the friendship grew, Father Mario 'told him everything that was said in the school and everything he knew'[8] about his fellow Piarists. This characteristic of ingratiating himself with locally influential officials and noblemen, at the expense of close and amicable relations with his colleagues had already been evident in his previous posting at Poli. As he grew closer to his new friend, Father Mario grew ever more distant from his own house and increasingly reluctant to become involved in any of the school activities. But within three months of his arrival, Father Mario began to use his new friendship to devastating effect.

A series of seemingly trivial incidents occurred, and each time Father Mario summoned the inquisitor to resolve matters in his favour. For instance, in the wake of his success with the Faustina scandal, Father Mario wished to continue hearing public confessions, but was assigned to other duties, perhaps to distance him from such public events and scandal. He begged his new friend to intervene on his behalf, and Father Muzzarelli obliged without hesitation. Although it was a public holiday and the church of Santa Maria de' Ricci was full to overcrowding, Father Muzzarelli suddenly arrived in full official regalia, publicly marched over to the confessional, and with great fanfare pulled out the other Piarist father who was on duty there, Father Luca di San Giuseppe – who was moreover a close relation of his – and installed his friend Sozzi in the booth. It was not only 'a great scandal to all those in the church', as a witness commented, but also a shocking infringement of the Piarists' right to self-government.

On another occasion the Florentine headmaster had been checking everyone's room, and as usual had discovered many forbidden things in Father Mario's cell. 'He removed from his room many sweet things, such as marzipan, rich fruit cake, crunchy biscuits, sugared almonds, and other such foodstuffs, and placing them on the table divided them up equally among everyone, including Father Mario. But someone – I don't know who – quietly laughed, because Father Mario knew that these things came from his room, so he made a scene, and went to the inquisitor, and said many inappropriate things.'[9] Once again, Sozzi begged his friend to intervene, and the inquisitor immediately imposed a ban on free travel by the Piarist teachers – no member could leave Florence without his written permission.

One night, several of the Florentine fathers managed to convince one of the older fathers that they had heard that at the upcoming chapter general he would be elected provincial, in charge of the whole region.

To celebrate the honour, the hopeful provincial scraped together enough money to provide a special meal, and the young fathers prepared a welcome prayer in Latin doggerel to invite all members of the house 'to appear at the feast with great hunger under pain of excommunication for those who do not comply'. Father Mario was offended by the use of the excommunication threat, which poked fun at the Holy Office of the Inquisition's most serious formula – but only after he had eaten his fill. Another visit to the office of his friend, Father Muzzarelli, ensued. A complaint was lodged with the Inquisition for 'use of certain flippant quotations'[10] and the school was dismayed to receive yet another official visit from a representative of the Holy Office.

The problems continued and although Calasanz thought about moving Father Mario elsewhere, initially he was still needed in the church and soon the inquisitor made it very clear he wanted him to stay so that he would be available to testify at the trial of Madame Faustina. Calasanz wrote several times forbidding anyone 'to use strange names or mocking nicknames' or to make any kind of jokes, from which one can safely assume that Father Mario had still not discovered a sense of humour.[11] He would later claim that his visits to the Florentine Inquisition were motivated purely by 'the grave danger to so many souls, and by zeal and honour and the glory of God'.[12]

Once again his strangely compulsive behaviour was noted: 'He used the confessional as a shop for all kinds of things, making a thousand little hiding places both in the confessional and in his room where he hid sweets, candies, marzipan, and all other kinds of foodstuffs, and ribbons and other presents for every kind of person.'[13] Calasanz asked the headmaster to remind everyone that hoarding food was not permitted and, without mentioning Sozzi specifically, asked him to take two colleagues and check everyone's rooms. 'Remove anything superfluous and make a note of it, because no one should have anything locked away.'[14]

This was standard procedure but for Father Mario it was yet another step too far and he later wrote to the Inquisition as part of a wider

accusation against the order, complaining that 'this visit basically consisted of nothing more than a search for information against me, since
I had the original copy of my complaint [to the Inquisition].'[15] Of
course the accusation that the visitors had removed private papers
belonging to the Inquisition itself – the 'original complaint' – was
guaranteed to excite the wrath of that organization, and it had terrible
implications. But what the visitors had actually found was Father
Mario's hoard of sweets. There was, of course, no mention of this in
Sozzi's reports to the Inquisition.

By now Father Calasanz must have realized he had a serious problem in the Florentine house, and in September 1640 he ordered Father
Mario's transfer to Narni. As a Spaniard, an Aragonese, Calasanz had
been born in a country where the Inquisition – though a rather different
organization in his homeland – was very powerful and feared, and he
must have been aware of the potential for trouble which Sozzi was
courting by drawing the Inquisition into the internal affairs of the
order. However, following his usual procedure, as soon as he heard of
the order, Father Mario once more scuttled around to his friend at the
Inquisition. His accusation this time was that the Piarists were trying to
ruin the trial of Faustina Mainardi and Canon Ricasoli, which had started on 9 August, by removing the star witness. Father Muzzarelli sprang
into action to protect his show trial. He provided Father Mario with a
sheaf of documents explaining how essential was his presence in
Florence and sent him hotfoot to Rome to make a formal deposition to
the Holy Office of the Inquisition, to the assessor, Monsignor Francesco
Albizzi.

Rome responded with heavyweight back-up. On 20 October 1640,
the cardinal secretary of the Holy Office, Francesco Barberini, wrote to
Muzzarelli: 'Having carefully listened to Father Mario, their
Excellencies [the cardinals of the Holy Office] have decided to send him
back, as you desired, but His Holiness [Pope Urban VIII], who has been
kept informed both by the letter you wrote to the assessor and by Father
Mario himself, recommends you to use dexterity, prudence and vigi-

lance in such an important matter, in order that all evil is uncovered.'[16] Sozzi was obviously making a name for himself in Rome. Now the Barberini Pope and his nephews, as well as the Holy Office of the Inquisition, were familiar with his problems.

'Just a case of brotherly persecution'

Pope Urban VIII, Maffeo Barberini, had been elected in 1623, the fifth son of a socially insignificant Florentine wool merchant, proud, insecure and anxious to enhance his family's position and prerogatives. As a youth he had attended a Jesuit school; he had written poetry and been interested in literature and the arts, and even when he had ascended Peter's throne, he still tried to set aside one hour a day to read poetry. Teodoro Ameyden, a Dutch lawyer who would later advise Calasanz on his legal position when the order's affairs were at their lowest point, wrote of Urban: 'He wished to seem a prince rather than a pontiff, a ruler rather than a shepherd',[1] and modern historians have agreed with that view: 'The Pope's concern to advance his lineage both materially and symbolically was the dominating political consideration of his reign.'[2] Papal relatives customarily acquired wealth and influence when their man was elected. One of the main differences from a traditional monarchy was the transitory nature of the kingship – the popes were in the main elderly and their reigns short – so their relations had only a short time in which to consolidate their fortunes and their futures. Urban, however, ruled for over twenty years. In that time he left his mark on Rome, so much so that his own physician, Giulio Mancini, would famously declare, 'What the Barbarians did not destroy, the Barberini did', outraged at Urban's order to strip the antique girders from the Pantheon portico to melt down and use to make guns and Bernini's enormous baldaquin in St Peter's. Castel Sant'Angelo was fortified to the point of impregnability to house 6,000 men; the Quirinal was surrounded by a protective wall; and all the while his relations built vast palaces and monuments throughout the city.[3] His close family consisted of two brothers and three nephews, and these were swiftly placed at the apogee of all power structures within Rome. Older brother Carlo, a 'wise and prudent financial administrator',[4] immediately became general of the Church, commander-in-chief of the papal armies. Urban's other brother Antonio Barberini, a pious and grave Capuchin, was dragged from his monastery and promoted to be a reluctant cardinal (known as San'Onofrio to distinguish him from his nephew of the same name).

The cardinal nephews fulfilled a vital role ('*nipote*' is the Italian for nephew, from which the expression 'nepotism' is derived), so much so that when there was no real blood nephew, popes were forced to adopt one, and contemporaries felt that in a system where all authority rested in one figure, a competent cardinal nephew was needed to access the pope and ensure a smooth administration of power. Carlo's eldest son Francesco, aged twenty-six, was nominated cardinal within two months of Urban's accession – his very first nomination to the cardinalate – and swiftly gathered up the reigns of power. A handwritten note of 1632 from the pope ceded him 'the government of our state, with universal supervision and broadest powers'. According to historian Laurie Nussdorfer, Francesco was 'intelligent, erudite, and a cultivated art patron'.[5] He had an apartment at the papal residence, as well as his own palace, and was physically as well as spiritually central to Urban's rule. The Venetian ambassador noted that he was 'closest to the ears [sic] of His Holiness'. He hid his true feelings, and while 'compliant and unobtrusive in Urban VIII's presence, he was vastly diligent and well-served in affairs of state by countless informants'. Nothing got to the pope without his knowledge. In spite of Urban's jealous guarding of his power, which limited his nephew's obvious autonomy, Francesco

Barberini was probably the most powerful man in Rome. A year after the family's accession to the papacy, the Piarists wrote to Cardinal Francesco asking him to be their cardinal protector, since 'it is difficult to succeed without the authority and holy prudence of Your Eminence'.[6] He refused the kind offer, but must have been sympathetic since, a few years later, he began to insist that the Piarists open schools in towns and villages where he owned substantial property. 'I can't say no,' said Calasanz, faced with a demand for three priests and two brothers to run a school in tiny Farfa, where the cardinal had an abbey, 'but I'll do as little as possible.' His stalling techniques worked on this occasion, but within a year or two six staff were sent to San Salvatore Maggiore, a small village under Barberini jurisdiction near Aquila. 'Since it would not have been wise to resist the cardinal prince,' noted one of the fathers, they were forced to agree. 'It is surrounded by mountains, which are usually covered in snow all winter long,' wrote Calasanz, who had not visited the school, but one of the teachers commented bluntly that it was 'a horrid place' and felt like being in the desert. The school closed down after two years.[7]

Taddeo, the second Barberini nephew, was appointed prefect of Rome when the position fell vacant on the death of the hereditary occupant. The Pope announced that Taddeo was to have ceremonial precedence over all diplomats, causing great ruckus and offence as ambassadors took alternative routes around town to avoid having to be seen to give way. The Venetian ambassador came face-to-face with Taddeo in a stand-off that caused ripples throughout the peninsula. On the death of his father in 1630 he was appointed commander-in-chief of the papal armies. His main function, however, was the continuation of the line, so he was promptly married to a wealthy princess, Anna Colonna, and endowed with many rich fiefs, becoming, according to Nussdorfer, 'one of the richest men of his time'.[8]

The youngest Barberini nephew, Antonio, became cardinal at the age of nineteen and proceeded to enjoy it. Described by Nussdorfer as 'high-spirited and fun-loving', he nevertheless held many public responsibilities in Rome and was appointed cardinal chamberlain of the Apostolic Chamber, over Spanish objections. His brother Francesco was keen to restrict his power, initially fearing competition, and the Venetian ambassador noted that 'he does not have a part in government, although he desires it'.[9]

It was the powerful Francesco Barberini and the pope himself who would play decisive roles in the future of the Piarists. As cardinal secretary of the Holy Office Francesco Barberini presided over one of the most feared instruments of the Catholic Church. The Inquisition or Holy Office had developed from the early ecclesiastical courts. In 1231 Gregory IX had commissioned a Dominican prior to enquire into those suspected of heresy, to convert them, or, if they proved recalcitrant, to condemn them. Initially entrusted to the Dominican Order – Domini Canes or the Masters' Dogs in the famous Latin pun – the Holy Office was reorganized in 1542 by Paul III as he attempted to combat the wildfire spread of Lutheranism. The infamous Spanish Inquisition, constituted in 1478 by Sixtus IV, acted with little reference to the central Inquisition based in Rome, and became synonymous in Protestant lands with cruelty and terror.

Under the next few popes the Holy Office was placed under the special command of six cardinals and given authority throughout the world. Its envoys could be sent anywhere and were given great powers to act immediately, against anyone, including archbishops and prelates. They could also call in secular forces to help. Under Paul IV (1555–9) its powers were extended to include immorality, 'crimes of sodomy, procurement, rape and prostitution, to which was added the crime of blasphemy and whatever came under suspicion of simoniac heresy, such as the sale of sacraments, etc'.[10] To cope with the increased workload, the number of cardinal inquisitors was increased.

Although later popes reduced the numbers of cardinals and the Inquisition's powers to concentrate on questions of faith, in 1588 the reforming Sixtus V made the Inquisition officially the most powerful and prestigious congregation. Maintaining the purity of the faith was the foremost priority. As well as all matters of heresy, phantoms, prophesying, magic, cursing and any form of divination came under the Inquisition's umbrella. It was an immensely influential and feared organization.

It was more cautious where sexual crimes were concerned. If, for instance, a suspect claimed that fornication was not a sin, this could be interpreted as a heretical statement and would therefore come clearly under the Inquisition's jurisdiction. Reclaiming concubines, bigamous relationships, witchcraft, and its association with sexual practices with the devil also fell under its remit. In the words of one of Caravaggio's most recent biographers, the Holy Office had 'clearly evolved from being a heresy court into being a court of collective morality ... it intellectualized social practices and applied the rule of suspicion, interpreting the various kinds of deviant behaviour as heretical'.[11] Inquisition cases throughout Italy – in Sicily, Modena, Sardinia, Venice – show that it intervened regularly in sexual matters during the late sixteenth and early seventeenth centuries.[12]

In 1965, at the end of the Vatican II Council, Paul VI changed its name from the Inquisition or Holy Office to the Holy Congregation for the Doctrine of the Faith, in an effort to dissociate it from the unpleasant and fearful connotations of the past. One of the procedural innovations introduced at that time was that authors of doctrinally suspect books were to be given a chance to defend themselves. The head of the Holy Congregation is still the pope himself, represented by the cardinal prefect – Cardinal Joseph Ratzinger since 1982 – and assisted by theologians and university academics. Critics nowadays accuse it still of being secretive, of accepting anonymous accusations, or imposing silence on the accused, and of censuring 'some of the most intelligent and creative people in the Church', theologians whom it considers to hold 'temerarious opinions', while failing to pay enough attention to child molesters.[13] The Congregation 'is the instrument through which the Holy See promotes the deepening of faith and watches vigilantly over its purity. Accordingly, it is the custodian proper of Catholic orthodoxy.'[14] According to Cardinal Ratzinger, 'Of course, we [the Congregation] preserve the right, by statute, to intervene everywhere in the whole Church.'[15] Naturally it is at the head of the official list of the congregations of the Roman Curia.

In the mid-seventeenth century, however, the Inquisition went by its old title, and was headed by the cardinal nephew. From the moment a traveller stood before the walls of Rome and was asked to show the Inquisition officer the books in his luggage before being allowed to enter the city, it was clear that there was a thorough measure of control.[16] The Holy Office or Inquisition still held first place amongst the official policing bodies. A practical handbook for inquisitors, the *Sacro arsenale*, first published in 1621, pointed out that 'since the Inquisition is directly delegated by the Holy apostolic see to know and decide on cases concerning the Faith and the Religion, and since it sits in place of the Supreme Pontiff, and represents the person of His Beatitude, its authority is enormous, its dignity is sovereign and its office is eminent.'[17]

It is probable that both the Florentine and the Roman inquisitors would have known this handbook, and even possessed their own copies, since a new edition had just been published in 1639, incorporating a new section on witchcraft. It pointed out that one of the main categories of enemy against whom the Inquisition would proceed – admittedly after heretics, magicians and blasphemers – was 'those who oppose the Holy Office, or its officials'.[18]

The wellspring for the Inquisition was denunciations, so Father Mario Sozzi was following standard procedure with his constant reports. The *Sacro arsenale* advised that anyone coming in with a denunciation 'be heard immediately, without deferring the appointment to another time'.[19] A special lawyer would be called and a written testimony be noted. As a general rule, a preliminary hearing would be held by the tribunal before any action was taken. At this point the suspect would probably be unaware that he was in trouble. If the preliminary charges seemed to be worthy of investigation, the suspect would be arrested, or sworn to appear before the tribunal, but not told the reason for the enquiry. He would usually be asked if he knew why he had been arrested, or if he had any known enemies. As questioning began, the subject would still be unaware of the full extent of the charges, nor was he entitled to any defence council. Torture was not permitted – providing the subject confessed spontaneously and named his accomplices, but if he was suspected of holding back any information, it was an acceptable form of interrogation. Persons found guilty could be executed, and although statistically death was unlikely, it was not impossible. In Venice, for instance, 'a dozen sodomites (including several clergymen)' were executed during the sixteenth century, usually by taking the guilty out to sea at night and drowning them secretly. Records for the Genoa Inquisition in one year show executions of twelve men and two women – three men for raping children, three murderers, three thieves, two homosexuals, one counterfeiter and one witch. As anyone accused would have known, torture and the death penalty – though physically enforced by the secular authorities – were real possibilities once the Inquisition was called in.[20]

Armed with his letter from Cardinal Barberini, an undoubtedly smug Father Mario Sozzi returned to Florence bearing the good wishes of the pontiff and the Roman Curia. Although his denunciations against his colleagues had failed to stand up to close investigation, his trip to Rome had been successful in that he had received support from the assessor of the Inquisition and the Barberini family itself. Sozzi's friendship with the local inquisitor had paid off and Calasanz's attempts to transfer Sozzi elsewhere had failed. But once back in Florence, Sozzi discovered that although the headmaster had been replaced in the wake of the distressing frivolity he had permitted, nothing else had changed. The teachers continued to be patronized by the Medici court, they continued to frequent Galileo's house, and they continued to live with what Father Mario considered a disgraceful lack of observance and respect.

Once more it was a trivial incident that ignited the explosion. It was carnival, a time during which the town succumbed to masked festivities, races, parties and excess drinking. Galileo had described it as a period when it was permissible 'to speak freely about everything'[21] and certainly some of the usual restraints on behaviour were relaxed. On 7 February 1641 the headmaster was delayed at dinner time and, after waiting a while, Father Giovanni Giuseppe di San Carlo read the blessing. He was not very well, and read the prayer in such a quiet and tremulous voice that the others in the refectory strained to hear. So quiet was the reading that no one knew when to say the responses, and a few of the teachers found this exquisitely amusing and began to giggle. At the end of the meal, one of the teachers went up to Father Ambrogio Ambrogi and asked, 'Did you laugh during the blessing?' Father Ambrogio replied, 'And who wouldn't have laughed! Why, surely laughing in the refectory isn't now a matter for the Holy Office?'

Father Mario overheard the comment and assuming, probably correctly, that it referred to him, exploded in anger. 'I'm a man of honour, I'm a man of honour!' he shouted. Father Ambrogio replied, 'Who mentioned anything about it? Of course you're a man of honour.' Once again Father Mario shouted, 'I tell you, I'm a man of honour!' but Father Ambrogio left the room, followed by Father Mario still protesting. Father Clemente Settimi tried to calm him down, explaining that it was holiday season, but Father Mario 'hearing such friendly words, suddenly turned like a tiger on Father Clemente and punched him hard on the temples, crying, "Are you against me too?"' Poor Father Clemente folded his arms and turned to the rest of the members present and said, 'You are witness. This father is excommunicated.' Hitting a fellow cleric was an excommunicable offence in canon law so, in theory at least, Father Clemente was correct.

Father Mario wanted to follow up with more blows against Father Clemente, but one of our brothers, Cesario [Landucci], interposed to hold him back, but then Father Mario hit him a few times, and caused him considerable pain, so being a young man he turned around to give as good as he got, but then he was held back by Father Angelo [Morelli] di San Domenico and others, so in fact Father Mario was never touched by anyone. But since the offended young man was struggling violently with the fathers who were holding him back, and showed every sign of wanting to revenge himself, Father Mario ran away out of the house without his hat or slippers, and went to the Father Inquisitor, and appeared in that way, excited and furious, saying to him, 'Look, Father Reverend, how the fathers have treated me! And all because I denounced Faustina to the Holy Office – since then they've been on my back, and they've mistreated me, as you can see![22]

This was how Father Berro, who was to become a bitter enemy of Father Mario, described events. But according to Sozzi (although he retold it in the third person), he had begged not to be sent back to Florence, fearing what would happen with the 'impassioned spirits' of his fellow fathers. And very soon after his arrival,

under the pretext that the said Father Mario was a spy of the Holy Office, the fathers – including the mathematician [Michelini] – beat him with fists and sticks, so that even though it was a bright midday in order to save his life he had to run and take refuge with the most reverend inquisitor of Florence. His face was so re-arranged that he had to stay indoors for a week such was the disfigurement. And since neither the superior nor the fathers themselves wanted him in their house he had to stay with a friendly priest for a month, and in all that time those fathers did not offer him so much as a glass of water. On the contrary, when they saw him in the streets in Florence not only did they not greet him, but they threatened him, and swore at him, and reported him to the ministers of the Grand Duke and to Monsignor Passionei, the nuncio, and all this was known to the Reverend Inquisitor of Florence.[23]

Of course he knew. Sozzi had run straight there from the refectory. The response came straight back – no one was to leave the house, under pain of severe punishment. The following morning the inquisitor appeared at the school in person, and once more Father Mario was put back into the confessional booth in the church, even though his colleagues thought he was excommunicated by virtue of having hit a colleague.

Florence was full of the gossip. A bare three weeks after the punch-up a letter arrived at the office of the Florentine inquisitor from Cardinal Francesco Barberini in Rome. As a result of the process against the fathers of the Pious Schools who had been maltreating Father Mario, the cardinal decreed that 'all the delinquents' were to be sent to Rome immediately and present themselves before 'the Supreme and Universal Inquisition', while a new batch of teachers were to be sent back to Florence so that Father Mario could return home and not be harmed. Fathers Angelo Morelli and Clemente Settimi, and Brother Riccardo Antonio were named as the worst offenders. Ambrogio Ambrogi was also transferred to Rome under the pretext that his mother was very worried by the turn of events.[24]

The Piarists must have journeyed to Rome with a heavy heart. As soon as he arrived, Father Clemente scribbled a brief note to Galileo, whose own last trip to Rome a decade ago had been made after a similar terrifying summons: 'After a wearisome journey we have arrived safe in Rome with the help of the Lord God.' A month later he finally managed to deliver a letter he had brought from Galileo to Evangelista Torricelli, and sent his greetings to the scientist along with the hope that he would be able to return very shortly. After a brief investigation by the Roman Inquisition the three Piarists were exonerated. In May Father Clemente joyfully notified Prince Leopoldo Medici that 'our process is finished with great satisfaction, and the gentlemen of the Holy Congregation have realized that it was just a case of brotherly persecution, and nothing to do with the Holy Office; and the one who caused it [Sozzi] will realize in time that he has not profited.' All the fathers were to return to Florence, even though some of them were reluctant, fearing further unpleasantness, since Father Mario was also ordered to return in order to bear witness in the Faustina trial.[25]

If the father general and the Florentine members thought that all would now be well they were cruelly deceived. Calasanz even wrote to the Florentine headmaster: 'I particularly want Your Reverence to keep on good terms with the father inquisitor, and I think in future he won't be against us, but rather favourable, though Your Reverence should take care not to do anything which annoys him.'[26] The Florentine Piarists would not, however, have any time to cultivate the inquisitor. Father Mario Sozzi must have received the news at the same time as the 'delinquent' Father Clemente. The tribunal had been deceived by 'a thousand lies'. He was to be sent back to a school full of enemies. The bruises he may or may not have received – depending on whose version one believes – had counted for nothing; the Inquisition had declared itself uninterested in this case of fraternal feuding. But he knew how to get the Holy Office's attention. The next accusations would not be so easily dismissed and the Inquisition would be forced to take him seriously.

'Galileo is the most important man in the world'

Father Francesco [Michelini] di San Giuseppe of the Pious Schools thinks that all things are made of atoms, and not of material and form, as Aristotle and all the others believe. He holds this to be true doctrine and publicly teaches it.

He also believes that the earth moves and the sun is still, holding this doctrine and others of Signor Galileo to be so true, that he thinks all others are false and worth nothing. He is very opposed to Aristotle, calling him very ignorant, and calling Signor Galileo an oracle. He preaches that the said Galileo is the most important man in the world and gives him other magnificent titles. Not only Father Francesco, but also his pupils, Fathers Ambrogio [Ambrogi], Clemente [Settimi], Carlo [Conti] and Angelo [Morelli] think and feel the same, and these fathers claim to be the most wise and intelligent fathers, and they mock the other religious and consider them ignorant.

They have managed to get the Grand Duke, and then Prince Gian Carlo to believe this philosophy too ... and he [Michelini] is teaching Prince Leopoldo not only these opinions, but others. They call it new philosophy and certain science and they have set up a school and want it to be taught, so the Grand Duke has said they are looking for scholars to teach, who are clever and poor, and they will give them a salary, as in fact Father Francesco has already done for two of them.

In order to achieve this school I know they have kept what books they could from Signor Galileo ... and if Your Reverence confiscates the chest, which is in the classroom where Father Clemente teaches mathematics, you will see that this is true.

Often he has talked to me about the doctrines and opinions of Signor Galileo, and particularly that the earth moves and the sun is still, and he thinks it is so true, even though it has been condemned as false that he said with his own mouth that His Holiness [the Pope] wronged Signor Galileo by condemning him, saying that he was motivated by an insult which he thought Signor Galileo had written ... [by casting Urban as Simplicius to promote the Aristotelian view in his *Dialogue*] and that when His Holiness understood that and was annoyed and angry, and also encouraged by Signor Galileo's competitors, particularly the Jesuits, he condemned these opinions of his as false. But Father Francesco says that His Holiness was wrong to condemn Signor Galileo.

Father Clemente claims that the world had no beginning and that everything was created and regulated by the Heavens and that there is no other creator or governor.

Father Ambrogio says that all bodies are composed of atoms. On the occasion I talked to him about colours he said there are no colours, which would conflict with one of the accidents that we profess about the most holy [Eucharist].

All the above-named say that there is no more true nor more certain science than that of Galileo, which is taught via mathematics, calling it new philosophy, and the true method of philosophy. And many times all of them, and especially Fathers Francesco, Clemente and Ambrogio, say that this is the real way to know God, and many times Father Clemente exhorted me to try this method.

... They say this philosophy is proven, and that this is the true way to convert heretics and know God. If you, Reverend Father, will go and investigate, you will see this is true, and also they hold other extravagant opinions more like Atheists than Christians.[1]

This was a challenge to its authority that the Inquisition could hardly ignore. Father Mario Sozzi was accusing his colleagues of believing in atomism, heliocentrism and anti-Aristotelianism, of denying the miracle of the Eucharist, and of considering the pope to be plain wrong, and of not only holding these views but of attempting to spread them. People had been burned for far less.

Galileo's heliocentric views were well known. He had also pushed atomism to the fore with the initially well-received *Assayer* in 1623, when he described the world of the senses as a dense movement of particles of matter. According to historian Pietro Redondi 'Galileo reserved the word "atom" and the concepts of infinitely small dimension and infinitely great velocity only for luminous, infinitesimal particles of discontinuous material, capable of penetrating sight.' He had avoided writing about atoms in *The Dialogue* of 1632, 'either out of caution or at the suggestion of his theological advisers', but a few months after its appearance, the Jesuits had – just in case – issued an urgent internal memo specifically prohibiting themselves from even mentioning the word.[2] Other writers who had written on atomism included Democritus, Epicurus, Lucretius, Ockham, Telesio, Bruno, Campanella and Copernicus. But all those on the list who were Catholic had been condemned by the Church, some with fatal consequences.

On colour Galileo had written, 'I think that tastes, odours, colours, and so on as regards the object in which they seem to reside are nothing but pure names and reside only in the feeling body, so that if the animal is removed, all these qualities are taken away and annihilated', in direct contradiction to Aristotle's writings in, for instance, *On the Soul*.[3] The denial of the existence of colours implied that Father Ambrogio had cast doubt on the Eucharist itself, the most important sacrament of the Catholic Church, since 'heat, colour, taste, smell, and the other sensible accidents of the bread and wine after the Consecration ... transform[ed] their entire substance into the body and blood of Christ',[4] and to hold that even one of the elements was non-existent, contradicted orthodoxy and represented a view firmly anathematized by the Council of Trent. To question the existence of colour was to re-open the whole transubstantiation debate and to lay oneself wide open to a charge of heresy, of supporting consubstantiation, of Lutheranism. It was to arouse the wrath of the Society of Jesus 'for whom Eucharistic apologetics were an essential preoccupation – the great inspirational motive for their Counter-Reformation struggle, their banner'.[5] In short, it was a very serious theological and political allegation.

By this time Galileo himself had been forced – at least on paper – to become more discreet, 'to succumb and remain silent about the attacks that have rained down on me in such great numbers, even on natural subjects, in order to suppress the doctrine and publicize my ignorance, but it is also advisable that I swallow the sneers, sarcasms and insults'.[6] Natural philosophy was banished, only mathematics and experiments were permitted. But to his Piarist disciples in the privacy of his house, when he thought no written trace would remain of his comments, he must have been more open, and they in turn had not held their tongues, at least in what they considered to be the confidential enclave of their own residence.

Whether Sozzi's attack was motivated by a desperate desire to be the centre of attention, the pursuit of revenge for perceived insults, an inferiority complex at his inability to keep up with his intellectually superior brothers, or perhaps, if one were to be charitable, a true desire for religious rectitude and orthodoxy, it is hard to tell. Perhaps he just wanted to impress his drinking companion, Father Muzzarelli, the Florentine inquisitor, or offer him another juicy case such as that of Faustina Mainardi, which could put Father Mario back in the limelight. Sozzi is painted very blackly in the documents of the order, and it is hard even from his own writings not to see him as petulant, vindictive, selfish and very dangerous to those around him.

Whatever his motivation, to be sure that nothing could go wrong with his accusation, Father Mario sent copies to both the Florentine and the Roman Offices of the Inquisition, marked for the attention of Father Muzzarelli and Cardinal Barberini. And if the inquisitor wanted confirmation of any of this, Father Mario recommended he ask the current procurator general, his friend Father Stefano Cherubini, who was already notorious within the order.[7]

Within ten days of reading Sozzi's latest and most serious accusations Cardinal Barberini wrote to Father Muzzarelli in Florence: 'On receipt of this, call Father Clemente of the Pious Schools and exile him from the city under pain of being sent to the galleys and other punishments at the jurisdiction of this Holy Congregation, by whose order tell him to come to Rome and present himself to the commissioner of the Holy Office.'[8] Michelini and the rest of the fathers were not mentioned, since they were perhaps too closely associated with the Medici court for the Barberini to risk offending.

But these were serious threats and they affected not just the Piarist Order but also the Medici princes. The grand duke and his brother were accused of protecting and even fostering heretical beliefs, and they sprang into action to limit the damage. Letters were immediately sent from the Tuscan court to Cardinal Sacchetti and to the Tuscan ambassador Francesco Niccolini in Rome, instructing them to do all in their power to 'stop these persecutions once and for all'.[9]

The pressure must have been successful for the case was quietly dropped, which was an extraordinary outcome to such serious accusations. Father Clemente wrote in great relief to Prince Leopoldo on 14 December that he had once again been completely exonerated by the Holy Office, even though it was true that he was friendly with Galileo and had not been very respectful of the Inquisition. Meanwhile, back in Florence the case against Faustina Mainardi and Pandolfo Ricasoli drew to a close and, thanks to Father Sozzi's immaculate testimony, both were condemned to 'perpetual prison': life imprisonment.[10]

Once more the Florentine house could look forward to peace and quiet. Surely now that the reason for Father Sozzi's presence in town was over, he could be quietly transferred elsewhere and the school could continue with its daily life – the ever-growing classes, the School for Nobles and most importantly for some, the scientific research with Signor Galileo up in Arcetri.

But for Father Sozzi the time for vengeance had finally arrived. Fresh from his triumph at Faustina's trial, he returned to Rome and arranged to meet with the Roman inquisitor, Monsignor Francesco Albizzi. He realized that Father Sozzi deserved a reward after all his sufferings: the alleged physical abuse by his fellow teachers, the essential evidence he had provided to put the criminals behind bars, and perhaps to compensate in part for the failure – at least for the time being – of his accusations of Galilean heresy. The reward would benefit the Inquisition too, for they would have a well-placed friend in an influential position. The new provincial in Tuscany, in charge of all the schools in the region, was not to be appointed by the father general. It was to be an appointment made by the Holy Office of the Inquisition itself. It was to be Father Mario Sozzi.

'A sublime nothingness'

The members of the order greeted the appointment of Father Mario Sozzi to the position of Tuscan provincial with incomprehension. Not only had the Inquisition intervened in a manner that was quite unprecedented for any order, infringing the jurisdiction of the father general and his assistants, but also such an important province had been put under the control of such an unsuitable man. The cardinal protector, Alessandro Cesarini, Bishop of Viterbo, who had taken on the job two years earlier, intervened at the highest levels, pointing out that not only could Sozzi not be entrusted with a position of influence, but a case could even be made for putting him in jail, perhaps for lack of obedience and general trouble-making.[1]

But nothing could be done. Father Mario claimed that the order had come 'from the mouth of His Holiness himself, promising that he would never lack his protection, nor that of his Eminencies, his nephews'. Calasanz realized that the pope must have been privy to the decision, even if he had not actually initiated the process. 'You know that the Holy Congregation of the Holy Office, which usually does not give orders without the knowledge of His Holiness, has ordered that Father Mario return to Florence as provincial ... and that he can elect his members as he chooses, which I have obeyed with good grace.'[2] To Michelini in Florence, Calasanz wrote, ' I find myself with my hands bound ... The will is not lacking, but our forces are impeded.'[3] Father Mario had been given the position as a reward for his help in the Faustina denunciation, but had then had the temerity to send back the licence, demanding fuller powers, which had been granted. Not only was Father Mario in control, but he could start with a clean slate, getting rid of all the teachers who hated him – and whom he hated – from the Florentine school, and requesting whoever he wanted from wherever they were currently teaching. It was a disastrous state of affairs, for the new provincial was completely ruthless in his demands. From the Rome house alone, for example, he summoned eleven members. When he asked for a further seven and the father general demurred, explaining that this would wreck the teaching and the curriculum of the Rome school, Father Sozzi instantly complained to the Holy Office that Calasanz was being uncooperative. Although he had taken eleven staff he failed to send any back, and classes in Rome were severely disrupted.[4] He also wanted Father Luigi from Genoa, Brother Giovanni from Pisa and Padre Simone from Pieve di Cento.[5] He wanted Father Giacomo, who was Calasanz's private secretary.[6] He wanted Father Domenico Antonio, who taught a special music class in Rome 'to enable poor boys to earn their bread', even though no other school was permitted to teach music, and there was no other teacher who could carry on Father Antonio's work.[7] In pursuit of his ideal team of teachers, Father Sozzi did not care what impact his selections would have on the rest of the order.

Calasanz was forced to write a humiliating letter to the Tuscan schools, not only informing them of the new appointment but also 'derogating, annulling and declaring of no value any order, privilege, faculty or licence both in general and in particular of any sort which we have conceded in the past to any religious, whether superior or subject within that province, unless it be first confirmed by the [new] provincial'.[8]

On 22 March 1642 a lawyer arrived from the Inquisition at the Roman school in San Pantaleo, insisting that 'without any discussion

all those fathers from the said Order be sent to Florence that have
been requested by Father Mario ... under severe pain, at the arbitra-
tion of the Holy Office.'[9] The only example of someone actually
wanting to work with the new provincial at this point was Father
Glicerio Cerutti, who wrote to Sozzi directly – something forbidden by
the rules of the *Constitutions* – to ask if he could come to Florence
from Vercelli.[10] Unsurprisingly, Cerutti would become one of the
principal troublemakers as the order spiralled downwards towards
disintegration.

It had become impossible to cross Father Mario without entering
into direct confrontation with the Inquisition. He was given a special
licence, as Father Clemente Settimi wrote in warning to Prince
Leopoldo, 'to demonstrate that he is favoured by the Tribunal [of the
Holy Office], and the licence contains this clause: *to share its duties and
voices,* which in summary seems to mean no less than that if he fears anything in Florence, he can invoke the Holy Office and claim that he is its
man'.[11]

The assessor at the Holy Office who had supplied the licence to
Father Mario was to become one of the Piarist Order's most dangerous
enemies. Francesco Albizzi was born in Cesena in the Papal States in
1593. He had studied civil and canon law and received his doctorate at
the tender age of seventeen. Three years later he married a young
widow and over the next decade they had five children. Meanwhile he
worked as a lawyer with modest success, but on the death of his wife in
1623 he abandoned secular life and joined the Church. Leaving his children to the care of nearby friends, Albizzi left Cesena for Rome where
the Barberini Pope had just been elected. On his arrival he was put in
contact with the young cardinal nephew, Francesco, and was soon
offered a good job as an auditor general in Naples. After other similar
postings to Madrid and Cologne he fell out with the cardinal he was
serving at the time, and returned to Rome where he was invited to
become an assessor at the Holy Office, again through the good graces
of Francesco Barberini.

The Inquisition was headed by the pope who acted as president, and by the cardinal nephew as secretary. Then came the Cardinals' Commissions, which judged cases, supported by various theologians, who acted as advisers. The two important executive officers in the Inquisition were the commissary, who was always a theologian, and the assessor. This role was, in Francesco Albizzi's own words, 'a tough job'.[12] It involved preparing trials and summaries, organizing the meetings, sorting out which parts of the meetings should be held in secret for only the cardinals, taking minutes, meeting with the pope and the rest of the Congregation every Thursday afternoon, then drafting any orders and decisions resulting from those meetings, sending them to be checked by the cardinals if they were important, organizing that they be recopied and sent to the relevant destinations; in summary the whole administration of the legal business of the Holy Office. Albizzi claimed he was so busy 'that he did not have an hour to waste', but he obviously relished the role since he took over even those meetings that were supposed to be presided over by his colleague, the commissary. Needless to say, Albizzi immediately came into conflict with his colleague, the Franciscan Vincenzo Maculano, a military architect who was promoted to cardinal in 1641, a good few years before Albizzi made the grade, and the enmity lasted for life. With the job came a sumptuous apartment in the palace for each official. A French doctor visiting in 1645 noted they were 'magnificently lodged as though they were prelates', although in the cellars of the building, out of earshot, were the prisons, which several of the more senior Piarists, including Calasanz, would soon visit. There were usually at least fifteen prisoners held here, many prior to being shipped off to the galleys, some of them for years, such as the poor Neapolitan nun, Sor Giulia, who was held from 1609 until 1645. The daughter of an artisan and a converted Turkish slave, Sor Giulia had been arrested aged twenty, accused of an early form of quietism (heretical religious mysticism). In 1615 she admitted to 'disorders with a priest' and was sentenced to perpetual imprisonment, leading Albizzi to joke in 1645 that he had been passed over for promotion because Sor

Giulia wanted him to stay on at the Inquisition as her 'indivisible companion'.[13]

By 1642 Albizzi already had a few ongoing cases to deal with, as well as his everyday administration. He was secretary of two special commissions into Dutch and Irish affairs, he was a corrector at the penitentiary and, from 1640, he became a judge in civil cases at the Inquisition. In that year he also started to deal with the Jansenist heresy, a doctrine based on predestination, the denial of free will and the belief that man, though depraved in nature, is unable to resist God's grace. The historian Ludwig von Pastor wrote: 'Jansenism was born of the desire to discredit the Jesuit Order and historically the new heresy can best be understood if Jansenius is viewed as the antithesis of Ignatius of Loyola, as the contradiction of, and a reaction against, the Jesuits' teaching on grace, their ascetical and moral theology, their principles on the frequent reception of the Sacraments and their strong attachment to Rome.'[14] Albizzi discussed it with the official theologians, although he had no knowledge of theology and apparently very little interest in it. However, he always favoured the Jesuits, from whom he received a pension, a policy that would soon cause great problems for the Piarist Order, and this bias came out strongly in his handling of the Jansenist case. In August 1641 Albizzi organized the first move against Jansenism, the suppression of Jansenius's book *Augustinus*, but included in the suppression document a final clause that threatened French royal power and would lead to great conflict. Later Albizzi would become a cardinal and write on the legal aspects of his work; the rarity of the surviving volumes would seem to indicate a small print run.[15] It was while Rome's response to Jansenism was taking up much of his time that the Piarist problem began to edge onto the corner of his desk.

Albizzi seems to have been a self-important and unpleasant man who got on badly with nearly all his colleagues. His portraits show a plump, double-chinned man, with a thin nose, a goatee beard and unruly hair springing out from his slightly cocked cardinal's cap. His gaze is hard and he is turned away slightly, as if suspicious of the artist.

An anonymous contemporary, who observed him twenty years later, when he had been promoted to cardinal and was about to go into conclave to elect a new pope, wrote this ambivalent verdict:

What a strange character! Monk and very learned, mystic and almost atheist, of relatively severe habits but excessively free in his language, very over-sensitive as to his person but rips up others; sarcastic, petulant, full of whims, not respecting anything, not fearing anyone, sacrificing justice, law and truth for a witticism; scornful of the whole world, and believing himself strong, brave, friendly, seeking to get to the bottom of things and call them by their name; knowing everything, being everywhere and always in the right place, mixed up in everything, ripping away veils; mocking all and sundry on any subject; generous or miserly, keeping his word, but never keeping it secret, dreaded and respected, good for everything and incapable of nothing ...[16]

His past showed he was ambitious, intelligent, efficient. Events would prove him vindictive, avaricious, vainglorious, and interventionist – when someone needed to be arrested, Albizzi would lead the guards in person. According to Franciscan historian Father Lucien Ceyssens, who wrote a biography of Albizzi, he had no classical knowledge, little intellectual curiosity and read sparsely. No one could disagree with him. When a French envoy, Jean Bourgeois, dared to contradict him in 1645, the results were immediate: 'I saw a sudden change in his face. His cheeks became inflamed, his eyes glittered, his lips grew pale and trembling ... I knew I'd made him angry.'[17] Albizzi was always interested in money, and many of his letters to Cardinal Barberini deal with his expenses and his need for full recompense, and then a bit more. Ceyssens, a specialist on Jansenius, is clearly unimpressed with his subject: 'Always talking without listening, giving himself airs about knowing everything, even in theology and patrology, Albizzi terribly over-valued himself, to his great cost and to the cost of those around him.' His final conclusion on Albizzi's legacy is so terrible it is almost anachronistically Wagnerian in its damnation: 'His writings have no resonance, his poetry is scorned, his library had no future, his palace was dilapidated, his belvedere demolished. Even his name barely survives; his inscriptions have disappeared or become illegible, his biography remained buried in the dust of the Malatesta Library ... His *oeuvre*, one must alas recognize, was an error, a fatal failure for himself, for the church, for his era. According to Pope Alexander VII, a sublime nothingness.'[18] And so it would prove for the Piarists, as Albizzi began to take a personal and fatal interest in their activities.

'You are prisoners of the Inquisition'

It was Francesco Albizzi's sensitivity to slights to his person, but particularly to the prestige of his Congregation, that would prove one of the main stumbling blocks. In his *Autobiography* he would write, 'He who offends the officials of the Holy Office, is said to commit an atrocious crime, and will be atrociously punished,'[1] lending this statement of his own views the sonorous quality of a biblical commandment. It was this over-developed sense of his own and his office's prestige that Sozzi was able to exploit to the full. Every time the Piarist needed a protective reaction he could accuse his colleagues of slighting the Holy Office, and Albizzi would come charging to the rescue.

The father general went to visit Monsignor the assessor to explain the problems Sozzi's requests for staff in Florence were causing for the rest of the Order's schools. Albizzi listened to him 'with great benevolence', told Calasanz he understood the problem, and ordered that Sozzi's requests all be fulfilled without further delay. Reasonable explanations were of no interest to this prelate.[2]

Father Mario had arrived in Florence 'all vainglorious and distracted' and immediately ordered that news of his appointment – with all his supplementary powers duly underlined – be read out to all the staff. 'He began his rule with great magnificence,' commented Father Berro. He instantly embarked on a round of ceremonial visits – to the grand duke, to the archbishop, and of course to his great friend, Father Muzzarelli, the inquisitor. Again according to Berro, he was so enchanted by the trappings of his new position, that he spent all his time visiting. 'He especially visited the rooms and antechambers of the Most Serene Grand Duke and often he was seen there without any reason for his visit, just wasting time in vain discourse and pleasantries.' Soon some of the officials became suspicious, or perhaps just irritated at his presence, as did the grand duke, and Sozzi received a message that 'The Most Serene Grand Duke would prefer that Your Reverence does not visit his palace so often, and only comes when he needs something, and that he pay attention to matters concerning his province.' At this point, again according to the same hostile source, Father Mario did the opposite:

Where previously he had gone to the palace, for instance, three or four times a week, he now started to go six or eight times, showing that he paid no attention to the warning sent to him from the Grand Duke, and being spotted by His Highness whenever he walked from one set of rooms to another, or whenever he entered or left the building. And when he couldn't find anyone with whom to chat, he just stood around observing everything, and always chewing like an ox as usual.[3]

One of Father Mario's main enemies had always been Father Francesco Michelini. As the teacher and leader of the other Galilean Piarists and as a great friend, not only of Galileo, but even more significantly of the Medici grand duke, Father Sozzi had denounced him above all others as the ringleader. But Father Michelini, whom the duke and his brothers called Father Mathematician, seemed to benefit from a kind of diplomatic immunity, 'living at court and with great liberty'[4] and had never been summoned to answer for his teachings before the Roman Inquisition, even though he was clearly and frequently fingered by Father Mario. The consistently strong protection the Medici offered the Florentine Piarists was to a great extent motivated by their friendship for Michelini. When the new provincial arrived in Florence at the end of January 1642 to take up his position, one of the main people he hoped to destroy was the Father Mathematician, in spite of repeated promises to Calasanz to treat him with 'love and benevolence'.[5] But it had long been clear to everyone that life was going to be dramatically different under the new regime, and Father Michelini had prepared his bolt-hole. The death of Galileo on 8 January merely made that decision easier. As soon as he had heard the news of Sozzi's appointment, Michelini had organized – with Calasanz's complicity – that he be summoned away to travel with the Medici princes. A new school had recently opened in Pisa, very conveniently and with excellent access to Prince Leopoldo and the university, and Michelini transferred himself there, out of earshot and reach of the new provincial.[6] Reports from the Tuscan ambassador noted that the members of the Pisan school were leading 'a good and exemplary life'. He also warned that the duke should not get too mixed up in Father Mario's affairs, 'if he doesn't want to get involved in an embarrassing tangle'.[7] But he also warned the duke that if Michelini was ever summoned to Rome by the Inquisition he would encounter grave problems.[8]

By pure coincidence, one of the intellectual heirs to Galileo, Robert Boyle, was in Florence at the time of Galileo's death. Aged fifteen and travelling around Europe on the Grand Tour, the future physicist and chemist was not only introduced to the delights of the brothel during his stay in town, but, 'being at that Time in the Flower of Youth' with a fresh and untrammelled complexion, he was 'somewhat rudely storm'd by the Preposterous courtship of two Fryers [friars], whose Lust makes no Distinction of Sexes'. He had gone out unaccompanied and was hard put to escape – 'not without Difficulty, & Danger'. These 'gown'd Sodomites' and their 'Goatish heats' had apparently put him off sex for life.[9] However, the problems of the Florentine Piarists at that moment were linked to personality and ideological clashes, rather than their morality.

The Pisan school now became the focal point for an anti-Sozzi rebellion, in spite of many calls from Calasanz to submit to the inevitable and not to give Sozzi any excuse to call in the Roman Inquisition once more.[10] The new foundation, which had only opened the previous January after strong pressure – and considerable financial support – from the Medici dukes, claimed that it had never answered to the provincial, even before the new appointment, but had always reported directly to the general and the cardinal protector. The Tuscan ambassador in Rome, Francesco Niccolini, visited the cardinal protector, Cesarini, to try to sort out matters and found him at his wits' end. He knew that Father Mario would not listen to him, but would try to visit Pisa to impose his authority, since he enjoyed the special protection of the Holy Office, and was an obstinate, headstrong man. In fact, during the course of the visit, Niccolini discovered that the cardinal was fed up with being the protector of such a troublesome bunch of 'barefoot priests', and was beginning to make moves to distance himself from the Piarists. He was a member of the committee of the Holy Office, but was increasingly sidelined by the Barberini, and had begun to think that the whole problem of the Piarists was becoming far more trouble than it was worth.[11]

Once he had settled into his role in Florence, Father Mario decided to visit the rest of the schools under his control. Fanano, Guglia and Pieve di Cento, the smaller schools that formed part of his province, opened their doors to him and received him correctly, but they must have been unconvinced of his good faith, for a few weeks later they all decided to join with the Pisan school and call themselves an entirely new province, Lombardy.[12] Father Calasanz was kept informed of proceedings, but did not condone the rebellion, although naturally he was later accused by Father Mario of lending it his support 'with secret intelligence'. As usual, when faced with problems beyond his personal control, Sozzi fled to Rome, to try to put his case to the Holy Office and the Barberini once more. According to him, the Tuscan – or rather Lombard – Piarists treated him like 'a thief, a rogue, and a spy ... a rebel against the Father General, and a destroyer of the Order'.[13] According to Father Berro, he arrived in the Eternal City 'brimful of so much rage, poison and hatred, all based solely on his pride, wild fancies and passions, with letters virtually dictated by him from Father Muzzarelli, so that no words emanated from his mouth, but rather thunderbolts, when he wanted to recount to anyone the things that had happened to him.'[14]

At the Office of the Inquisition Sozzi was received by the assessor, Monsignor Francesco Albizzi, and presented the letters from his Florentine counterpart, Father Muzzarelli:

And then, vomiting out his poison, which had generated in his brain and concentrated itself in his heart, he said that what the Grand Duke had done and the insults received from him by Father Mario, were all the fault of the venerable Father General [Calasanz], since he claimed that His Serene Highness [the Grand Duke] had been spurred to action by letters from the Father General and that the insults received were all carried out on his orders.[15]

While investigations were underway, Sozzi remained lodged at San Pantaleo, but he observed no rule:

He went in and out as he pleased; he did and said what he wished. He tortured the reverend founder and general, and his venerable father assistants as a cruel tyrant does to his most menial slaves, swearing at them even in public, calling them proud, hypocrites and liars, and similar insults. And they were forced to be patient in order not to annoy the most illustrious assessor, who had been taken in by the letters from the Reverend Muzzarelli and was treating him with great favour.[16]

Sozzi had also managed to draw to himself a gang of similarly disillusioned Piarists, prime amongst whom was his main ally, Father Stefano Cherubini.

In April 1642, Cherubini had finally been stripped by Calasanz of the office of procurator 'for just cause', and sent away to Chieti on pretence of sorting out some legal problems. Describing events later, Calasanz admitted knowing about Cherubini's original 'wicked practices' with pupils in Naples, but claimed that out of respect for the offender's

family he had permitted him to continue as procurator general, with
particular responsibility for the legal problems of the Nazarene College,
which were proving very complex, until his ongoing behaviour showed
that in spite of a change of scenery he was continuing with his old
habits of abusing young boys.[17] The usual wheels of patronage and pressure swung smoothly into motion and before very long Calasanz was
requested – or more likely ordered – by Stefano's brother, Flavio, to
summon the errant priest back to Rome on urgent family business. Now
Stefano settled into companionship with Father Mario. Together they
ignored the restrictions of the order, ate well and revelled in a certain
liberty and lack of humility, which they had clearly been craving.

The cardinal protector, Cesarini, meanwhile refused to meet with
Father Mario but sent his deputy, Sebastiano Gentile, Bishop of Terni.
The meeting went very badly, and Sozzi 'responded with such insolence
... and spoke so badly about His Excellency, the cardinal protector of
the Order and about the venerable founder and general, saying that he
had such and such material in his hands not only to punish the Father
General, but also to destroy the Order, adding other nonsense against
His Eminence'.[18] The bishop was amazed and shouted at him, 'What, is
this how you talk about a cardinal of the Holy Church, born a prince,
and your superior!' and departed abruptly, promising to let the cardinal
know the extent of Sozzi's temerity. The threat of blackmail by Sozzi
annoyed the cardinal so much that he took two actions. First a counter-
accusation was drawn up against Father Mario, accusing him, amongst
other things, of breaking his vows. Unfortunately this accusation is one
of the many burned in a huge purge of incriminating material that fed
a bonfire years after the events in 1659 when the Piarists were trying to
clean up their history.

The other action that Cardinal Cesarini, furious at hearing of Sozzi's
insolence, took on 7 August 1642 was to send his auditor, Count
Corona, accompanied by a secretary, to San Pantaleo to search through
Father Mario's room and remove any incriminating material. In the
presence of witnesses, the room was unlocked – though according to

the *Rules* of the order it should never have been locked – and a detailed inventory was made of the contents. 'Various things were found that were neither necessary nor convenient for a priest, but they did not find the hiding place where he kept the least worthy things,' commented one father. As they left, Father Mario was heard to mutter that 'they had not found the good things, and other such boastful words'.[19]

Hearing this report a few hours later the cardinal protector was determined to go one step further and carry out a search of Sozzi's person and force him to reveal his hiding places. When Father Calasanz heard news of Cesarini's intentions, he sent word via his secretary to beg the cardinal not to pursue this course of action, knowing well that Sozzi would do his utmost to ensure major retribution from his friends at the Holy Office. But the cardinal's blood was up, and when Calasanz came round in person and begged him to think again, he only replied, 'Father General, I have made enquiries as to whether Father Mario has any official position with the Holy Inquisition and I have been informed that he definitely does not, nor any immunity whatsoever, and he is my subject and I intend to carry out the search this evening, so be patient.' And even when the old man fell to his knees and begged him not to carry out this dramatic intervention, the cardinal still stuck to his decision.

That evening the auditor, Corona, was dispatched once more to San Pantaleo, this time with a lawyer as a concession to the father general's concerns. Father Mario was called and given the express order 'to hand over all writings, items and money which he had on him, and to say where the rest were hidden'. He replied that many things were with the assessor Albizzi and handed over a few items, which were carefully noted down by the lawyer. He pulled out a sheaf of papers and said, 'These things belong to the Holy Office.' Corona replied that His Excellency was a member of the Holy Congregation – Cesarini was on the cardinals' committee – so he would be able to take care of it and evaluate it. Father Mario made some resistance, but the auditor was determined, and he was forced to give way. The lawyer locked and sealed the papers into a special box. Later it would transpire that the document in question was a simple inventory of the sacristy, carried out by order of Muzzarelli and signed by him, but by then the actual contents were irrelevant. Father Mario was ordered to stay within the school walls, but he demanded and was given permission to attend the Holy Office, claiming he had urgent business there. As indeed he did.

Father Sozzi was incandescent at the events of the day. Encouraged by a couple of friends, including Father Stefano Cherubini, that same evening Sozzi wrote an emotionally charged note to the assessor, Francesco Albizzi, informing the Holy Office of what had happened, emphasizing the confiscation of the Inquisition documents, and not mentioning the loss of his own property. The *Sacro arsenale*, the popular handbook for inquisitors, was very clear on the seriousness of the matter. It advised immediate action against 'those who offend denunciators or witnesses examined by the Holy Office, whether with blows, with insults, or with threats'. And it went on to attack 'those who steal writings, or books, or any other thing which belongs to the Holy Office'.[20] An attack on a witness was an attack on the Inquisition which was an attack on the supreme pontiff, which was an attack on the very heart of the Catholic religion itself.

Although the search had been carried out at Cardinal Cesarini's request and by his men, Father Mario's account blamed Calasanz for the whole episode. The next morning, 8 August 1642, he went round in person to underline the gravity of the offence ostensibly caused by Calasanz to the dignity of the Inquisition. The assessor presented Sozzi with a pen and paper and asked to write a formal complaint. Sozzi then left for Signor Orsino de' Rosis's palace, which was just opposite San Pantaleo, and waited for events to unfold. The assessor immediately told the Barberini nephew, Cardinal Francesco, about the insult to the dignity of the Holy Office. Given the speed with which events proceeded that day, everyone involved must have been rushing around Rome from door to door to resolve the issue. The papal nephew reported the matter to the pope, and the order went out immediately to arrest and incarcerate the guilty parties.

At midday Monsignor Albizzi arrived at San Pantaleo in a carriage, accompanied by a squadron of guards. Entering the sacristy, Albizzi halted on the threshold and 'in a loud voice and with supreme authority' cried out, 'Where is the general?' When Calasanz appeared, the assesor demanded that the assistants and the other leading figures of the order be immediately summoned to his presence. Of the four assistants one was absent and one was sick. The other two, Fathers Pietro Casani and Giovanni Garcia Castiglia came hurrying to the scene. The secretary general, Father Giacomo Bandoni, was holding Mass in the attached church and was hastily summoned. Albizzi acted viciously throughout. His guards lined the walls in silent threat, and as the old men knelt before him, presumably terrified, and certainly confused and uncertain, he held his head up high, maintaining the supremacy and importance of the organization he represented. He stalked up and down the sacristy, barking out orders with ill-concealed impatience as the priests cowered before him. Even when he was assured that Father Buonaventura Catalucci, the fourth assistant, was truly sick, he insisted on visiting his room to check that he was really in bed and too unwell to be moved. Then returning to the sacristy, he announced the words that must have struck a chill into the hearts of many men before: 'You are prisoners of the Inquisition.' No further explanations were provided. Calasanz would later write, 'I was taken to the Holy Office without knowing why.'[21]

While Albizzi was checking on the sick man, some of the younger Piarists had run to the neighbours for help. The Marquis of Torres and Prince Pietro de' Massimi, summoned from the next-door palaces by the desperate cries of the priests, came rushing to lend their support. But the assessor was inflexible. His only concession to the noblemen was to agree that the four old men would not be chained. However, when the prince and the marquis begged that the old men be allowed to ride in a carriage, the assessor flatly refused. As criminal suspects they should walk through the streets in their shame. As he mounted his carriage, the assessor shouted to the prisoners, 'Onwards to the palace of the Holy Office', and then settled himself back in his seat. The procession set out from the main door towards Piazza Pasquino. Two by two – Calasanz, aged eighty-five, with Pietro Casani, aged seventy, in front; Giovanni Garzia Castiglia and Giacomo Bandoni, striplings of sixty, behind – preceded and flanked by uniformed guards and followed by Monsignor Albizzi and his attendants in his carriage. As the midday sun of a Roman summer burned down, they walked past the booksellers of Parione, past the governor's palace in Monte Giordano, through the crowded shopping areas and on over Ponte Sant'Angelo. There, Calasanz, overcome by the heat and the long humiliating walk at the hottest hour of the day, was assailed by thirst and was permitted to pause at a fountain to moisten his lips, before the procession continued through Borgo and towards Piazza San Pietro and the palace of the Holy Inquisition.

And from the window opposite San Pantaleo, in de Rosis's palace, Father Mario Sozzi looked down 'to see to what depths the founder and creator of the holy habit that he himself was wearing had been reduced'. He was so joyful and jubilant at his achievement that Signor Orsino de Rosis was revolted and told him to be quiet. 'But Father Mario laughed and was very satisfied.'[22]

CHAPTER SIXTEEN

'A brief is to be prepared.
But secretly'

The procession of old men halted in the courtyard of the palace of the Holy Inquisition. Monsignor Albizzi descended from his carriage, ordered the prisoners to go up the stairs and await him in an antechamber. He soon joined them and the preliminary questioning began: 'Where are the papers which you removed from Father Mario yesterday?'[1] Father Calasanz meekly replied, 'Monsignor, most illustrious, I don't know anything about this, and neither do these fathers. Cardinal Cesarini, our protector, sent Count Corona, his auditor, and everything was done on his orders. And he took everything away with him to give it to His Excellency.' Albizzi was not convinced: 'You will not leave here until I have in my hand all those papers which were taken from Father Mario yesterday.'

Some of the other Piarists had meanwhile run to Cardinal Cesarini to tell him of the terrible events and to beg him to intervene. The cardinal sent for Count Corona, who still had the documents, but he had 'gone to a garden for recreation' and was nowhere to be found. As the prisoners waited at the Holy Office,

their souls were very joyful since they were suffering in innocence, but their bodies were very troubled, since they had not eaten for twenty-eight hours, and the heat was very great. They felt faint from weakness and tried to stretch out on the benches in the room, since they could no longer keep themselves upright, nor sit down. They begged one of the assessor's guards for a bit of water to refresh themselves, but no carafe arrived, and nothing else was offered.

Finally, as evening began to fall, Count Corona arrived, bringing the papers. He had returned from his expedition to find urgent messages and had immediately leaped into his carriage. The imprisonment of the general of the Piarist Order and his colleagues was over. Cardinal Cesarini, whose actions had precipitated the arrests, sent a carriage to the Holy Office and the old men were allowed to return to San Pantaleo, exhausted and shaken by their arrest.

But for Albizzi and Sozzi the matter was not over. Shortly after, a lawyer arrived from the Holy Office, bearing a warrant for the house arrest of the old men. None of the principals of the order was to leave their rooms without the specific permission of the Sacred Congregation, and more particularly that of assessor Albizzi. After several pleading letters, Albizzi conceded that the principals could attend the adjacent church and attend Mass, but they were not to leave the building.[2]

Father Calasanz wrote to Cardinal Francesco Barberini, explaining that 'with regard to the documents removed from Father Mario, neither the general nor his assistants nor any others are in any way to blame, since this action was done by the express will of his Eminence the protector',[3] and although Cardinal Cesarini backed him up, he was increasingly irritated by the whole business and inclined to back off completely. The pope held a meeting the following week at the Quirinal, to which Cesarini was either not invited or chose not to attend, and although Calasanz and his colleagues were released from house arrest, the Pope and the assembled cardinals announced their full approval of the actions of Monsignor Albizzi.[4] Any paperwork belonging to the Inquisition was to be instantly returned; Father Mario's extrajudicial position was approved – he was not subject to Calasanz's jurisdiction – and the rebel Lombard province was to be brought to heel. No one was to come to Rome without written permission; no one was to leave their own province. The cardinal protector quietly resigned, having not only completely failed to safeguard the interests of his protégés but having made the situation worse by further antagonizing the Inquisition. At a moment when the order really needed a strong protector to look after its interests, it no longer had a special voice at court.

A new man was needed to sort out the rebellious Tuscan fathers, and Father Mario Sozzi and Monsignor Albizzi knew just the right person. Father Stefano Cherubini had been promoted by Calasanz after the disgraceful events in Naples, first to visitor general and procurator general, through the direct intercession of the pope. Since being stripped of the office of procurator a few years earlier, for once again behaving badly with young boys, he had been at a loose end. Now his friends put his name forward as the candidate of their choice for commissar to sort out the 'Lombard' problem. Within a week of his release from the Inquisition, Calasanz signed the licence for Father Stefano's appointment. Presumably he felt he had no choice, but it was to prove disastrous. Together Fathers Mario and Stefano drew up an indictment of the disobedient houses and gave it to the father general to sign, threatening him that the Inquisition would intervene once again if he refused.[5]

Meanwhile, relations between Barberini Rome and most of northern Italy were reaching a point of open warfare. The spark that lit the fuse was Castro, a large and wealthy feudal territory, within the Papal States on the borders of Tuscany. The Barberini had been interested in acquiring it for several years. When Odoardo Farnese, the Duke of Parma and Piacenza, the owner of Castro and thus the pope's vassal, over-extended his finances, his bankers, who probably included the Barberini, pressed for immediate payment. Odoardo came to Rome in November 1639 to try to resolve the situation, but the relationship deteriorated into a series of petty arguments and quarrels over precedence with the nephews and from there degenerated into a more serious row, so that by the time Farnese burst into the pope's apartment, accompanied by armed retainers, to try to present his point of view, the situation had become irredeemable. Odoardo left Rome and began to put Castro onto a military footing.[6]

In March 1641 the Apostolic Chamber, the papal financial department, headed by the younger cardinal nephew, Antonio Barberini, revoked the Duchy of Castro's right to export grain, thereby cutting off any chance of repaying the debt. Farnese hoped for help from Richelieu in France, but none was forthcoming. Both sides started to build up their armies and fortify their castles, and in September, 12,000 infantrymen and 3,000 cavalry left Rome and swiftly captured Castro, led by one of the other papal nephews, Taddeo. A few months later the Apostolic Chamber announced that Farnese property in Rome was confiscated and to be auctioned off. In reply, Odoardo expelled foreign members of religious orders from his territories and pawned his wife's jewellery to raise more troops, shrugging off the inevitable excommunication, which arrived in January 1642.

Other Italian states were watching with great concern. Since 1598 the Papal States had absorbed Ferrara and Urbino, where the ruling families of Este and Della Rovere had failed to provide a definitive heir to the succession. Such dynastic acquisitiveness was worrying. Now, as the Barberini strengthened the fortifications near the borders of Tuscany and Venice, these states came together with others, and in August 1642 concluded a mutual defence pact and sent money to support Farnese. As Calasanz was being arrested by the Holy Office, Pope Urban was hearing bad news from the frontiers of his state. Giacinto Gigli, a Roman diarist, noted: 'The Emperor, the King of France, the King of Spain, the Venetians, the Grand Duke of Tuscany and the Duke of Modena have joined together and made known to the Pope that they do not want him to make war in Italy, that the Pope should make peace with the Duke of Parma.'[7]

Meanwhile, in Tuscany, Ferdinand II, the Medici grand duke, encouraged by his brother Leopoldo and their favourite mathematician,

Father Francesco Michelini, made clear their support of the rebel Piarist schools, which were refusing to recognize Father Sozzi's authority. In the context of a state of war between Rome and Florence, the Pisan school was directly forbidden by the duke to obey any order coming from Rome, or to receive any superior sent from Rome,[8] which, of course, suited the Lombard fathers perfectly.

In September Farnese invaded the Papal States near Bologna and, as the defence 'scattered like chaff' before him, he marched towards Rome, meeting with little resistance. With Odoardo encamped on Lake Trasimeno less than 100 miles away, Rome flew into a panic. The pope transferred from the Quirinal to the better-fortified Vatican. Heavy taxes were levied and troops were raised to defend the city, but there was little confidence that they would be able to withstand a serious attack. Gigli noted that many horses were commandeered and men were ordered onto them, but 'they did not know how to make the horse go … and many fell off and broke their legs, and had to ride off in that state, dejected and in pain'.[9] Calasanz noted that the vineyards had been cut down around the outside of the walls so that the cavalry could maneouvre, as well as on the inside, and the papal army numbered 5,000 cavalry and 15,000 infantry. He was more sanguine than Gigli about Rome's defences: 'The city, thank the Lord, is well-provisioned and with many people on horse and on foot to defend it if necessary.'[10]

However, in October, Odoardo Farnese lost his nerve and withdrew, as Cardinal Antonio Barberini approached with his army. Meanwhile Father Mario had travelled through the war zone and arrived in Florence on 4 November. He was unaware that it had been decided at the highest levels that if he dared to show his face in Tuscany, there would be trouble. The grand duke had written to Leopoldo, 'His Highness wants you to tell that father from the Pious Schools … that he should go and do his business outside our state' and again a few days later, 'His Highness fully approves that Father Mario of the Pious Schools be ordered to leave the state within twenty-four hours and not dare to come here, because he will be punished, and the Marchese

Gonzaga [of Mantua] has already been warned. His arrogance and impudence are truly unbearable and damaging.'[11]

So no sooner had Sozzi reached the school gates, armed with his letters of support from Cardinal Barberini, than he was swiftly expelled, sent flying rapidly northwards by accusations of trouble-making and spying for the enemy Barberini. At the border with Modena he was also refused entry, Duke Francesco d'Este having been warned of his approach by the Medici as promised.

Once again Father Sozzi sped back to Rome to complain to the Inquisition. He, Sozzi, an important ecclesiastic, appointed directly by the Inquisition and the pope, had been forced to flee for his life, while the Medici court and its Galilean heretics mocked the powerlessness of the Holy Office. Monsignor Albizzi, the assessor, was mortally offended by the treatment meted out to his favourite – or in his own words, his 'particular friend' – by the Tuscan court.[12] He summoned the ambassador, Francesco Niccolini, to protest against the expulsion, which he blamed on the envy and spite of Sozzi's colleagues, but which had resulted in an unacceptable infringement of the dignity and reputation of the Holy Office.[13]

In compensation, Calasanz offered Sozzi the provincialate of Rome. Father Mario refused this sop. He was now aiming higher. He openly accused Calasanz of conspiring with the Medici, the Este and the Farnese against the Barberini, as well as having lost his memory. 'He's a senile old dotard, who no longer knows what he does, who no longer remembers the things he has ordered, and who writes letters ordering one thing one day, and the contrary action later in the day, so that the schools and the provinces are very confused ... He has no brain any more and is no longer fit to govern the Order.'[14]

According to Father Berro, the Inquisition sent some gentlemen to test Father Calasanz, to see if he really was senile, 'but separately and individually they talked to him at various times about different subjects, and realized that the accusations were false, that although the reverend founder was eighty-five years old he had a very sound head, an excellent memory, very wise discourse, that he was on top of what he was discussing, and the gentlemen were very impressed'. Calasanz's letters of the time show no sign of senility – rather they demonstrate his usual grasp of detail and his customary inability to delegate. Mostly they depict a man who sees events spinning out of his control and who, faced with the strength of important organizations, whether it be the Cherubini family network or the Inquisition, was powerless to respond and was forced into making foolish decisions and appointments. Whether Calasanz was senile or not, he was undoubtedly very old, and his grasp of the Piarist empire – thirty-six schools spread over six provinces – was no longer as firm as it had been. Even if Berro's tale of the gentlemen who came to test his mental agility is true, it still had no effect on the assessor.

Monsignor Albizzi planned his next step, and it was a dramatic one. He wrote to Marc'Antonio Maraldi, the secretary who prepared the papal briefs. 'By Order of His Holiness a brief is to be prepared. But secretly. Creating Father Mario [Sozzi] di San Francesco vicar general of the religion of the Mother of God, because of the great age of the Father General and for other reasons which move the spirit of His Holiness. The brief is to be given to Monsignor Assessor of the Holy Office [Albizzi himself].'[15] Father Mario Sozzi was to be promoted to the very governorship of the order.

By the end of December 1642 Monsignor Albizzi had the brief in his pocket, and rumours of a new title for Sozzi had begun to reach Calasanz. However, the old man thought it would be an honorific title 'just for pomp', since surely as general he was still in charge. In fact, Calasanz had read the situation very badly. As the brief made very clear, it was his own position that was to become honorific, while Father Sozzi was to run the whole order.[16]

On 15 January 1643, as armies marched around Italy and the pope threatened to excommunicate those who dared to help the Farnese Duke of Parma, the Holy Office promulgated the decree *In causa Patris Marii*. In the presence of Pope Urban VIII, the Barberini nephews, several other cardinals and Monsignor Albizzi, Father Calasanz and the existing assistants were suspended *in absentia*, and the father general was replaced by Father Mario as the new first assistant general, to govern the order in association with a specially appointed apostolic visitor. The visitor was to try and sort out the serious long-term problems within the order, while Father Mario was to concern himself with the day-to-day administration.

A few weeks later the old general and the whole household of Rome were summoned to the domestic oratory to hear the verdict. The vice-regent of Rome, Giovan Battista Altieri, read out the decree to the assembled fathers. A gasp of horror must have gone around, for no one had known the worst. Although an apostolic visitor held out the hope of some kind of resolution in the future, for the time being Father Mario was in full control. There was no legal or canonical procedure to offer a way out. The pope and the Holy Office of the Inquisition had spoken. No explanations were provided, no defence could be offered. Father Mario's time had come.

'Do you know anything scandalous about your superiors?'

The new apostolic visitor was a Somasco priest, Father Agostino Ubaldini, a forty-one-year-old inspector of the Holy Office. The Somaschi had been founded a century earlier and specialized in running orphanages and seminaries. Father Berro commented that 'the visitor, Father Ubaldini, clearly demonstrated both his piety and the nobility of his blood by the way he carried out the visit, showing great reverence towards our Reverend Father founder and general, and also respecting the other priests.'[1] Father Calasanz noted that he seemed to have many qualities, and his letters reflect a modest and conscientious character.[2] To supplement Father Sozzi, the visitor immediately appointed three new assistants, Fathers Santino Lunardi, Stefano Spinola and Giovan Francesco Bafici, blameless men of good reputation who would not last long. Father Ubaldini himself seems to have approached his new task with enthusiasm and an open mind. He too would not last long.

He started the visit in formal fashion. First the brief of authorization was read aloud to the household and then the inspection began with the church and the sacristy, where all was as it should be and nothing untoward was found. Suddenly Father Ubaldini turned to Father Mario and requested the keys to his room. 'It was a complete surprise and totally unexpected,' commented Father Berro in his *Notes*. Although his rooms had already been controversially inspected twice, being illegally locked both times when items not permitted in the *Rules* had been found, on each occasion Father Mario had been able to turn the situation to his advantage. He must have thought he was safe now that he was the first assistant, and once again his room was locked. But Father Ubaldini was not to be gainsaid, and Father Mario was given no opportunity to tidy his room or hide any evidence. Accompanied by his secretary, another Somasco Father Muzio Carracciolo, Father Ubaldini entered Sozzi's room. There he discovered 'many things unworthy of a priest – in addition to money, food, sweets and all kinds of edible things and enough drink for many people, embroidered gloves, women's adornments, wigs, hairpieces, very fine precious ribbons, superb rosaries for women and other devotional things in abundance, of which an exact inventory was made, and the visitor was absolutely amazed'.[3]

Nothing similar was found in any of the other rooms – 'they breathed an odour of total poverty, clean but very poor'. Father Ubaldini drew up a detailed report, which he sent to the Congregation of the Holy Office. According to Father Berro, 'it was truthful, and completely summed up what he had seen, and touched with his own hands, saying that all evil and unrest was caused by Father Mario'.[4] The report was never seen again. Meanwhile, on 13 April, he summoned the household of San Pantaleo together to read out the most salient points of his investigations. Apart from Father Mario's room he had found nothing wrong that was not trivial. For instance, library books were to be promptly returned; teachers were not allowed to go out into town singly but only with a companion. So as far as Father Ubaldini's apostolic visit had progressed, the only problem had been Father Mario. The rest of the Piarist headquarters had passed the inspection.

It seemed that Father Ubaldini was preparing to visit the provinces, when suddenly, a bare two weeks after presenting his preliminary report on the Rome house, and only six weeks into his investigation, he 'renounced' the job. One can only assume that Francesco Albizzi had sacked him, displeased at the moderation of his findings and the criticisms of his protégé, for a replacement was ready and announced that same day. Father Berro blamed not only Father Mario but also the current political situation and Calasanz's ongoing correspondence with the Medici princes, the enemies of the Barberini, for Ubaldini's departure after his favourable report. On 29 April 1643, Father Silvestro Pietrasanta took over as apostolic visitor. Father Francesco Baldi, one of the teachers at the Piarist Nazarene College, later wondered about the rapid change: 'I don't know whether His Holiness ever knew [about the new appointment] because it seems to be a sign of frivolity to appoint someone to a position and then without any reason fire him and elect someone else.'[5] The Piarists lost one of their closest allies as the Tuscan envoy, Niccolini, fled Rome on 29 May, without even taking leave of the pope, such was the dire state of relations between Rome and the rest of Italy as the War of Castro rumbled on. One of the last letters between Niccolini and the Tuscan court warns that 'only bad actions can be expected from Father Mario', along with another warning to the Medici grand duke not to become involved with him in any way.[6]

Father Pietrasanta was a Jesuit, a member of an order that did not view the Piarists with particular favour. Also founded by a Spaniard, Ignatius Loyola, one hundred years earlier, the Jesuits were considered the elite among religious orders. Dedicated to obeying every papal command, and ultimate defenders of religious orthodoxy, the Jesuits had acquired a reputation for intellectual superiority. In Messina a damaging rumour had spread that Calasanz was a Jesuit reject, but in fact he had a great respect for the Society of Jesus and had integrated much of Loyola's *Constitutions* into his own version. He and the Jesuit general, Father Muzio Vitelleschi, exchanged friendly correspondence, and were mutually deferential when they met in the street.

However, it was in their attitudes towards the poor that the differences between the two orders were most apparent. While the Jesuits aimed to teach rulers and noblemen, the majority of the Piarists' pupils were poor. The Jesuits begrudgingly acknowledged that their teaching could if necessary be 'accommodated to the intelligence of children and ignorant persons', while Calasanz specifically targeted those very sectors 'with great patience and charity'.[7] In some towns the two orders were in direct competition for resources, as Father Berro had found to his cost when he joined an anti-Jesuit riot in Sicily aimed at preventing the opening of a new college. In central Europe there had also been some competition for patronage and resources. Calasanz had always tried not to offend the Jesuits, claiming that 'our schools won't bother them at all because most of our pupils will be learning to read, write and do arithmetic, and those who know grammar will go to the Jesuits anyhow'.[8] So the Piarists would be left with the younger children, or 'those who can't afford the level of clean clothes which are needed in those [Jesuit] schools'.[9]

The Galileo affair had also placed the Jesuits and the Piarists on opposing sides. While the Florentine Piarists, with Calasanz's quiet approval, became ever more closely associated with the disgraced scientist, Galileo's opponents were in the ascendant in Rome. With the heliocentric view now banned, the Jesuit College of Rome under Orazio Grassi became the leading centre for the orthodox pursuit of mathematics and astronomy. The centrality of the Jesuit role in Galileo's downfall was acknowledged by the school's professor of mathematics and astronomy: 'If Galileo had known how to keep the affection of the fathers of this college, he would live in glory before the world and none of his misfortunes would have occurred, and he would have been able to write at his pleasure about any subject even, I say, about the movements of the earth.'[10] Once the Piarists became friendly with Galileo, and associated with his atomist views of the Eucharist (as Sozzi had stated in his accusation to the Holy Office in 1641), they had inadvertently brought on themselves the potential enmity of the powerful Society of Jesus.

To offend the Jesuits was politically dangerous too. Giovanni Ciampoli, author of a contemporary *Discourse on the Court of Rome* advised that one should always remain on good terms with them: 'For hate or passion or spirit of contradiction, or because of natural inclination, one should never try to antagonize a commonly esteemed religious order, like that of the Jesuits today.'[11]

Other known enemies of the Jesuits were friends of the Piarists. Gaspar Schoppe and Tommaso Campanella were both renowned for their anti-Jesuit feelings. Their association cannot have enhanced the relationship between the two orders. Campanella had even written a sonnet entitled *Against Hypocrites*, which clearly targeted those 'With the name of Jesus marked in front'.[12]

So when it became known that a Jesuit had been nominated to oversee the internal troubles of the Pious Schools, there were many who thought this an ominous development. As Father Berro said, 'They have put the sheep right into the wolf's mouth'.[13] The visitor's own claims that 'the Company of Jesus professes charity and prudence, not politics, and through charitable motives always inclines towards conservation and not destruction of religious Orders, according to the axiom *do not do unto others what you do not wish done to you*' aimed to reassure the anxious.[14]

Monsignor Albizzi was closely associated with the Jesuits. His favourable opinion was encouraged by a life pension from the Society of Jesus, which was wealthy and could afford to purchase his favour. His interest in the Society is borne out by the provisions of his will, which stipulated that when his legitimate heirs died (he had had five children before being widowed in 1623) all his possessions should go to the Society. Perhaps the real mistake the Piarist Order made was not only in retaining worthless priests such as Mario Sozzi and Stefano Cherubini, but in not developing real political and financial influence. The poverty of the order, which would so trouble Mario and Stefano (both of whom preferred a more luxurious way of life), meant that it could not afford the favour of men such as Albizzi. Cherubini, however, would later recognize this and reach an arrangement with the assessor. This was a shrewd move, for as Father Baldi, teacher at the Nazarene College, said, 'everyone knew the power the assessor had with the rulers at that time; the terrible information he gave directly to

His Holiness [the pope] about all the religious orders, calling us all disobedient and refractory.'[15] Meanwhile Albizzi must have been fairly clear about the sort of verdict he anticipated with the appointment of the new visitor.

Father Silvestro Pietrasanta was a well-established preacher, the author of many works, poems, elegies, heraldic treatises and devotional material. He had been in Germany for nearly ten years in the service of Cardinal Caraffa, then rector of the Jesuit college in Loreto, before returning to Rome and working for the pope on many important and delicate missions. He was hostile to Galileo's ideas and a few years earlier had written that 'the flaws in the character of a magnanimous prince are no more real than the sunspots, which … are mere illusions caused by the vibration of the "opticum specillum"', which did not bode well.[16] Nevertheless, the new visit started well. Father Pietrasanta sent out a circular to the schools introducing himself. The assistants, the same fathers who had served with Father Ubaldini, also sent out a circular asking people not to listen to 'immature gossip of little judgement'. The aim, they explained, was 'to establish in our Order universal and particular peace, both internal and external, useful and necessary both for the service of God and the health of souls, and for the continuation of our Order'.[17] Feedback was very positive and many of the schools, including that of Florence, wrote encouraging replies.

But it soon started to go dreadfully wrong. A week after the assistants sent out their circular, Father Mario wrote to Father Berro with a bald statement of his aims: 'This organization has been, and still is, holy and good. But it has not been well led. Now with considerable efforts by me I hope that we will be able to fulfil my desire, which is to provide a structure for this Order, because it has never been given one … I have subordinated my own interests for the universal good of this Order, and my aim is to sort it out, not to destroy it.' These words obviously shocked Father Berro for he peppered this page of his *Notes* with question marks. That Father Mario, whose experience of running anything amounted to a few days as head of the Poli school, and his time with the honorific title of 'provincial' (for which he revealed no useful qualities), and whose grasp of grammar even was tenuous, should try to sort out the order's problems and restructure the organization clearly struck him as ludicrous.[18] Within a month the three assistants – Lunardi, Spinola and Bafici – were disgusted with Father Mario:

We declare under oath, that after having accepted our positions [as assistants], and governed for the space of one month, we are forced into this action by the bad conduct of Father Mario [Sozzi] di San Francesco and we cannot support such a man to the detriment and ruin of the whole Order. We are unable to persuade him to govern well because of the backing he receives from Monsignor Assessor of the Holy Office, so that whenever we propose something that is not to his liking or his whims, he threatens us with the said Inquisition. Thus we have taken the decision to renounce our assistantships, which we hereby renounce.

The 'bad conduct' they complained of was not specified.[19] Father Pietrasanta persuaded them to continue in post for a few more months, but the situation subsequently deteriorated still further.

Without informing the other assistants, Father Mario then offered the job of provincial and headmaster of Rome to his friend, Father Cherubini. With plentiful access to the young boys conveniently under his care, and the prestige of a provincialate, the position was perfect. The three assistants were offended at the lack of consultation and horrified at the elevation of someone like Cherubini, but when one of them, Father Santino, complained to Father Pietrasanta, the visitor exploded. 'He jumped up raging,' wrote the other two assistants, 'not only against Father Santino, but also against us innocent and silent ones, and he treated us all as rebels and disobedient towards the Holy Office, without having had any occasion to do so, neither from us nor from Father Santino.'[20] Perhaps the apostolic visitor was feeling defensive about his decision to permit the notorious Father Stefano to take such a responsible position. The three elderly fathers were instantly relieved of their positions. No replacements were appointed. From now on there was only one assistant, Father Sozzi.

Sozzi was now free of constraint and could rule as he pleased. Father Cherubini was immediately re-appointed procurator general, the position from which he had been ignominiously fired by Calasanz only a few months earlier. Fathers whom Sozzi considered hostile were posted to obscure schools where they would be denied close contact with the apostolic visitor. Mario's friend Giovan Antonio Ridolfi della Natività was recalled from Tuscany to act as secretary to Father Pietrasanta, a move that filled the rest of the order with foreboding. Father Giovan Antonio was 'not only young, but very free and susceptible to temptation, so that our superiors had often had to eject him from some place or other and subject him to frequent punishments'. He was inexperienced in government and teaching, and his morals and way of life were considered suspect by many members. In an earlier posting to Moravia he had shown himself to be indiscreet and unreliable. 'No one really trusts him,' wrote a colleague, 'and we consider him to be someone in whom you cannot entrust your secrets for fear of your own ruin.' He was, according to the same correspondent, 'furious, impassioned and restless', and desperate to leave the order and live freely in lay society.[21] When in January 1643 Calasanz sent him a pious letter, advising him how to guide his soul into the harbour of eternal happiness, he sent back a curt note saying, 'Since I have never given Your Reverence cause to write to me, and do not consider myself deserving of such a letter, I am sending it back since it must have been addressed to me in error.'[22] The striking lack of courtesy clearly showed that Calasanz had lost any authority over at least a certain section of his membership.

Ridolfi saw his job as closely controlling who had access to the visitor, filtering his correspondence and ensuring he only received what Sozzi and his companions wanted him to read. The Roman members had hoped that the Jesuit would take an independent man from outside the order to this sensitive position, but with Ridolfi in control all information was fed back to Father Mario, so no confidential matters or reports could be sent to the apostolic visitor without his knowledge. Father Pietrasanta tried to reassure the members by appointing a Jesuit father in each town to whom the Piarists could entrust sealed letters, which would be delivered by the Society of Jesus to Pietrasanta 'in his own hands', but in fact Father Ridolfi seems quickly to have established an iron grip on the visitor's sources of independent information and even letters that had travelled via the Jesuits ended up in his hands.[23] Nor could anyone make an appointment with the Jesuit without first explaining to Father Mario or one of his adherents what they wished to say.

Father Pietrasanta was no longer in the best of health, so he relied on others' reports for an accurate representation of the state of the order outside Rome. Unfortunately these visits were usually carried out by Father Mario's friends. The German provincial was aghast at the choice of visitor:

Who for the love of God did you send? Maybe an old man exhausted by his duties running the Order? Maybe a penitent of good reputation and renown, as would have been convenient, reasonable and necessary? I don't want to say too much since this letter will be shown to the whole Sacred College, bishops, princes and others, but even though these men [chosen to be visitors] had reached a reasonable age they had never been given any governing duties within the Order, but had rather been punished and kept down because of their free way of life. I need say no more.[24]

These colleagues and advisers were 'the most dissolute and lax men that one could possibly find'.[25] One of Sozzi's first actions, barely three weeks after being appointed, was to name Father Nicolò Maria Gavotti del Rosario as visitor. Gavotti was to inspect the province of Liguria, which included the schools of Genoa, Savona, Carcare, and the recently founded Cagliari in Sardinia.

Suspiciously, Gavotti had never stayed in one school for very long and Calasanz had received many complaints about his behaviour, but his influential patron, Cardinal Sacchetti – himself a close ally of the Barberini – had protected him through the years.[26] He had a great reputation for enjoying lay company, and for leaving the house and going out into the streets alone, which was strictly forbidden by the *Constitutions*.[27] From 1639 worse rumours began to follow him, mysterious comments in the correspondence such as 'it's a pity that boy took it so badly', to which Calasanz initially responded by suggesting that Gavotti be sent away from the school on a short break: 'Let us proceed with subtlety and charity so that no one says or suspects anything.'[28] In Savona he was suspected of altering the accounts in his own favour, but his cardinal's protection once again kept him inviolate. Calasanz asked the Neapolitan provincial, Father Giuseppe Fedele, to see if he could find out any more, only to discover that 'the more one digs up about Father Nicolò Maria, the more one discovers in Naples and elsewhere'.[29] As the complaints against Gavotti began to reach a crescendo Cardinal Sacchetti ordered that the Piarist devote himself entirely to his patron's business affairs, although he still remained in residence in the Neapolitan school.[30]

It was there that something terrible seems to have happened in October 1641, the month that Sozzi denounced the Florentine fathers for Galileanism. The father provincial wrote ominously to Calasanz:

I have often asked Your Reverence to remove Father Nicolò Maria from here for just reason ... Now I have discovered a very serious matter, which, when it is discovered, will result in great disturbance for the whole Order. I am not going to write about it, but wait to tell you face to face. But I beg Your Reverence not to wait that long. By the first courier call him to Rome and remove him from here. It is not a matter to sleep on. May this serve as a warning to Your Reverence.[31]

A week later, the headmaster, Father Francesco Trabucco, took up the call: 'For the love of God, do not forget to remove that blessed father, unless you want to hear very disgusting things.'[32] When Gavotti was still there a few weeks later, Trabucco wrote again, in even stronger terms:

As for removing from Naples the one I wrote to you about, do as you please, but I beg you not to complain to me later if you suffer something that will give you great disgust, because these are not things which are done in a house where I am regularly, but [may happen] outside, and they are ugly and of great importance. And I would write them to you, if I did not fear that the letter might be opened by laymen, not by our own religious, which would not matter so much.[33]

None of them specified exactly what the issue was, other than to say it was scandalous, disgusting and involved lay matters. It is hard not to conclude that the problem was of a sexual nature, for the earlier financial irregularities had not provoked such an outcry, nor such heavy indications that Gavotti's actions would cause disgust. Calasanz bowed to pressure and recalled Gavotti to Savona. However, at the time it did not suit Father Nicolò Maria to leave Naples immediately, and although his letter was full of protestations of obedience about how 'I would immediately have obeyed your instructions were I not prevented by the bad weather', he also pointed out that the cardinal wanted him to stay in Naples and deal with his legal affairs for the time being. He kindly suggested that another father be sent to Savona in his stead.[34]

In January 1642, just as the order was beginning to come to grips with the implications of Sozzi's promotion to provincial, matters suddenly took an urgent turn, and Gavotti and his brother Vincenzo were forced to leave Naples in a great hurry, and set off for Genoa, where the provincial was less than happy to receive him.[35] Whatever it was that had made an urgent departure imperative, one can assume it was something disgraceful. Given the reputations they carried with them, and their later behaviour, a safe assumption would be that they probably enjoyed relationships with young boys and men from outside the order, and that they made no secret of their behaviour. Once installed in the Ligurian capital, the Gavotti brothers and their entourage began to indulge what one of their worried colleagues, Father Giovan Luca Rapallo, called their 'love of ruin and free life' once more.[36] After Sozzi

appointed Vincenzo to the position of provincial, their behaviour knew
no bounds. They bought themselves new clothes and smart shoes, and
traipsed around town 'like a group of soldiers, loving ruin and free living'. They behaved no better in school: 'In the provincial's room there
are always four or five of them, and always a boy, and that does not
seem appropriate to me,' wrote the same observer.[37]

Father Nicolò Maria Gavotti was already, according to Father Berro,
'quite well known', by the time he was appointed visitor in August 1643,
'not so much in the province of his birth [he was born in Savona in
northern Italy] but throughout the rest of the order, and especially in
the Neapolitan houses'. The suggestion had come from Father Stefano
Cherubini. 'Father Nicolò Maria,' wrote Berro bleakly, 'was worthy of
improvement in many areas, and was an accomplice of the said Father
Stefano, and through their particular interests he was recommended to
the Jesuit apostolic visitor.' Clearly Cherubini and Gavotti were allies
and shared 'particular interests [*particolari interes[s]i*]'.[38] Both had already
been in trouble with the mainstream of the order, and Gavotti was
known as Cherubini's 'individual companion', according to Berro,
while Calasanz too had admitted he had 'nothing of the religious about
him save his habit'.[39]

By the time he reached Sardinia in October 1643 to continue his
duties as visitor, Father Nicolò Maria Gavotti had cast off his impoverished cleric's uniform of rough cloth and sandals. Father Vincenzo
Berro reported that he arrived 'not as a poor religious of the Mother of
God of the Pious Schools in sandals, but dressed rather as a soldier
or an actor, since underneath he wore a collar edged with gold, a pair
of stockings also trimmed with gold and so many other vanities that,
although I can remember them in detail, it makes me blush to describe
them'.[40] By the time Father Gavotti had finished his visit – which after
all was supposed to check on observance and morale – he had acquired
so much luggage that it required 'the shoulders of fourteen youths' to
carry all his purchases down to the port for the trip back to Rome.
Several holy relics encased in marble, four donkeys, wine, Indian

roosters, linen, money and huge quantities of edibles formed the bulk of his luggage. And if the Cagliari teachers were not already irritated by this display of ostentatious shopping, they could console themselves with the reflection that the many cheeses, salamis, pomegranates and other foodstuffs had been bought with their own revenue from their school funds and with money donated by their local patrons. Apart from the relics and four sheep's cheeses, which he gave to the Savona school as he passed through on his return trip, the rest all went to his relative's house, presumably for his own consumption.[41] 'He is one of those people who desire the recognition of his family and who do not care for the honourable actions which should speak for a priest,' noted one of his colleagues, Father Baldi.[42] He also took with him a gaudy young man, the bastard son of a local captain, to bear him company on the long sea journey onwards. 'The Lord help our poor Order,' wrote the Sardinian headmaster as he told Calasanz about the new depths to which the Piarists were sinking.[43] As Gavotti sailed away with his loot, a small tartan – a single-masted ship with a large lateen sail and jib – was captured just off the coast of Sardinia by the Turks. It carried cloth from Livorno, which had been destined to provide new clothes for the Sardinian teachers, and was now lost. The headmaster commented bitterly that although eight of the staff were virtually wearing rags after Gavotti's visit, there was now no money left at all to buy any replacement cloth.[44]

In spring 1644 Father Nicolò Maria Gavotti annoyed the Genoese school with his lack of observance and 'free way of life' so greatly that, although they wanted in principle to obey the apostolic visitor, the entire staff were so outraged by his behaviour that they refused to receive him any more.[45] Later they accused him of seeking revenge and punishment for earlier imagined insults and of being not only incompetent but 'a man of terrible reputation' who had scandalized the local population.[46] It was only in 1662, many years later, that the pope himself would personally banish Gavotti from Rome because his 'secular intrigues' had caused 'a terrible stench to everyone nearby'.[47] At this time, however, Gavotti and his brother were strongly supported by one man, Father Ignazio Guarnotto di Giesù, who sent an official letter in support of Vincenzo Maria Gavotti, whom he claimed to find very prudent and religious, and fully informed about all his past habits.[48] Since these 'past habits' included Father Ignazio's activities in Naples, from where he had been abruptly removed to Genoa after encouraging his pupils to fondle one another, the comment was revealing. A promotion to the priesthood had followed swiftly on Ignazio's transfer and another to the headship of the Genoese school, one of the most important run by the order, shortly after Calasanz's removal from authority. As well as writing in strong support of Gavotti, Ignazio also recommended Father Stefano, whom he found 'very deserving' of all honours, regarding his actions with 'universal satisfaction' and announcing that if he had had to elect anyone for the post of superior, Father Stefano would have been his first choice.[49] His was a lone voice.

In Naples Father Giovanni di Rosa was initially appointed as provincial in May 1643.[50] However, he soon began to uncover some sordid scandals. Within a week of his appointment he was pointing out to Sozzi that Father Gioachino Gallo, headmaster in the tiny school at Bisignano, had been frequently accused of 'wicked practices with a youth'.[51] He would obviously need to be replaced but the Roman superiors failed to see any urgency in the request.[52] Five months later di Rosa was more insistently pointing out to Father Sozzi that 'a man of his character should not govern one of our houses'. As well as being suspected of dishonesty and drinking, 'he has returned to his old friendship with that boy or youth, which Your Reverence knows was already being rumoured, and is still being talked about by our members and by laymen'. His warning was clear this time: 'If this father is not removed from Bisignano, things will happen that will pain not only Your Reverence and me, but also give great offence to God.'[53] Yet again his letter was ignored, although by this time Sozzi was very ill. A year after di Rosa's first warning, he wrote to Father Stefano Cherubini about Father Gioachino: 'They say that he has had wicked practices with a youth called Timoteo. He has solicited one of our lay brothers, etc. In conclusion he is more suited to prison than to be superior. And if Your Reverence doesn't remedy this by removing him, either all will leave Bisignano, or they will smash his head in.'[54] Other correspondence confirmed the accusations that Father Gioachino was involved with a certain beardless Timoteo, for whose upkeep he even went so far as to sell many books from the school library, a chasuble and a breviary.[55] If Timoteo was still beardless nearly two years into his relationship with Father Gioachino, he must have been young indeed at the start. Di Rosa was planning a special investigation, leading to a trial of Father Gioachino, when he was suddenly removed from office by Father Stefano in September 1645.

In his stead came another friend of Fathers Sozzi and Cherubini, appointed as visitor to the Neapolitan province, Father Glicerio Cerutti della Natività, the only man to volunteer to join Sozzi in Florence when he had been appointed provincial by the Inquisition, and another close associate of Cherubini. The case of Father Gioachino and his young friend Timoteo was quietly shelved, as the new visitor prioritized the task of enriching himself with sumptuous goods. He too 'was well-known by everyone, and had been the source of great merit for the Father General for putting up with him, though he often scolded him, since by nature he was stupid and talkative, very contrary to the Father General, and very like Father Stefano degli Angeli and Father Mario'.[56] He too ate and dressed very well, again contrary to the original *Rules* of the order. 'With great avidity he accumulated things and money to send away such as chests of pomade, flasks of perfume, necklaces and pendants of crystal and similar things, as well as crates of sweets, caskets and boxes, half a barrel of wine.'[57] Cerutti would survive the order's black years and be remembered by archivists and historians in later years. In 1659, years after the deaths of Sozzi, Cherubini, Calasanz and many of the other important figures of this period, Cerutti would build a huge bonfire using the order's most controversial papers for firewood. Father Berro in particular would be furious, and as he wrote his *Notes of the Foundation* he would often bewail 'those two big boxes which I left in Rome, thinking they were in a safe place ... but which were burnt by someone who should have protected them with his own blood'.[58] Had he known Father Cerutti was in charge of them, he probably would not have left them there with such misplaced confidence. But in the mid-1640s Cerutti very much enjoyed his duties as visitor, and shipped his trophies back to Rome for enjoyment at greater leisure.

The third visitor was Father Giovanni della Beata Vergine, who, despite his complete inexperience, was charged with visiting his own province of Naples. The schools in Tuscany and the breakaway Pisan house where Father Francesco Michelini had taken refuge were not inspected at all at this time, since relations between the Medici and Barberini families were so strained.

The visitors chosen by Sozzi and Cherubini to inspect the schools of the order were without exception a group of men with bad reputations. It would stretch the definition to call them a paedophile ring, not only because this would be an anachronistic term, but because the surviving evidence is insufficient. But they were certainly not a fit group of people to be placed in charge of the spiritual and physical welfare of thousands of boys. There are simply too many contemporary references to ignore. Their priorities lay more with their own physical enjoyment and material enrichment than with any spiritual obligation towards their religion or their habit.

Meanwhile, Father Pietrasanta in Rome was receiving information filtered by the secretary he had appointed, Father Ridolfi. Those who would be unsympathetic to Father Mario were not invited to write or to visit Rome, or their letters were censored. Of the hundred or so Piarists in the city, Pietrasanta managed to speak to only twenty-five. And of the houses visited outside Rome – by visitors whose credibility and behaviour was suspect – he received reports from only seven of the thirty, and several of those would arrive too late for integration into his final summary. Father Berro commented, 'I personally know that the depositions of many important priests of our Order were listened to because they had been summoned, but because they did not speak according to the aims of Father Mario and the visitor, nothing was written down.'[59]

The apostolic visitor had sent the schools a questionnaire with some thirty leading questions. The influence of Father Mario and Father Stefano is quite clear:

Does it seem to you that the damage has proceeded from too great an expansion, or that the teachers are too overwhelmed with fatigue?

What do you think about going unshod, sleeping without sheets, and dressing so poorly?

Do you think there are too many fasts and what about standing up to eat the evening meal?

Do you think the Order can continue without any sort of income?

Do you think some schools should be abandoned?

Do you know anything scandalous about your superiors, or about the other members of staff?

How are the vows of chastity and obedience observed?

Does this way of life create any threat to chastity?[60]

Father Mario and Father Stefano had their own agenda for the reform of the order. Out would go the radical poverty, the ascetic way of life, the accompanying home of children, the daily chores, the strict fasts. Father Stefano had always had problems observing the rigid dietary and clothing rules; Father Mario had always managed to secrete clandestine sweets and foodstuffs in his room. But as time passed, others in the order began to approve some reforms along these lines and observance started to slip. Father Vincenzo Berro, after criticizing the visitor Cerutti's profligacy, acknowledged: 'The truth is, however, that here everyone hates this Holy Poverty, and does not want to wear discoloured clothes, let alone darned and torn ones ... I don't think that in the whole of Naples more than eight or nine wear woollen shirts. In winter almost all wear shoes ... At table and in the house all you hear and see are poor behaviour and inappropriate language. Many eat as they please under various pretexts ...'[61]

Initially Father Mario Sozzi enjoyed his life as a ruler. Father Giacomo di Santa Maria Maddalena, who had been Father Calasanz's secretary for many years, was sent away and the old man's books were removed. Calasanz's correspondence was censored, and when some of the fathers managed to get a complaint to him that he had not answered their letters, the erstwhile father general replied that he always answered if he received the letter, and that thus they would know if the letter had been correctly delivered by his response. His keys to the archives and to various rooms were confiscated. Even his personal items were removed, most importantly the heart of Glicerio Landriani, which the old man had treasured in his room as a revered relic from his early Piarist colleague and potential saint. According to some faithful fathers, Calasanz deferred to the younger man, kneeling before him to ask his blessing and permission whenever he wanted to go out. The old father general seemed resigned to his fate. 'Father Mario gives orders exactly as he pleases,' he noted sadly in September 1643, two months after the sacking of the other assistants, and even orders ostensibly signed by the apostolic visitor had been drafted by Sozzi.[62] At this point he made no effort to summon any kind of diplomatic support against the trend of events. Father Berro noted that he never tried to arrange a meeting with the Spanish ambassador or with any other princes or influential members of court who might have stirred themselves against Sozzi's machinations. Even when a princely supporter sent him 100 scudi, a substantial sum, to help him mount some kind of defence, he merely thanked the donor and turned the money straight over to Father Mario, who took it joyfully, and counted Calasanz back a few miserly coins with which to buy himself a holy picture since his own collection had been removed. Whether the lack of any attempt at a defence showed a saintly resignation, or simply passivity, the resulting humiliation of the erstwhile father general was a triumph for Sozzi and his colleagues.[63]

But the first assistant's luck was about to run out. A few days after

Calasanz had written that Father Mario Sozzi ordered everything his own way, the latter noticed some marks on his body. Within a fortnight his skin had erupted in an ugly covering of scabs that flaked from his body at the slightest touch. Father Berro wrote that the disease was 'stomach-turning and shameful'. The doctors argued about the diagnosis. One of the Piarists commented with *Schadenfreude*, 'The Lord who looks into our hearts and gives a just reward for our deeds, sent Father Mario such a bad disease, that starting from the pudenda, it covered him completely in a very short time, so that he became one huge scab, which was variously diagnosed by the doctors.' Some called it *sorus*, a kind of fungal growth usually found on the underside of leaves, others leprosy. Historians are divided about the medical diagnosis. Leprosy or syphilis are possible diagnoses, but Sozzi's steep decline seems too fast a progression for either of these. Others suggest some kind of rampant staphylococcal or streptococcal infection. The most recent Piarist historian, Father Severino Giner Guerri, thinks that Father Mario died of the ferocious cures that were inflicted on his body. Medical opinion suggests that he developed extensive psoriasis, succumbing to fulminant progression, with infection and dehydration finally killing him.[64]

The disease progressed with horrible rapidity and even though Father Mario had had 'the constitutional strength of an ox', according to one colleague, he sank quickly. No expense was spared to cure him. 'The doctors treated him and medicated him as though he were a supreme and absolute prince, not sparing any cost, even though it was enormous.'[65] Initially he was fed with expensive delicacies. Then the cures became more bizarre as the patient and the doctors became more desperate. 'To cure himself he took purges, and the doctors applied many remedies, even giving him wine containing viper poison, baths, they put him in a calf slit alive down the middle and all was in vain. The doctors said that it was a terrible leprosy but the more remedies they applied, the more it grew. When they changed his sheets, they found handfuls of scales.'[66] All this cost a fortune: 'Viper wine is very expensive because you have to kill the vipers first, and to supply them alive costs a great deal,' noted Father Berro.[67]

He was moved in a covered carriage to the Nazarene College at Capo le Case where the air was considered better and where there were pleasant gardens, and some remaining vineyards. A new kind of bath with oils made of precious ingredients was prescribed. After being purged, Father Mario sat in his bath for the required length of time, and at first it seemed to have worked. 'He came out very handsome, and all the scabs stayed behind in the bath,' wrote Berro, 'and he and his friends were very encouraged, and very joyful, and Father Mario himself wrote to me to tell me about it and about his recovered health.' But the respite was brief and the encrustation grew back. Once again the bath cure was tried and proved effective and the scales fell away. But by the following day, his whole body was crusted over once more. Once again a heifer was purchased and slaughtered in a nearby room and the warm fresh meat was wrapped around Father Mario's body, but to no avail. It seemed that the time taken between the death of the beast and wrapping up the patient's body was too long, and the effect of the lukewarm meat too feeble. So a large ox was purchased, brought to the Nazarene College and slit open in the patient's presence. 'Without the animal even being skinned, Father Mario was enclosed naked within the ox, and remained there for some time as determined by the doctors.' Once again, there seemed to be some temporary relief but then a regression. Father Berro thought it ironically appropriate that someone with the constitution and even the physiognomy of an ox, and a similar habit of continual mastication and rumination, should attempt a cure through that animal. And he slyly noted that not only was a huge amount of money wasted in an attempt to expiate Sozzi's sins, but when the Piarist fathers later ate the meat of the ox afterwards, no one became sick.[68]

Father Mario's skin hardened progressively, until his face was a mask and he could no longer even move. All doors were closed, no one was to be admitted and he no longer left his room. He summoned the apostolic visitor, who had left Rome on some private business, to his bedside.

Father Pietrasanta returned in haste and, according to an eyewitness, was in time to hear Father Mario's dying requests: 'I no longer have any hope of life but I beg you not to forget Father Stefano [Cherubini] degli Angeli, for I greatly fear that if I die he will suffer some serious humiliation if the Father General returns to govern the Order, since he has been so close to me, and has been my adviser.'[69] Apparently Father Albizzi of the Holy Inquisition also visited and Sozzi asked him too to take care of Cherubini, and was told 'that he could be sure that they would not let him suffer in any way, but rather they would help him and make him his successor'. Sozzi's concern for the future of his friend while on his own deathbed indicates the close relationship between the two men.

Calasanz also visited twice but was refused admission. Father Berro reported that 'from Father Mario's answer you can see that although he had lost his strength and his life, he had still not lost the malice and the aversion in which he held the reverend founder, and he sent a message that he would not dream of bothering him'. He did not wish to be seen in such a terrible state by the old man he considered his enemy. During his last days he confessed to Father Stefano and then, on 10 November 1643, a bare six weeks after the onset of his disease, the thirty-five-year-old father, who had worked so closely with the Inquisition, died.

The body was in a terrible state. 'I saw the body of poor Mario all burnt up, like a roast pig, and one could not distinguish the form of his limbs, because the legs and the arms had shrivelled up, as though they had been burnt, so that his friends, though they mourned him, were afraid to look at him,' wrote Father Caputi, and Father Berro added, 'Once Father Mario was dead, they opened him up and found his entrails cooked as though he had been roasted in an oven, and his heart was so little and densely knotted that it had almost lost the shape of a heart.'[70] Whatever the disease, it was certainly considered by many of his colleagues to be divine justice.

When Piarist historians recount the dreadful details of the death of Father Mario, they usually spare a word for Father Giovanni Muzzarelli, the Florentine inquisitor who had been the first to hear Sozzi's denunciations of his colleagues. A few months before Father Mario fell ill, Muzzarelli was also struck by ill-health. A huge cancer grew above his left ear, 'so large it almost hung down to his shoulder, and the shape and size of a salami', as a fellow countryman described it. The inquisitor heard of a famous surgeon in Lucca and had himself carried there in a litter from Florence via Pescia and Pistoia in the hope of a cure. However, when the authorities in Lucca heard that he was arriving with such a terrible cancer, 'they feared some damage to the public if he entered the city', and sent orders that he be stopped at the gates. There the famous surgeon visited him, took one look at the growth and said, 'Father, you need to think about your death, and make your peace with the Lord for there is no way to heal you, and you are finished.' Muzzarelli had himself carried back to Florence and there he apparently repented of his behaviour towards the Piarists:

I fear that I bought this terrible disease for myself by the protection I gave to that wicked Father Mario, whom I well know to be a scoundrel, but he was recommended to me by influential people, and by red berets [cardinals], so I could do no less. And I should have received a summary of information into the life and behaviour of Father Mario, which I requested many times but never received, so I could have shown it to the people who had recommended this rascal with such warmth.[71]

In August 1643, just as Sozzi was beginnning to notice the first scabs on his body, Muzzarelli's cancer killed him.

After the postmortem on Father Mario, the body was sealed into its coffin and taken to the church of San Pantaleo, where it was buried without public ceremony at night opposite the chapel of Saints Giusto and Pastore. Today there is no sign of the tomb. But the death of the virtual ruler of the Piarists did not signal the beginning of a new and better dawn. No sooner had Sozzi drawn his last breath, than Father Stefano Cherubini immediately began to give orders as to his colleague's burial as though he were already the father general of the order. Unmourned by the majority of the Piarists, even his close associates seemed to lose interest in Sozzi as soon as he was dead. Designated successor on Father Mario's deathbed, the new 'universal superior' would be a man of even less integrity.

'Unworthy of such a position'

The apostolic visitor, Father Silvestro Pietrasanta, presented his findings on 1 October 1643, shortly before the death of Sozzi, to the special Cardinals' Commission, which also included Monsignor Albizzi. He had been appointed six months earlier to try to sort out what the authorities perceived as the Piarists' fundamental long-term problems.

The order was acknowledged to be a useful and praiseworthy organization, he wrote, but the regime was too severe for teachers to cope with the rigours of teaching, and there was obviously much unrest amongst the members.[1] Clearly Father Pietrasanta thought his task was completed and he would move on to the next project, but Albizzi thought otherwise. The cardinals decided to defer a final decision until they had more information.

While Father Sozzi lay dying, rumours about his successor were already spreading, aided by Father Stefano Cherubini's behaviour, which was clearly that of an heir-apparent on the cusp of succession. Father Mario's rule had been poor, but his key adviser for the worst aspects of his policy had always been Father Stefano. The cardinals began to receive desperate letters begging them not to appoint Cherubini, 'for the general disrepute of his life', and offering to supply signed depositions and evidence about his past.[2] However, the morning after Sozzi's death, only hours after his secretive night-time burial,

Monsignor Albizzi proposed Father Cherubini to the cardinals as his successor, although the announcement was kept secret for several months.[3]

Meanwhile, Father Pietrasanta, still in post as the apostolic visitor, was simultaneously reassuring the members in Rome that Cherubini's position would only be temporary, and that he hoped all would be sorted out by Christmas, and preparing a letter for circulation throughout Europe to inform the members of the order of the appointment of their new universal superior. Father Stefano organized a meeting with Father Calasanz at which, according to Father Berro, he apparently threw himself at the old man's feet and begged him to support his position. In the interests of peace, and as a temporary solution, Calasanz agreed to do so. Cherubini then also sent out a circular explaining how reluctant he was to take over the position, and how he hoped it would only be for a short time, until 'this tempest has calmed itself, and I can return to my peace and quiet'. He promised to take advice from Father Calasanz and asked all the members to support him in their prayers.[4]

A few weeks later Pietrasanta summoned all the members of the Roman household to hear the latest decision of the cardinals and the assessor. The public bell was rung; the Piarists assembled. The visitor began by expressing the hope that they would accept what he had to say and warning them that if they did not they would have to suffer the increased wrath of the inquisitorial assessor. By the time he came to read out Albizzi's conclusions, which he wrapped in a great deal of self-justification, the members must have known that they would not be pleased with the results. Cherubini was confirmed in his position for the foreseeable future; there was nothing temporary about his appointment. Anyone who had anything to say could come individually and talk to the visitor in a neighbouring classroom. 'One or two went,' wrote Berro, 'but without much hope of satisfaction, because according to his usual false promises he placated them, telling them to have patience for yet another short period of time ... He led us all by the nose, and betrayed us with honeyed words.'[5]

Far from supporting him, the order, with very few exceptions, was disgusted by the appointment of Cherubini and demanded the return to authority of their founder, as the correspondence arriving at the Rome school soon showed. The new appointee was known to have behaved disgracefully with pupils since at least 1629, some fifteen years earlier. He had repeatedly betrayed the trust laid on him as a priest and as a teacher. Time after time he had been promoted away from the scene of his crime. There is no record of him ever expressing a word of remorse, guilt or reform. The members had kept silent through many years, but this appointment to universal superior, over the head of the ancient founder, was a step too far.

How could anyone with a brain [wrote Father Francesco Baldi, teacher at the Nazarene College in Rome] believe calumny of an old man of eighty-seven years, founder and general of an Order begun with exemplary rigour and austerity, and acclaimed for its charitable work throughout the world and much in demand everywhere. He and his four assistants are honoured by laymen, especially crown princes, and even the Emperor himself, as men deserving of great respect and credit. And to be deprived by one of their subjects who was found unsuitable even for the lowest of positions twenty years ago, and by a few of his adherents, and maintained in some still respectable ministry solely to please some of his relations until the discovery of matters so prejudicial to the honour and reputation of the Order, that he was then removed ... I don't want to say more because the prudent will understand what I have to say without any further gloss.[6]

Such partial circumspection would soon be thrown to the wind.

The archives show that letters, memos and petitions poured into the Cardinals' Commission. There is no possibility that the cardinals or the assessor of the Holy Office of the Inquisition could have been unaware of the strength of feeling provoked by Cherubini's appointment. Even after the bonfire of 1659, in which one can assume the most incriminating documents were destroyed, a mass of material remains to bear witness to the revulsion felt by the members of the order at the unsuitability of their new leader. For example, thirty-one fathers from the Rome house, starting with Calasanz, wrote to the cardinals: 'We beg that as they love peace and the good progress of this Order, Father Stefano degli Angeli must not be elected or confirmed, or anyone proposed by him, unless firstly information is sought about his life and customs, with sworn statements from those giving evidence, and we offer to swear about the afore-mentioned father, that he is unworthy of such a position.'[7] Each father's full name and position was solemnly subscribed so that the list included almost the entire household, united against the new appointment.

How could this have happened? Why did Pietrasanta, Albizzi and – higher up the hierarchy – the Cardinals' Commission, the papal nephews and even the pope, accept the appointment of such a profoundly unsuitable figure?

Other memos streamed in as the news spread. The communities of Ancona, Carcare, Genoa, Fanano, Florence, Pisa, Narni, Pieve di Cento, Moricone, Norcia, Frascati, Poli and Naples joined with Rome to express their disapproval and frustration, until 325 signatures, from an order comprising around 500 members, were counted against him. Father Berro noted that 'in Naples he stank'.[8] Father Pietrasanta was furious at the outcry, and refuted all the allegations with great vigour. He declared that the attacks on Cherubini caused 'great damage to the reputation and credit' of those who signed them, but apparently refused to take them seriously, even though they were so numerous as to be impossible to ignore.[9] Maybe Albizzi, Pietrasanta and Cardinal Roma, the president of the commission, did not even show the rest of the cardinals this flood of protest, for it is hard to conceive that they would persevere in their support of a man who had outraged so many. But the Church authorities paid no heed; Cherubini was confirmed as universal superior.

Once in post he was shown the accusations against him and the emollient tone taken in his introductory circular soon changed. Initially he claimed that most of the fathers must have signed the petitions without knowing what was written in them. For instance, he wrote to Father Berro:

If Your Reverence was told that this memorial is in my favour, you are excused, but if you really know the contents you are worthy of reprehension, since Your Reverence could never swear that you have seen me carrying out an unworthy action ... Your Reverence has always had a good relationship with me and in all your problems you ran to me for help. I cannot believe that you have carried out this action, since I never took you for an enemy.[10]

But when he was assured that not only Father Berro but almost all the fathers and brothers from Naples had signed in full knowledge of the contents, he became far more aggressive.[11] Father Baldi complained to Cardinal Roma: 'Monsignor Assessor has shown [Cherubini] ... the memorial presented to Your Eminence with the signatures of a great number of fathers ... And it has resulted in great inconvenience because the person named in that document as being unsuitable to be the superior – but who is currently the superior – goes around attacking and punishing this one and that one, asking why he signed against him.' Baldi went on to say that not only did this prove the biased nature of Monsignor Albizzi, but that Albizzi had taken bribes from Father Cherubini. 'We are sure of donations made by the same person (whom we publicly declare unfit to govern, to his discredit) to the aforementioned prelate, in order to retain his position.'[12]

This is perhaps the core of Albizzi's motivation. His biographer declared that he 'always had his hand outstretched, or rather both hands, to receive pensions from both sides'[13] and a simple explanation for his actions at this stage would be that he was bribed by the Cherubini family. He was also jealous of the privileges of the Holy Inquisition, which he always considered pre-eminent. The anti-Galilean nature of Sozzi's main accusation, and what he considered an ongoing reluctance by a stubbornly sovereign religious order to obey the dictates of his office, galled him. But according to Father Baldi, it was a matter of pure financial corruption. Albizzi's reputation as a man who could be bought is also supported by his acceptance of an annual pension from the King of Spain of 3,000 scudi at the same time as he was receiving a pension from the French king, although the interests of these nations were diametrically opposed. Add that to his Jesuit pension (which may have further influenced him to look unfavourably on the Piarists and more inclined towards Pietrasanta and the Society) and it becomes clear that the Monsignor's finances were extremely healthy.[14]

But the pressure Father Stefano Cherubini exerted on the hierarchy was not purely financial. He also pulled all possible family levers. Father Baldi wrote one of the few surviving documents that pulled no punches:

We see, we understand, we know and we can even touch with our hands how [Father Stefano] and his adherents, companions, relations and friends work directly and indirectly to keep him in that position, which he should not legitimately hold. And how many presents and donations from his relations are made by intermediaries to ministers at the heart of the palace, so that the business should be agreed by His Holiness and by Cardinal Barberini in favour of the said Father Stefano, who having control of the Order's finances can manage it to his own pleasure without anyone even knowing.

He concluded that Father Pietrasanta paid more attention to his career prospects than to the wisdom of his decisions. 'Because it was not convenient for him to say: "This is the order from the [papal] palace; this is what the rulers want; this is what that prelate desires, and if I go against them they could remove me from my post and so I would lose my reputation in this world."'[15] Father Berro, viewing matters from Naples, but corresponding closely with several fathers in Rome, was even less charitable. For him the matter was simple and unacceptable. It was not that Father Pietrasanta was swayed by his superior, Albizzi, or by pressure from the papal court or members of the Jesuit Order. It was a more purely emotional reason: 'All our problems stemmed from the fact that Father Pietrasanta loved Father Stefano too much.'[16] Since there are no direct accusations against Pietrasanta of sexual impropriety, it could be that this was a purely fraternal affection.

Whatever the reasons – a combination of misplaced fondness for a colleague, concerns about a future clerical career, judicious bribery, family influence, bureaucratic incompetence, a reluctance to come to terms with the seriousness of the accusation – the authorities permitted a known child-abuser to be appointed by the Inquisition, acting on behalf of and with the knowledge of the papacy, to the position of universal superior of a respected religious order whose mission was to teach young boys the principles of literacy and religion. In spite of 325 signatures pointing this out, Monsignor Albizzi presumably pocketed his bribe, Father Pietrasanta swallowed any doubts he might have had, and Albizzi and the Cardinals' Commission followed their initial inclination and confirmed the forty-four-year-old Father Stefano Cherubini as superior. The pope approved the appointment and a brief made public in February 1644 but dated 11 November 1643 (the very day after Sozzi's death) sealed the issue.

Another memo signed by some 200 Piarist fathers from all over Italy – the reaction from the members over the Alps took a while longer to arrive – was recently found in the archive of Cardinal Francesco Paolucci, the secretary to the Cardinals' Commission, so there can be no doubt that the information was received:

We all demand the re-establishment in his office of our Father General [Calasanz], very well known in this city … Finally we would ask Your Excellencies to consider that the present government of Father Stefano degli Angeli is not acceptable, since he has been known to be harmful to the Order not only through the great discredit of his person towards priests and laymen, for his behaviour and way of life, but also for the way he throws away money received as alms in unnecessary expenses, both for food and clothing. Also for having placed the Order in such a situation that it has lost excellent representatives, and for having made it odious through the many useless and superfluous quarrels he has created and continued in order to keep himself in the position of procurator general, from which office he was deposed at the last Chapter General, having been suspended already by the Father General for reasons, about which we remain silent out of due respect ... And since we hear from many in great authority that Father Stefano degli Angeli is to be elected vicar general, or placed in some other high position within the Order, we beg you not to permit it, unless you first take juridical information about the life and customs of this person, or of others proposed by him. And furthermore we beg you not to give any credit to what he says, or what his adherents propose, with regard to sorting out the Order ... Prostrate at your feet we beg you to re-instate the Father General and founder.[17]

The pleas were to no avail.

The new superior, once confirmed, went on the offensive, writing to Father Patera in Naples, 'If it comes to finding proof, we will see and hear great things; because for the sake of my honour I will show you all up as audacious liars and fraudsters. And this will be easy for me, given my innocence, which is well known by those who will have to judge me.' Two weeks later he wrote again to the same father, 'I thought you had studied logic, but I see I am mistaken, or you have forgotten what you learned, since you draw certain indirect and false conclusions, which you could not in any way sustain.'[18] But he could not stem the flow of criticism.

Finally – fifteen years too late – Father Calasanz himself felt forced to make a deposition, setting out bluntly what he knew of Father Stefano:

I, the undersigned, testify that when Father Pietro [Casani] of the Nativity was provincial of the Pious Schools in the kingdom of Naples, I was frequently informed of the wicked practices [cattiva prattica] that Father Stefano degli Angeli, at that time headmaster of the Pious Schools of Duchesca, did with some pupils, and to avoid the scandal, which could have occurred if the parents of the youngsters had heard about it, I took him away from Naples and brought him to Rome with an honourable title out of respect for his family. However, I ordered the above-mentioned Father Pietro, provincial, to collect information secretly, and having done so he sent the package to me with Signor Felice de Totis, who bearing the package found that I had at that moment gone out to hear Mass in our church of San Pantaleo. So he entrusted the package to the said Father Stefano, so that immediately I had finished Mass he should give it to me personally, but he, suspecting what might be contained in that package, went with it to his house and there opened it. Seeing the information, or process, the same day in the evening Signor Flavio Cherubini [his brother] and Signor Felice de Totis, excusing himself as best he could, then brought me the open package. Seeing the matter uncovered, to avoid greater inconvenience if such a matter were to be published, out of respect for his family, we drew up a document in which I agreed that the said Father Stefano would not be harmed in any way, or some such words, but I did not say that the things contained in that process were untrue ... And I have never wanted to give him another position such as provincial or headmaster, even though I have been requested to do so by important people, but my conscience would never let me do it.[19]

It could not have been clearer. Calasanz had known all along that Cherubini was molesting boys, but had kept it secret, and kept him away from children as far as possible, until now. The document was read out at the next session of the Cardinals' Commission. There was absolutely no reaction. Father Cherubini remained universal superior.

'Messing around with boys'

With the installation of Stefano Cherubini, the order began to fall apart. Memos and letters of protest continued to arrive in Rome and, as the German province heard the news, Piarist voices from across the Alps were added to the outcry. From Nikolsburg in Moravia, the fathers wrote, 'No attention was paid to the previous life he led, contrary to all religion ... As headmaster or as procurator general he never even attended prayers, punishment sessions, or disciplinary hearings, so ... given that he was never a good subject, how could he be a good superior?'[1] Cherubini's past failings were clearly universally known within the order and many houses refused to acknowledge his new ascendance.

However, the new leader had a plan. He drafted a set of new *Constitutions*, designed to mould the order more to his way of thinking. For instance, the aim of the order, under the new rules, would be 'to use every possible diligence to teach free and for the love of God, without any wage', whereas the original *Constitutions* imposed an obligation to do so, not just an attempt. Each school would be run independently, and Cherubini spent some time discussing the eating arrangements, which were to be much more luxurious than before. In the prologue, he criticized the earlier *Constitutions* for being 'too rigorous and austere, and impossible to observe'. The new rules would enable the workers 'to labour more and happily, and fruitfully with Heaven's blessing in the Lord's vineyard'. Father Berro's interpretation of this section, knowing the author, was unsparing: 'Note, reader, the substance of this prologue, the malice of the author. The aim of writing these new *Constitutions* is solely to escape the mortification of the flesh, and give oneself over to the convenience of eating well, drinking well and messing around with boys [*practicare con regazzi* (sic)].'[2] Calasanz was of course completely against any relaxation of the rules. But as the order bickered its way through 1644, the new *Constitutions* sat awaiting papal approval while the Barberini pope dealt with other matters, including impending bankruptcy and rumours of a tax revolt, the hostility of nearly all the neighbouring states, an unwinnable war and his own approaching death.

As Pope Urban VIII entered the last months of his reign, an anonymous document began to circulate. Historians of the order have accused Fathers Cherubini or Pietrasanta of authorship, but the most recent scholar of the order, Father Severino Giner Guerri, pins the credit on Monsignor Albizzi.[3] It accuses the Piarists of endless examples of disobedience and of 'a complete lack of subordination and subjection to the apostolic see and its supreme tribunals', in other words, to the Inquisition. According to the document, Cardinal Barberini himself said, 'This is an Order which grew and spread by always disobeying', spreading outside Rome and teaching advanced subjects, which it had no right to touch. It protests at the lack of acceptance within the order of the new superior, and goes on to attack Father Calasanz for not being able to prevent himself from meddling, even when suspended from duty. The solution, the document explained, would be to reduce the order to a congregation without a central headquarters or loyalty, which could just work directly in each town or city which needed a school.[4] Perhaps the difficulties with the new universal superior were beginning to make the whole project seem just too troublesome for the authorities. This was not what the faithful followers of the old father general wanted to hear, and it was worrying that this was the kind of advice that had been 'whispered to the Pope'.[5]

But the Barberini era was drawing to an end. After a series of military reverses in the War of Castro and 'great complaints and much murmuring' from the Roman populace about the huge tax increases, which were seen to benefit only the papal family – 'instead of suffering they double their gain' wrote the diarist Gigli – a peace treaty ending the war was signed in March 1644, returning the fief that had been the source of all the conflict to the *status quo ante*. Millions of scudi – a colossal sum – had been spent to no effect; as the great German historian Ludwig von Pastor gloomily summarized: 'Thus ended the War of Castro, which cost little blood but a vast amount of money, benefited nobody and inflicted grievous injury on all concerned.'[6] In late July a rumour spread that Urban had received the last rites. A few nights later, processions of prisoners in chains were seen being led out from the jails in preparation for their release on the pope's death. And on 29 July 1644 the news tolled forth from campaniles throughout the capital that Urban was dead. The next day the news sheets reported that His Holiness had been sick for several days of 'catarrh with dysentery' and that after giving up his spirit to his creator at the age of seventy-seven, his ring and seal had been smashed in accordance with the ritual at the death of a pope.[7] Orders had immediately gone out to board up his statue on the Capitol and to place squads of soldiers in strategic positions around the city. A nearby statue, unprotected in the Jesuit College, did not survive. The Dutch lawyer, Teodoro Ameyden, friend of Calasanz and hostile to the Barberini, noted with satisfaction that 'The Pope died at quarter past eleven and by noon the statue was no more.' There was an outburst of popular hatred. Gigli wrote, 'During this time the people vented themselves against dead Pope Urban VIII and the Barberini, with injurious words, and with the pen, writing of him every evil; wherewith were published an infinite number of compositions in Latin and in the vulgar tongue, in prose and in verse, so that I do not believe there has ever been anything like it.'[8] Calasanz noted that the Romans embarked on a brief spree of murder and insult until rigorous edicts clamped down on the lawlessness.[9] All curial business ground to a halt awaiting the appointment of a new pontiff. Father Stefano Cherubini was annoyed, and wrote that, 'Our business had just reached its desired end, but then the death of the Pope put silence to everything.'[10]

But encouraged by the Barberini fall from grace, the majority of the Piarists permitted themselves a faint glimmer of hope. A new pope could look at the case with a fresh vision. The rumours of poor observance amongst members, which had influenced the dead pope and his nephews, could now be overcome.[11] 'There is a time to be silent and a time to talk,' wrote Father Francesco Baldi a couple of weeks later at the head of a lengthy call to arms. He ended with a despairing cry, 'Oh God, how many times has our Father General said clearly to the visitor and the other cardinals that this Father [Stefano] so praised by the visitor is not suitable to govern, given the damage to his reputation within the Order?'[12]

The armies of the Grand Duke of Tuscany and the Viceroy of Naples were waiting on the borders of the Papal States 'in order to guarantee the freedom of the conclave', and to underline the desire of their rulers that Taddeo Barberini and his French mercenaries be dismissed forthwith. The conclave opened on 9 August and dragged on through the unhealthy Roman summer as Spanish interests fought against French ones, and ex-nephew, Cardinal Francesco Barberini, sought to provide for the future of his family. Several cardinals succumbed to malaria, including the main French candidate, and finally in September a compromise candidate, Giovan Battista Pamphilij, was elected as Innocent X. He was a thin and ugly seventy-year-old with a straggly beard, and Velázquez's portrait of him a few years later shows the suspicious glint in his eye, which would only increase with age. His way of life was pious and moderate, his moroseness already renowned and 'he soon proved not only hot-tempered but also erratic and unreliable; his anger would flare up unexpectedly and rash decisions could then be made'.[13] Innocent had been a member of the Cardinals' Commission investigating the Piarists, but he had never attended any sessions. He had been strongly opposed to the War of Castro, so it was ironic that on Odoardo Farnese's death in 1646 and the subsequent murder of the Bishop of Castro in 1649, Innocent's troops would capture Castro without difficulty and forthwith raze it to the ground. The Barberini nephews meanwhile fled to Paris, their palaces and wealth confiscated, although Francesco and Antonio would return some years later.

After that experience, the new pope's possession of only one nephew was considered to be a great point in his favour, although his sister-in-law, Olimpia Maidalchini, would shortly emerge as the target of much of Innocent's nepotism and the equal in rapaciousness to her predecessors. She was the rich widow of his elder brother, and her wealth had formed the basis of Pamphilij's own climb up the papal ladder. He did nothing without her advice, to the point where contemporaries referred to her as the 'Papessa' and a modern Catholic encyclopaedia refers to his dependence on her as 'the great blemish on his papacy'.[14] In one of those seemingly trivial twists of fate, which in fact would change the history of the order, Calasanz had a few years earlier fallen out with Donna Olimpia. Her confessor at that time had been a Piarist, Father Pietro Andrea di Jesu Maria. Unfortunately the Piarists' then cardinal protector, Alessandro Cesarini, demanded that Father Pietro Andrea be transferred to head the school in Norcia. At the time it seemed a strange request – normally the cardinal protector did not bother with such mundane staffing decisions, especially for such a minuscule school in an impoverished village. Calasanz had agreed to the cardinal's plea. Donna Olimpia, however, was very keen to retain the services of her confessor, and asked her brother-in-law, the future pope Cardinal Pamphilij, to intervene. He duly summoned the father general to an audience. When Calasanz heard how attached the lady was to her confessor and that Cardinal Pamphilij was personally asking for him to stay in Rome, he told the cardinal that he would immediately beg Cardinal Cesarini to change his mind about sending Father Pietro Andrea to Norcia. When he heard the name of Cesarini mentioned, Pamphilij immediately said,

'No, Father General, I want this favour from you directly; if you are able to grant it, all very well. If not, I do not want any involvement with Signor Cardinal Cesarini.' Calasanz replied, 'The departure from Rome of Father Pietro Andrea is an absolute order from our eminent cardinal protector. But if Your Eminence would leave it to me, I will beg him, and I'm sure he will grant me this favour and the lady will be happy.' Pamphilij dismissed the offer: 'Father General, if you cannot grant this on your own authority, my sister-in-law will have to find other confessors, but I absolutely do not want you to speak of this to Cardinal Cesarini.'[15] And that was the end of Donna Olimpia's attendance at the Piarist church of San Pantaleo.

In later years the sermons given by her confessor, the Jesuit Father Oliva, in her palace would become the most important social events in Rome, attended by all who mattered, so in retrospect a great opportunity was missed and an important enemy made. It would become clear that there had been a bitter feud between Pamphilij and Cesarini; the latter's request must have been motivated by spite, and by sending away the lady's favourite confessor, Calasanz had been seen to choose his side. It would not be forgotten by the lady and her important brother-in-law. Father Berro commented that this had 'put a flea in the ear of the most illustrious and most excellent Signora Donna Olimpia' that she would never forgive. Even after the Queen of Poland wrote on Calasanz's behalf to Donna Olimpia, begging her forgiveness for the earlier insult, the lady remained hostile. When the order later needed help, Pamphilij would reply, according to Father Berro's account: 'Those fathers of the Pious Schools have a cheek asking for favours. Don't they remember what they did to my sister-in-law when I was a cardinal?'[16] And by then Cardinal Cesarini had died so there was no one who could explain that the Piarists had been merely innocent bystanders.

On 23 November 1644 Innocent X was inaugurated. An enormous celebration was held on Piazza Navona, a child's stone-throw from the

Piarist school, as a great Noah's Ark perched on Mount Ararat was built in front of the Palazzo Pamphilij in the centre of the piazza. The classes must have been empty, the streets outside packed, as a dove, the symbol not only of peace but of the new papal family, flew down with an olive branch in its beak to Noah and set off a magnificent firework display.[17] The Barberini bees were well and truly routed, and English diarist John Evelyn, then in Rome, commented, 'Thus were the streetes this night as light as day, full of Bonfires, Canon roaring Musique pla[y]ing, fountains running Wine in all excesse of joy and Triumph.'[18]

Father Stefano Cherubini also displayed 'no small signs of joy' at the choice of new pope since Cardinal Pamphilij's auditor for the last few years had been a member of the Cherubini family, and he seemed set to continue in the post. Moreover his brother, Flavio, was still at court and in favour as an increasingly important lawyer.[19]

Meanwhile those fathers hostile to Cherubini began belatedly to mobilize some political support. Bernardo Panicola, the Bishop of Ravello, wrote and visited everyone he knew on behalf of the beleaguered order. 'I have done what I could,' he wrote. 'I cannot put it to paper.'[20] He complained that Father Stefano was 'slippery as an eel' but his pride surely meant he was heading for a fall.[21] The Viceroy of Naples, and the Spanish and Tuscan ambassadors were asked to intervene, though the Florentine ambassador, Bali Gondi, was rather irritated by the whole matter. He thought Father Baldi's call to arms had rebounded, and that he was 'rather restless and so embittered against Father Cherubini and the assessor that ... the Order could suffer'. Baldi had also failed to understand that among so many other more important items of business between the Medici grand duke and the papacy, the order's affairs would be 'suffocated by more important matters'. Calasanz, however, was beginning to understand the situation, and wrote sadly to Father Berro, 'The Pope is daily offered so many pieces of business of great importance, that it is no wonder that the resolution of our affairs drags on so long ... in comparison our business is minuscule.'[22] With small matters such as the aftermath of the War of Castro, the political situation with regard to the rivalry between France and Spain, the machinations of Mazarin and the Barberini nephews, to say nothing of the last gasps of what would become known as the Thirty Years War, it is little wonder that the pontiff was rather preoccupied.

Calasanz himself found it impossible to get an appointment with the new pope for several months, although he frequently went to the Vatican and queued and begged various officials (some of whom he knew and who had previously been sympathetic to him). Eventually he was allowed in to kiss the pope's feet, and to hear the ambiguous – though gratefully received – message from the pontiff: 'We have nothing against you.'[23]

The Congregation of Propaganda Fide, whose energetic secretary, Francesco Ingoli, was a friend of the order, a stickler for law and known to be hostile to the Jesuits, was asked to intervene.[24] This congregation, founded in 1622, the same year as the Piarist Order, had two aims: to spread Catholicism to new areas, and to fight heretics in areas supposedly already Catholic. The Piarists had been running schools in Germany since 1640 to great effect. Each year the congregation compiled a summary of conversions of heretics and the Piarists had done very well. In 1644, for instance, they had notched up 198 saved souls, and Ingoli was very happy to support their work in both deed and in supportive letters.[25]

Father Calasanz also met with King Ladislaw IV's resident, Giovanni Domenico Orsi, and letters soon began to arrive from the kings of Sweden and Poland. The Polish monarch had not been greatly appreciated by the Barberini pope. In 1641 the nuncio to Poland, Onoratio Visconti, had not been promoted to cardinal, despite strong support from the king; in 1643 the royal candidate was again passed over, leading to a formal rupture between Warsaw and Rome. The nuncio was told to hand in his passport, the Polish envoy was recalled from Rome. It seemed that any letters of support and pleas for resolution for the Piarist problem addressed to the pope went straight to the office of Monsignor Albizzi.[26] Finally the king wrote in his own hand, and asked

Orsi to present the letter to Innocent during an audience. He pointed out the damage that would be done to schools in his kingdom, and requested, as a personal favour, that Monsignor Albizzi, 'of whose dislike of them, and of my own affairs, I myself have seen clear signs', be removed from the case. He begged that Calasanz be restored, and if he was now too old (as the founder was then nearly ninety years old), he be supported by some suitable assistants.[27] The audience did not go well. The pope replied that he was happy to hear that the fathers were useful in Poland, but that he was 'very well informed of their actions, and knows how they behave'. He continued, 'Monsignor Assessor only dislikes the bad things they do, and they have no reason to complain of him if they do not annoy him, but it is a badly organized Order and not much good.' Father Orsi, who reported this meeting verbatim to the king, backed off hastily at that point, for fear that His Holiness would say something irreversible and block all future efforts. The following week he met with Monsignor Albizzi, but again could only report further failure to the king. Albizzi had completely ruled out restoring Calasanz, whom he called 'a decrepit old man, and much too obstinate', pointing out that the order was now very well governed by a man to whom he had entrusted the job.[28]

And that man was enjoying himself. Father Pietrasanta, nominally in charge of the order as apostolic visitor, noted that Cherubini governed 'with prudence, quiet dignity and gave good satisfaction', but most of the members of the Rome community thought otherwise.[29] Now that he was in command, the order's dull routines could all be ignored – the fasts, the communal prayers, the weekly disciplines – in fact all the aspects of religious life that were so important to Calasanz and his colleagues and which Cherubini had usually avoided. From his earliest days in the order he had always found it hard to get up in the morning for 'mental prayers' and Calasanz had had to have him woken and accompanied.[30] Now, with his group of friends – Nicolò Maria Gavotti who had scandalized Naples, Sardinia and Genoa; Ridolfi, who as secretary had kept uncomfortable information from the apostolic visitor, and who now bought himself some spurred boots, a pair of breeches and a tight-fitting jacket;[31] Baltasar Cavallari, and Antonio Lolli, nick-named della Farina after his role in the Neapolitan flour-smuggling affair, an illiterate bricklayer with thieving tendencies – Cherubini went out to parties. Nearly every day his brother Flavio visited him and brought him gifts.[32] With his friends he planned 'expeditions in car-riages even in public, amongst their friends, masquerades on the Corso and throughout the city of Rome, during which unworthy excursion they were arrested once by the guards, and all paid for by the house of San Pantaleo, treated like a private purse'. Once the carriage's axle broke and the fathers tumbled out and were recognized sprawling on the road by passers-by – all the more serious since according to a spe-cial regulation of 1624, clergy were supposedly forbidden from travel-ling in closed carriages.[33]

At the Nazarene College, the nobleman's seminary, which also came under Father Cherubini's administrative mantle, the universal superior could allow himself free reign. This college was one of three special institutions for noble children, which the Piarists had agreed under pressure to create – the others were in Florence and Nikolsburg in Moravia – and which had specific criteria for entry. The Nazarene College had been founded as a result of a legacy from Cardinal Michelangelo Tonti, who had investigated Calasanz's request for his congregation to be elevated to the status of an order back in 1621.[34] So convinced had the cardinal become – after his initial scepticism – that he had changed his will on his deathbed later that year in favour of the new organization, to the dismay of his relatives, who tried desperately to keep Calasanz away from the cardinal in the last hours of his life, showing him into an antechamber where he was forced to wait for five hours while they hoped the cardinal would expire. Tonti had, however, hung on and finally the relatives, realizing Calasanz would not go away, had been forced to show him in. 'Oh, Father Giuseppe,' cried the car-dinal. 'Why didn't you come? I've been waiting so long, and I've had you called so often, and you never came.' Calasanz was unwilling to throw the blame onto the relatives, so the cardinal continued, 'I've changed my will, I've established the Nazarene College, and I've made it my universal heir, and your Order will take care of it. Are you pleased, Father Giuseppe, are you pleased? If you don't like it, tell me and I'll do it as you wish.' Father Calasanz then replied, 'It's fine, it's fine, you did very well. Your Excellency should calm yourself and attend to your soul now, since you have sorted out your affairs.' Thus reassured, the cardinal lay back, and a short while after expired in Calasanz's arms. His relatives were obviously furious at this turn of events; they removed as much of the furniture and goods as they could carry that day, and sold off the rest at the door of the palace. They continued to challenge the last-minute will for half a century, even going so far as to fire shots at the Piarist fathers with an arquebus.

Nevertheless, and in spite of the ongoing litigation, which involved petitions to the pope and claims for payment for the cardinal's funeral expenses and his gravestone, the college was eventually established and opened its doors in 1630. Pupils were to be of legitimate birth, aged between twelve and eighteen years, healthy, well-behaved, intelligent and poor, and when they left the college 'could study any sort of science in any university, without being obliged to take orders, or any other obligation'.[35] Needless to say, the 'poor' qualification soon went by the board as places in the college became increasingly sought after. The final selection was the responsibility of one of the highest courts of the Church, the auditors of the Rota, a legal body consisting of twelve senior ecclesiastics, all with doctorates and at least three years' legal experience, representing the pope in various legal tribunals and advisory councils, who were initially not that enthusiastic to take over the duty.[36] Competition for the few places was intense, with at least eight boys vying for each place. All came highly qualified with recommendations from at least one cardinal. The pupils studied grammar, humanities, rhetoric and Greek, more advanced subjects than in the normal Piarist schools. They also wore a uniform, a striking peacock-blue tunic worn over a tawny, ankle-length cassock with a red strip, over linen

trousers. 'There is no college in Rome where the pupils are better treated than in the Nazareno,' wrote Calasanz in earlier years.[37] This treatment would soon include the special attentions of Father Cherubini.

Among Cherubini's first modifications to the curriculum at the
Nazarene College was an instruction that a new style of theatre pro-
duction be performed. Gone were the modest devotional recitals,
instead he demanded comedies 'of such extravagance and so little
shame for those poor young boys that they were studying love, rather
than virtue and literature'. Years before, Calasanz had forbidden such
things, saying, 'Do not think of putting on any productions, because I
am resolute in not permitting it, since I know how little fruit they bring
... it may seem a good thing, but think of it as a temptation, for the
pupils are diverted by these things which please the senses and they
deviate from their studies.'[38]

But for Cherubini, pleasing the senses was no bad thing. He organized an illicit revenue stream from charitable donations and financial
transfers from various funds to finance the college's productions as well
as his expensive lifestyle, and soon landed the house at San Pantaleo
with over 1,000 scudi of debt. All in all, Father Berro was appalled,
accusing Cherubini and his gang in strong words of 'blackening the
purity and candour of the Order and of so many pure and holy souls
with their fetid and infamous filth'.[39]

Cherubini was also looking to his future. In an effort to prevent any
more investigations into past scandals, the 'unworthy' Father Glicerio
Cerutti della Natività was again dispatched as visitor to Naples, where
the first rumours of Cherubini's activities had initially arisen. The osten-
sible reason for the visit was to sort out the Naples school, but he also
carried with him a list of responses to the questionnaire that Cherubini
considered unsatisfactory, with a brief to discover which fathers could
be considered trustworthy. More importantly still, his mission was to
limit any damage caused by evidence from those who had known of
Father Stefano and his activities earlier and who might be considering
testifying against him. Father Berro, based in Naples, saw Father

Glicerio unloading beautiful fruits, sweetmeats, rich fruitcakes, silks from Hormuz, brocades, silk stockings, belts and other tempting objects. He also took 100 ducats from the main Neapolitan school accounts and a large amount from the other school on the outskirts, while from the neighbouring Posilippo school he removed two barrels of an expensive wine, claiming it was for the venerable founder (although it never reached him). Father Glicerio went on a judicious present-giving spree, distributing money, cakes and precious silks amongst the courtiers and officials whose friendship, influence or silence might need to be secured.[40] Meanwhile, as the money drained through the universal superior's fingers, fathers throughout Italy and Germany struggled to keep their schools running and their pupils focused on learning.

But as the years dragged on, the order remained in limbo. Since the appointment of the first apostolic visitor in January 1643, through the many sessions of the Cardinals' Commission, the death of Father Mario, the appointment of Father Stefano, the death of the old pope and the installation of the new one, little real progress in sorting out the future of the order was made. In July 1645 the apostolic visitor, Father Pietrasanta, presented his third report to the cardinals. He summarized the state of the order, pointing out that there were some 500 members in forty schools around Italy and central Europe. Surprisingly, he presented a favourable report and recommended the return of the eighty-eight-year-old Calasanz as father general, to be supported by six assistants, one for each province. However, despite calling for the founder's restoration, the memorandum also contained a breathtakingly partial account of the problems within the order that deflected all blame from Father Stefano: 'By the singular grace of our Lord God, no serious case of any lack of observance has occurred in the Order, nor of public disorder, which might have brought scandal or even suspicion to laymen or to the Order, nor has any important excess come to my notice to the detriment of the three essential vows of the Order, and particularly that of chastity.' In one relatively succinct paragraph, Father

Pietrasanta of the Society of Jesus discarded the enormous number of serious complaints he had received about the way of life of his chosen superior. He went on to compound the lie:

It was claimed that there was some reluctance to receive Father Stefano degli Angeli as superior of the Order even though he was deputed with a [papal] brief, but the whole thing had its origins in the passions of some members, and in reality I received letters from all the houses of the Order accepting and recognizing him as their superior, and since then he has governed with prudence and peace, and given great satisfaction. Only here in Rome there seems to be some reluctance to recognize Father Stefano as their superior, and even me as visitor, so that it has frequently been necessary for me to resort to Your Excellencies and use your support. These members are few, and once removed from Rome with the supreme authority of Your Excellencies we hope the matter will be resolved; we will give the names of these to Monsignor Assessor [Albizzi].

In fact, of course, almost all the houses had written in protest, not in support. It is not clear why a highly respected priest like Father Pietrasanta would have tried to steer any blame away from Father Stefano, of whom he was perhaps too fond, while trying to re-establish the order to an even keel.

Whatever the truth of those few paragraphs, the overall report was favourable, and the Cardinals' Commission, meeting on 18 July, decided to restore the old father general. His supporters rejoiced. However, Father Ridolfi, secretary to Pietrasanta, friend of Sozzi and Cherubini, visited Monsignor Albizzi on the evening of 18 July and 'told him thousands and thousands of excessive things about the Father General and about the assistants', which, as Father Berro elegantly put it, 'dropped the stone in the well with his evil tongue'. Albizzi hastily convinced the cardinals to delay the announcement until the pope himself had had a chance to reconsider. Meanwhile he, Albizzi, could work on the pontiff to ensure that Calasanz's reinstatement would not happen.[41]

As the summer heat began to fade in the Eternal City, the cardinals met again. Cardinal Roma, the chairman of the Commission, had always been hostile to the idea of teaching the higher sciences to the poor, and was now showing signs of being fed up with the whole matter of the Piarist Order and its troubles. As a man who did not believe in even the basic mission of the Piarists, he had hardly been a sympathetic judge. The Tuscan ambassador visited him a few days before the next session and reported back to Florence that yet another cardinal had little desire to continue being involved, and was keen to spend some time in the country avoiding the issue.[42] Next he visited the pope, who 'revealed himself to be better informed than me' but impatient about the whole subject of the Piarists to the point of hostility.[43] The ambassador was bombarded by letters from the members, one of which, unsigned, suggested a fantastical resolution to the problem. If only the Tuscan duke and the Polish king would ban all Jesuits from their territories for a hundred years, then the Jesuit visitor, and all the Society of Jesus, whom the order were increasingly beginning to blame for their problems, would suddenly change their tune and start to support the Piarist schools. For the Tuscan ambassador it was simply a sign of how desperate and far removed from reality some of the Piarists had become.[44]

A group of young fathers from San Pantaleo decided to take matters into their own hands. The uncertainty over their future was too much, and they were also suffering from increasingly poor living conditions, verging on penury and hunger, while Cherubini and his colleagues lived luxuriously in the adjoining rooms. On the second night before the feast of Epiphany, 5 January 1646, some twenty members went to St Peter's, knowing that the pope would be present. After the liturgy they entered the palace and positioned themselves where Innocent was bound to pass. As he came close they threw themselves to their knees and two of the Genoese members, Father Gabrielle dell'Annunziazione and Brother Luca di San Bernardo, cried out that the order had been waiting now for three years, and begged him for 'justice and a rapid solution' to the order's leadership and constitutional crisis, while pressing a petition at him. He replied with a snap, 'Go, you will be dealt with very soon' and, with the assembled princes and nobles marvelling at the scene, it was clear that the pontiff was not pleased. When Calasanz was told about their actions, he too was unimpressed.[45] Brother Luca replied that if spending the next few months in the wind and the rain on the steps and ante-chambers of the cardinal deputies' palaces would help, he was quite prepared to do so.[46]

By February 1646 the Rome community of Piarists had reached desperation. The visitor had recommended reinstatement of the old general; the cardinals on Albizzi's instruction had refused to ratify the decision. The pope could not decide; meanwhile Cherubini was still nominally universal superior. In the absence of any leadership the order was drifting. Foundation requests went unanswered, cries of financial desperation from outlying schools were ignored, discipline and the religious *Rules* fell away. The observant and the conscientious tried to continue with their teaching and routine, others explored avenues to escape from their legally binding vows, or concentrated on their own physical enjoyment.

Pietrasanta was irritated that the fathers had tried to take matters into their own hands by approaching the pope directly. He wrote a menacing letter, noting that the order had always been disobedient to the pope, that the school in Pisa under Michelini was still refusing to acknowledge the validity of central authority, and that the recommendations of various apostolic visitors over the years had been ignored. 'I finish by reminding you that in religious life pure obedience is a virtue, and lacking this, particularly towards the Holy See, it may be necessary to undo and dissolve the Order itself.'[47] It was an ominous threat.

The fathers reacted in fury and wrote back to Father Pietrasanta in ferocious terms:

It seems to us (with due reverence for the dignity of your person) that with this letter not only do you not lighten your conscience, but rather burden it still further, while either because of faulty information or because of an over-

abundance of affection for Father Stefano – who though he may be your colleague in office, yet he is your underling in the visit – or perhaps because of
other even more occult reasons, you have accused the whole Order of disobedience towards the Holy See and independence and a lack of total subordination to the vicar of Christ. Since this is a matter of too much importance since
we are accused of being schismatic, we thought it right herewith to reply to
your letter, so that you can modify the opinion which you seem to have formed
of us.

They went on to accuse him of refusing to investigate the life and habits
of Father Stefano, even when faced with the united opposition of all the
Rome fathers. 'It seemed incredible that the eminent cardinals would
have given supreme government of this Order to a person so universally considered excessive, as the numerous complaints demonstrated.'
And they accused the Jesuit of being supported in all this by Monsignor
Albizzi, 'who in this case, possibly motivated by something unknown
to us, so much favours the said Father Stefano'. Moreover, in a bitter
comment that indicated they had virtually lost hope of any resolution,
they launched a further accusation against the visitor:

We have been trying not to listen to those who say that your Order wishes
from political motives to destroy ours. On the contrary we should all be happy
that the number of workers who labour on the vine of the Lord increases, and
since we have such faith in the integrity and rectitude of the Society [of Jesus]
we tried never to pay attention to those who said of you that we could not
hope for justice, but should rather fear some great damage and ruin.[48]

It may well have been that these serious accusations against
Pietrasanta and Albizzi proved to be the deciding factor. For the whole
Roman community to accuse the apostolic visitor not only of being
politically motivated and badly informed, but also of unreasonable
favouritism towards a man of such dubious lifestyle – whose reputation
and unsuitability were clear to all, even though the visitor had refused
to investigate – was shattering in its effect. On 9 March Monsignor

Albizzi once more sent a draft to the secretary of the papal briefs, Monsignor Marc'Antonio Maraldi, for him to prepare the required legislation. The brief *Ea quae pro felici* was ready a week later and on 17 March 1646 Signor José Palamolla, the secretary to the cardinal vicar arrived in San Pantaleo. The members were summoned to the domestic oratory, and Palamolla slowly read out the brief. Then he took the document – the printed version would only be ready a month later – and departed. He must have left a shocked silence. The order was finished. It was to be suppressed, closed down. According to the visitor himself – conveniently forgetting the history of the Knights Templar several centuries before – there had never been a case like it in the history of the Church.

The order was reduced to the status of a congregation, with no solemn vows. The only reason given was 'serious disagreements' within the order. The priests were free to leave for other orders, if they could find any to accept them. Those with private means of support could return to their families. Obviously no new novices could be accepted, and even the current ones would be unable to finish their noviciate since there was no longer anything at the end of it. The schools and houses dotted around Italy and Germany were to be subject to their local bishops, and it was up to them whether the schools sank or continued. The administration of the Nazarene College was to come fully under the authority of the Roman Rota, a local judicial body. There was no more father general, no more visitors, no more central organization.[49]

Father Mario and Father Stefano's efforts had overshot their target. They had wanted to reform the order by relaxing its austerity, and they had wanted to rule the order to enjoy the power and the privileges it brought. But instead they had destroyed it completely.

'We are in a most confused silence'

The order was stunned. The visitor's last report had been so positive, while the brief itself provided so little reason or explanation for such an unprecedented and drastic action. As the schools gradually heard the news the letters began to arrive.

Some gave themselves up to uninterrupted mourning for several days, and not only paid no attention to what they were eating, but couldn't even swallow their food, so blackened were their hearts with grief. Others were so terrified they could make no sense of it, especially in those early days, and remained comatose thinking about it, not knowing to whom to turn, nor on whom to lean. There were very few who made a virtue of necessity and gave thought to organizing their departure.[1]

Rumours spread that all members would be forced to return to their parental homes under pain of excommunication, or forced to become secular priests, or be beaten up by the police if they walked the streets in their Piarist uniform, or be reduced to teaching catechism at Sunday schools. It was claimed that the pope thought the Pious Schools were a harmful institution, damaging to the Christian Republic, through educating poor children in grammar and humanities and raising them above their station. The local news sheets were full of the suppression, and in the streets pupils from rival schools ran after the teachers shouting mocking insults – 'Excommunicated! Warrant they won't be here next week' – so that the fathers stayed indoors unless absolutely necessary.[2] Many, including Calasanz himself, were overwhelmed with bitterness and blamed the Society of Jesus, seeing Father Pietrasanta simply as a Jesuit who had seized a golden opportunity to shut down a rival.[3] The papal nephew Cardinal Camillo Pamphilij, secretary of state and son of Donna Olimpia, was forced to issue a denial of this rumour to the apostolic nuncio for Poland, Giovanni Torres.[4]

Although Calasanz received some expressions of sympathy, initially no one was willing to tackle the pope directly about the matter and risk his possible displeasure.[5] Cardinal Fabio Chigi, who would be the next pope, told the Piarists in confidence, 'This brief was written with little thought, they have really done well to destroy an Order for no reason.' However, he too refused to intervene immediately, although he promised his aid in the future should it lie within his power.[6]

Calasanz himself was simply overwhelmed by the enormity of what had befallen his order: 'We are in a most confused silence,' he wrote.[7] 'I cannot believe that something so useful and so greatly desired by the whole of Europe and praised even by heretics, could so easily be destroyed by human malice.'[8] With his advisers he realized there was no point begging the pope to reconsider his decision: 'We are not present-ing a memorial to the Pope because we understand that everything goes to Monsignor Assessor [Albizzi] and so it would be a waste of time and effort.'[9] The situation seemed irrevocably bleak.

Within a few days of the publication of the brief, Father Stefano Cherubini put in an application to leave the Piarists. He had hoped to be confirmed as lifetime headmaster of the Nazarene College, with a rea-sonable income to support his lifestyle, but at the last minute that had fallen through. Events had, presumably, not gone according to his plans:

Now that Your Holiness has reduced this Order to a Congregation with other limitations [Cherubini wrote in his application, referring to himself in the third person] he has gained the hatred of almost all the members, as though he were

234

the cause of all that Your Holiness has done, calling him destroyer and enemy of the Order, and threatening to kill him. And as he cannot live safely and quietly with these religious because of the hatred they bear him and the obvious danger to his own life, being forty-seven years old, he desires to live quietly for the rest of his life and not condemn his soul.[10]

Instead he would wear the habit of a secular priest, as free of any disciplinary authority as anyone in the priesthood could be. His 'patrimony', in other words his family fortune, would support him and he would be subject only to the distant permission of a local bishop. On the back of his application it says 'recommended by Monsignor Albizzi', and so his request was rapidly granted. The normal 7 gold scudi fee for issuing such a brief may even have been waived. Having got his exit permit, he then decided to keep it hidden away in case of a real emergency and stay in San Pantaleo for the time being, so he cannot have felt too fearful of the threats to his life. Cherubini was the first to request departure, and the first to be granted it.

But the rest of his circle was not far behind.

There were some of our members who, as the saying goes, wanted to keep both options open, and these were in particular Father Mario's and Father Stefano's adherents. They requested apostolic briefs to make themselves secular priests, but then did not use them, while several months passed, and they lived meanwhile exactly as they pleased ... without doing any of the work of the Pious Schools, still less observing our old *Constitutions* for praying or exercises in mortification ... All they wanted from the religion was to wear the habit, and use it as a cloak for their dissolution, and the school as a shop-front for their business dealings.

One of the members wandered the streets composing sonnets, and 'virtually serving the idle rich young men of Rome as a jester, just so he could eat and drink well.'[11]

The behaviour of Brother Filippo di San Francesco, a colleague of Father Stefano's, was particularly unpleasant. Released from his disciplinary restraints, and encouraged by Cherubini, he would go out on the town, returning completely drunk and in a terrible state. Father Berro described a typical night's entertainment:

On one of the many occasions, Brother Filippo ate with some gentlemen in a certain hostelry and after dining well everyone was very jolly. To crown his buffoonery they filled his hat with natural excrement and the lowest human ordure, and when it was full of this soil they crowned him with it since he had exceeded all the rest of them in eating and drinking. But then, having covered him with such solid and liquid material both inside and out, they found the smell he exuded rendered him insupportable; and since it was late and dark they returned him to San Pantaleo, and they had to change his clothes and his hat, and they tried to wash his jacket, and put him to bed and left his jacket outside to dry off.

On another occasion Brother Filippo accepted a bet to drink massive quantities of snow-cooled liquid while driving around Rome in a coach with his friends. Snow was big business and the right to supply Rome with the refreshing white crystals was sold off by the Papal States as a highly protected monopoly to the highest bidder. During the winter the monopoly-holder built up snow deposits in the hills around Rome, packing them properly to insulate them, and defending them against all competition. The general treasurer repeatedly issued edicts preventing anyone except for the appointed tax collector from making such snow deposits, and further edicts permitted the monopoly-holder to carry arms in order to protect his business.[12] The new Piarist regime was proving to be a good customer for snow. To the amazement of all spectators, Brother Filippo managed to knock back twenty-eight carafes of the chilled drink, before his stomach rebelled and he 'filled the carriage from his nether parts, and sullied the rest from his mouth', so much so that his friends quickly abandoned the coach and ordered the driver to take him home, where he stayed in bed for several days 'out of himself.'[13] Such drunken and public cavorting obviously did nothing for the reputation of the disgraced order.

The notorious Father Nicolò Maria Gavotti meanwhile established a sort of tavern in his room, where many rowdy friends would congregate and buy drinks, before going out into the public piazzas to continue their evenings. He set up a shelving arrangement above the window of his room where he stored the bottles, flasks and glasses he needed for his new venture, where to the irritation of the majority of the house, they could be seen by anyone passing by. One day, just before morning prayers, Father Berro, who slept nearby, was awoken by an almighty crash and rushing to the window was gratified to see that the whole lot had come cascading down onto the roof below. Father Nicolò Maria immediately demanded an inquiry to discover who had sabotaged his business and one of the cardinals friendly to the Cherubini family actually sent his auditor, Camillo Paglia, later the inquisitor in Naples, to investigate, but no culprit could be found. Father Berro later wondered whether the Lord himself had intervened to remove such an obvious sign of decadence.[14]

But throughout the schools of the erstwhile order the fathers and brothers were struggling with personal decisions. In Tuscany, all the Galilean Piarists left, with the exception of Father Angelo Morelli, who continued to run the school in Chieti. He remained a Piarist until his death in 1685 and was instrumental in the order's rehabilitation. Clemente Settimi requested permission to leave the order in October 1646, to the irritation of Michelini and Calasanz with whom he refused to discuss the matter, and accepted a lucrative offer to teach in Siracusa, becoming Don Clemente, and then disappearing from the records.[15] Francesco Michelini was awarded the chair of mathematics in Pisa in 1648. Seven years later he abandoned his chair, and then the priesthood altogether. By now he was suffering badly from gout, arthritis and colic, and became increasingly involved in several get-rich-quick projects involving lemon-based therapeutic cures for various diseases. His one important work was published in 1664, *A Treatise on the Direction of Rivers*, and he carried out some work on Venice's lagoon problems, before dying in poverty in 1665. Salvatore Grise, 'having learned within the Order what talent he has',[16] had left a few days before Sozzi's Galilean denunciation of 1641 and Ambrogio Ambrogi left the following year, both having been removed from Florence as a result of Sozzi's machinations. Father Melchiorre Alacchi had accused Ambrogi of 'carnal vice' and when he initially mentioned he would like to leave the order, his headmaster commented that that would be 'good for him and good for the Order'.[17] Ambrogi became an engineer and mathematician to the papal troops, although after a few months in the field he became very sick and died in hospital in 1645. Carlo Conti and Domenico Rosa left the order when it was suppressed. Domenico's brother, Salvatore Rosa, had already left the order before its fall and became a painter of great importance, while his written works would make their way onto the Index of Prohibited Books some years later.[18] Conti had already written a book of poems published in 1642 under a pseudonym and left to continue with his literary career. Thus was the small scientific academy of Florentine Piarists dispersed and extinguished.

The other Italian schools, such as those at Poli, Moricone, Narni and Norcia, were supported by their bishops, who took them under their protection and continued to let them run more or less as before. Most bishops were supportive – after all, they wanted good schools in their areas. But there was an absence of new teachers, and inevitably a decline. Pieve di Cento was reduced to one father and three sick brothers; Genoa's staff fell from twenty to ten. In Turi the Bishop of Conversano made one Piarist novice serve as his cook, another as his estate manager, and all the while the fathers struggled to keep the school running. When a request came from Rome to leave them in peace, the bishop responded by moving into the school buildings with his entire household and staying there rent-free for several weeks. In Campi Salentina the visiting bishop simply took a candelabra from the church, claiming it as his right.[19] In Naples, where the school held over 1,000 pupils, there was a dispute between the secular and the religious authorities. Only six months later Naples would erupt in a massive anti-

Spanish uprising, mainly caused by the heavy burden of taxation, and led by the barefoot fishmonger, Masaniello. The cardinal and the viceroy would again be on opposing sides and the Piarist problem provided a foretaste of the far more serious events of the following year. While Father Berro approached the viceroy for support and received a promise not to publish the brief, two other members of his school, Neapolitan by birth unlike Berro, took a copy to the archbishop, Cardinal Ascanio Filomarino, and invited him to take over the school while most of the teachers were out watching a procession. He needed no second invitation and the deed was done. A new headmaster was appointed by the time the house assembled that evening for dinner. Over the next few days the other houses in the Naples area, including the noviciate, were also taken over. This led of course to internal factions and after one of these rows the Neapolitan teachers again visited the archbishop and complained that there were too many people for too few resources and too little income from alms. The archbishop immediately ordered all the non-native Neapolitans expelled from the territory within the next six days, under pain of imprisonment or worse, and the decree was posted at the doors of the Piarist school, residence, church and noviciate on 29 October 1646, along with details of four named foreign Piarists, headed by Father Berro, who was originally from near Genoa. The Piarists complained that of thirty-two staff, only four were truly Neapolitan, but the archbishop ignored them. The Florentines, Leccese, Genoese, Calabrians, and others from all over Italy were not targeted; only the four teachers most loyal to Calasanz and the old hierarchy were explicitly named.

Berro himself took refuge with the representative of the Duke of Modena, Count Francesco Ottonelli, relative of Calasanz's old colleague, for nearly a fortnight, before taking ship for Rome. However, he was cheated by the captain of the felucca on which he had booked a passage. He therefore set off by land but a few days into the journey realized that to travel from Naples to Rome by foot all alone was far too dangerous. On his return he spent a few weeks being shuffled from person to person, each time staying a couple of nights with members of the congregation whose confessions he had heard over the years. In most houses they could only offer him a wooden chest to sleep on, although occasionally they managed to find an old mattress to make it more comfortable. The weather was so terrible that the road and sea journeys to Rome were impossible. Throughout this period he was hungry, since the people where he was staying were generally poor and could only offer him a bit of bread or fruit. The other Piarist fathers never came to find him, and he avoided wealthier friends, such as the painter Aniello Falcone – soon to become an observer and hero of the Naples uprising – who could have lodged him, but who might have run a serious risk of discovery from the archbishop's spies.[20] After days spent hanging around in small churches or down by the jetty, or even on the beach at Chiaia, the weather finally improved enough for him to risk setting out with the postal courier. Armed with six ducats from the school, and a few other coins, Berro finally found a place with 'a really awful coachman, who treated me pretty badly. The roads were terrible, and throughout the journey there was continuous rain from the sky.'[21]

On his arrival in Rome Father Berro immediately fell gravely ill with a severe fever, which laid him low for several months. Cherubini and his circle voted that he be expelled immediately and only a plea to the higher authorities by Calasanz and his elderly colleagues in April 1647 finally resulted in permission to stay in San Pantaleo. In the autumn he was nominated secretary to Calasanz when the existing assistant, Father Gabriele Bianchi, became too ill to continue. Berro would stay at his side until the old man's death.

Some teachers saw the suppression of the order as a good opportunity. One teacher in Messina, hearing these rumours, took a wife, only for her to be declared a concubine shortly after. He was forced to flee to the mountains to avoid incarceration. In Rome, Brother Ferdinando di San Gieronimo went immediately to the local ghetto and sold his habit to a

Jewish merchant, but on his return to San Pantaleo was refused entry by the porter, who claimed he no longer knew him. Since he had renounced the uniform, he no longer had any right to be sheltered within the order's walls. Father Bernardino Testino seized the occasion to abandon teaching and become chaplain and confessor in a church in Palermo. Soon one of the elderly ladies whose confession he heard became very fond of him and adopted him. The widow's house was full of gold and silver and fine furniture and Father Bernardino became impatient to possess his inheritance. With the arrival of a fleet of ships in the harbour, he felt that his opportunity could be delayed no longer. As soon as he had confirmation of the date of departure of the fleet, he prepared a delicious meal of the widow's favourite foods, sprinkled on some poison and watched her expire before his eyes. 'And since there was no one else at all in the house, the ungrateful adoptee, the matricidal son, and most unworthy priest could at his liberty pack up the money, the silver, the gold and all the other things he desired and depart safely with the fleet, which soon set off with the infamous passenger.' The crime was not discovered for a few weeks, and the ex-Piarist was never heard from again, although Father Berro, recounting the tale, was hopeful that he had died a very horrible and painful death.[22]

In the aftermath of the suppression the school at Savona, near Genoa, also came to a very sudden and tragic end. The war magistracy had been storing 1,700 barrels of gunpowder in a ditch that ran the length of the bulwark of the San Giorgio fortress, thinking to have them conveniently to hand in case of emergency. Many in the city had expressed their anxiety about this, and they received frequent assurances that the situation was only temporary, the barrels would be moved shortly. However, in the middle of the night of 7 July 1648, Brother Agostino di San Carlo awoke suddenly from a deep slumber, and seeing the town on fire roused his friend Antonio di San Filippo Neri. Together they stumbled to the bell to ring a warning. Father Berro later heard the tale from Brother Agostino:

As they began to toll the bell, thunderbolts and lightning shafts fell on the city as all hell was let loose on Savona, and they felt an earthquake so terrible that the two clerics remained still and unconscious, unable to move as they seemed to be in the mouth of a great furnace, which burnt very splendidly, since nearly all the 1,700 barrels of gunpowder had caught fire and split the great tower of San Giorgio. Our two poor clerics remained like statues for a good space of time, and when they came to themselves again, they realized their danger and the ruin of the house around the campanile, especially since Agostino was still holding the bell rope. They didn't know what to do, and so without being really aware of their actions, they set off for the door of the house; but finding the staircase destroyed and the doorway so full of debris that they could not open it, they eventually managed to escape from the building, although they were very dazed.

The two brothers wandered around town for a few hours, Brother Antonio fainting from loss of blood from a head wound he had not even noticed in the earlier excitement and confusion. They tried to take refuge with the Servite fathers but their church was already full of victims and several of the fathers were themselves wounded. The brothers reeled onwards, and near the gates of the city finally found refuge with a lady who tended their wounds and put brother Antonio to bed. All around the city the windows and doors were blown out. The huge town gates themselves with all their heavy chains and bolts and keys hung wide open as if it were midday. Huge pieces of masonry had been flung several hundred metres across town. A total of 2,000 people were killed, and 500 houses were destroyed. Brother Agostino returned to the Piarist school but, as dawn broke, he could see that the whole building and church were completely destroyed, leaving only the base of the walls where the sacraments and some relics had been kept. Father Berro, whose own brother Pietro Paolo was killed in this explosion, went on: 'Imagine, reader, the blade of pain that transfixed the heart of this poor young man, seeing his house destroyed and his beloved priestly fathers buried alive.' As he watched in desperation, a child aged around six, completely naked, came crying from the building opposite and hurled himself to embrace Agostino's legs. The young cleric tucked him under his own habit, and since he had lost his own belt, the child could easily pop his head out from the opening, and so he carried him away to safety. Apart from the two brothers who survived, all five fathers who ran the Piarist school in Savona were killed. There was no room in the remaining churches even to bury their bodies. The bishop took the opportunity to announce that the school was obviously abandoned, and since the order no longer existed physically or juridically, the site should revert to his ownership under which he intended to establish a seminary. Meanwhile another order, the Discalced Carmelites, announced that the ruined buildings should be turned over for their use. A prolonged legal dispute continued for many decades thereafter.[23]

The non-Italian schools, meanwhile, strongly supported by their local noble patrons, held on and the local patrons also lent their diplomatic weight to the cause. King Ladislaw IV of Poland and Sweden told the papal nuncio he had no intention of permitting the brief of suppression to take effect in any of his territories. His bishops were notified of this decision and agreed with it, since they found the Piarist schools a useful weapon in the fight against Protestant heresy.[24] Jaroslav Borzita, Count von Martiniz, had been one of the two Imperial governors hurled through a window of Hrdčany castle onto a dung-heap in the Defenestration of Prague in May 1618 (a protest by Bohemian nobles against the Emperor's decisions that was one of the triggers to the Thirty Years War). He now also wrote in support of Calasanz. 'Your Order is without doubt an excellent work of God, serving him … This Institute of the Pious Schools has a good foundation, and infallible countersigns are these persecutions, which although annoying, are almost necessary, they will pass like flies, or rather stinging bees, giving us honey. As far as I can, I will help, and serve you most voluntarily.' The count still seemed to be suffering from the trauma of his defenestration, for he ended his letter to Calasanz with a request that if the old father knew of any 'efficacious remedies against melancholy, anger and cowardice, which I suffer from greatly during Mass, and at other times, without a good reason' he should send word immediately.[25]

Duke Jerzy Ossoliński, Grand Chancellor, whose sumptuous entrance into Rome in 1633 as ambassador to the papal court was still remembered with awe, and who played a leading role in political events in eastern Europe, also demonstrated his support. According to Father Berro, Duke Ossoliński

decided to go to Rome himself especially to ask the pontiff this favour, and he prepared everything for his journey, and said farewell to all his family and also to the kingdom and the king, and set off, with great pomp and circumstance as far as Warsaw, towards that delightful place called Italy, but in the morning while getting dressed to continue his journey to Rome, he was seized by an apoplexy, and a few hours later received the Last Rites and passed to eternity.

However, he had done all he could to help before his sudden death. He had written a tough letter to Cardinal Panciroli (who was unfortunately one of Cherubini's strong supporters), emphasizing the importance of the schools and the level of support they could expect from the local population and aristocracy. Initially, when the fathers had appeared in his house to say farewell to him, he had immediately prevented them from leaving, while he discussed the matter with the king and the senate, and had then brought the matter up at the next Diet. He told the cardinal that they lived 'in sincere poverty and with exemplary austerity and are venerated even by the heretics'. He enclosed letters 'from the king, the clergy and the rest of the republic in the sure hope that such great and unusual intercession will justify a change of decree by the Pope before God and the world'.[26]

The Polish bishops sent a petition, and Cardinal Franz Dietrichstein, who had been a strong supporter and helped create several foundations, leaned heavily on the willing Congregation for Propagation of the Faith to do whatever it could. In the Strasnitz school in Moravia the heretics were mostly Anabaptists; in Litomysl in Bohemia they were Calvinist and Lutheran.

These [children] are the real plants, where we hope for firmness in the true faith, because even when adult heretics convert, they do it under pain of punishment, so they are not well rooted, and they shake like trembling sticks, and often are uprooted at a mere puff of wind, or war, or change of government. But those who are irrigated by the dew of the true religion from an early age, when they are adult they will be like ancient oaks immobile before any tempest of diabolical opposition.[27]

King Ladislaw refused to give up. He instructed his special envoy to Rome, Domenico Roncalli, to visit all the relevant cardinals. He even asked him to try to bribe Monsignor Albizzi. Roncalli brought up the subject at his next meeting with Pope Innocent. He went right to the edge, threatening that the very loyalty of Poland to the papal see was in question. The pope was livid. Cardinal Panciroli described the meeting:

Roncalli replied that it seemed hard to him that His Holiness was resolute in losing the kingdom and the king of Poland by denying His Majesty the favours requested. This way of talking appeared very strange to the Pope, almost as though if he refused to grant these favours then the king and the kingdom would be alienated from the apostolic see, and lose the required veneration for the head of the Church. And it is certain that if all the other kings spoke in the way which Roncalli made the king of Poland speak, His Holiness said that the Holy See would be in a terrible state; but the other kings do not ask, nor have ever asked for the favours which this Majesty wants, nor when they are rejected do their representatives speak with the language which Roncalli used.[28]

Ladislaw's intervention served only to harden Innocent's heart.

The Tuscan grand duke had instructed his ambassador to visit the pope immediately when the brief was published. The Marchese Riccardi reported back that the pope was very hostile to the Piarists and he saw no hope: 'He told me an infinity of bad things about these fathers, saying that they had revealed a handful of filth [*una mano di porcheria*] about each other,'[29] which implies that he was familiar with

some of the more explicit reports. The suppression brief had only mentioned 'serious disagreements', but the pontiff must have known the
background to the decision.

Later appeals also came in from the Empress Eleanora Gonzaga,
attempting to change Pope Innocent's mind, but the answer was that
the matter depended directly on the pope who had already made his
decision. The advice was sent back via Cardinal Panciroli and the nuncio to the empress that the fathers be advised 'to be content and quieten
down, and not give any further irritation to His Beatitude since there is
no hope of achieving anything'.[30]

Soon those members who had decided to go had gone and the
schools were able to stabilize, admittedly at a lower level of staffing and
income, and with damage to morale and future training.[31] A pope does
not rule for ever, and the Piarists continued to hope that if they could
outlast this reign, and maintain their structures intact, they could appeal
against the suppression.

Father Cherubini could not wait. Yet again temptation stalked him,
this time in the Nazarene College where he was still in charge of the
seminary for young noblemen, and where he had recently introduced
his innovations in the form of risqué theatre productions. The well-bred
young students in their peacock tunics represented an elite selection of
attractive adolescents that simply proved too much for his fragile self-
control. Soon the news was known throughout the houses of the newly
demoted congregation. In Rome Father Bianchi spoke of 'something
unknown but spicy being discovered in the college [*non so che di aro-
matico nel collegio*]', after which Father Stefano renounced his position.
In July Father Carlo Patera wrote to Calasanz from Naples agog: 'I
understand that Stefano has been caught in the college by Brother
Orazio. I beg you, tell me how and what he did, because here everyone
has a lot to say. Father Vicenzo Maria [Gavotti] writes to a colleague
of his that all is calumny and persecution and therefore Monsignor
[Assessor Albizzi] favours him still more.'[32] He was so excited he no
longer even bothered to call the offender by his honorific title of

'Father'. Patera realized that Cherubini would have been very happy to continue in his position of responsibility had he not been forced to resign – after all he had been getting away with similar behaviour for nearly twenty years:

[His departure] was not real and spontaneous, as far as rumour indicates [he wrote] but insincere and forced; a term invented by the illustrious Auditors [of the Rota] to cover up his roguery. I beg you send me news of what has happened to him, because I wish that he had left ten years ago, then his roguery would not have ruined this poor Order. A thousand times I repent having left Rome and I am sick to the soul that I am not there now to go and ask Monsignor Assessor Albizzi whether these are [unfounded] persecutions, yes or no. I would also like to go to the Pope and make him realize how he has protected an infamous person; because perhaps if the Pope could clarify this truth to himself he would have some pity on us.[33]

While for some it was just another nail in the coffin of the organization, many took pleasure in Cherubini's fall. Father Vincenzo Berro wrote that at least 'now they will realize that the rest was not just the calumny of impassioned people', but had in fact been motivated by a desire to remove an immoral man from a position of too much influence.[34]

Where Father Stefano seems to have misjudged the situation was in the fact that the college boys were older and from wealthier families than his earlier victims. The usual Piarist pupil was aged between seven and fifteen, from a fairly modest artisanal background. The Nazarene College boys were a different matter. His latest victim reported the abuse to Brother Orazio Rinaldi, and soon some of the details were widely known. The auditors of the Rota, as the responsible authority and with a particular brief since they selected the pupils, were informed and came swiftly to investigate and interrogate the participants. As the truth emerged, Cherubini was exiled to the Frascati school, and the auditors were forced to ask Father Calasanz to suggest an immediate replacement.[35]

The scandalous news flooded through the city. In spite of this, the pope apparently remained adamantly fixed in his support for Cherubini. 'I am so amazed and confused,' wrote Father Berro, 'that the influence of so many powerful people in favour of our Order is worth so little to the supreme pontifex that he does not even recognize the calumnies which have been used against our so Holy Institute, and that after so many things have been discovered he *still* uses Father Stefano.'[36] Calasanz sadly pointed out that, 'There is no human aid that dares to speak up for us, so badly have not only the cardinals but also the Pope been informed against our Institute.'[37]

But now Father Cherubini did find himself alone. In spite of the pope's support, in the face of such widespread and widely acknowledged scandal his family could no longer defend him publicly. His connections probably protected him from legal pursuit or incarceration, and anyhow the authorities could hardly act when they had been warned so frequently of the situation and had chosen to ignore all the evidence. Frascati, hillside retreat of cardinals within striking distance of the Vatican, and stronghold of the Cherubini family, who had sponsored one of the first Piarist schools outside Rome there in the early years, was the perfect place to send the disgraced scion. It is unclear whether Monsignor Albizzi remained in contact with his friend during his exile. The Curia made no comment.

What did emerge from the pen of the Assessor of the Holy Office, Albizzi, was a vicious attack on the erstwhile congregation and its founder. Known as the 'Lengthy Account', it bore no author, but has been attributed to Albizzi, not only because of the depth of knowledge of the situation it revealed, but also because its views reflected those of the assessor and the papal court. It was probably written to justify the suppression, and it spared no blows. Piarist historian Giner Guerri described it as 'a small demonstration of the anthology of calumnies and equivocations with which Sozzi and Cherubini's circle had encircled the founder and the history of the origins of the Order'.[38] It started with a brief description of the origins of the organization under Clement VIII and Paul V, when 'the habit was modest and decent, but without bare feet; the institute was applauded and there was some point to it'. But then things went downhill. 'During the pontificate of Gregory XV, during which considerable importance was attached to those who affected sanctity, hypocrisy affected those who ruled Congregations and they rebelled to create a more austere habit, and to go barefoot, whilst intending also to leave the confines of Rome and her district.' Soon it became an order with ambitions to expand throughout Christianity, but the lack of subjects, the rapid expansion and the too severe way of life meant that new members of staff were accepted indiscriminately. It became clear at this point of the account – had his actions not already proved it – that Albizzi had a personal grudge against the founder. 'Father Calasanz, the general, ruled according to his whim, and filled the Order with a vile and incompetent rabble.' During the pontificate of Urban VIII, the disputes between superiors and the subjects in the order continued so that the pope had to suspend Calasanz, 'whose weakness or ambition caused the problem, and to call from all over Italy the subjects considered most suitable for government'. Under the visitor and his universal superior matters proceeded quite peacefully, Albizzi claimed, but on the accession of Innocent X, the quarrels and claims, especially by Calasanz to return to his previous dominion, were renewed. And it was at that point that it was decided to reduce the order to the status of a congregation.[39] Calasanz undoubtedly bore much of the blame for the administrative problems that faced the order, but for Albizzi to ignore the contributions of Sozzi and Cherubini so completely in his account was an astonishing feat by the assessor, whose own role was also brushed away. The 'Lengthy Account' was sent to Cardinal Pamphilij, the secretary of state, who forwarded copies to the nuncio in Poland. It was clear that in spite of Cherubini's latest disgrace, the opinion of the Curia, taking its lead from the pope and guided by Albizzi's poisonous information, was not going to alter.

A few months later Father Silvestro Pietrasanta, the apostolic visitor, fell gravely ill. He was fifty-six. For many years he had been suffering from kidney stones, and one of the criticisms of his visit had always been his lack of good health and his subsequent failure to inspect any of the houses outside Rome. Now the pain was so great that he decided to let the doctors operate. The date chosen was the feast of the Invention of the Holy Cross. The general of the Society of Jesus wrote to Father Nicolò Maria Gavotti to request that the Piarists pray for their visitor; he himself offered 500 Masses to ensure a good result. Every one of them failed. Against the advice of the surgeon the Jesuit fathers had given Father Pietrasanta an opiate, although it is not clear whether he was given the sedative before the operation, or afterwards to quieten his cries and permit the other fathers in the dormitory to sleep in peace. At all events, the operation on 3 May 1647 was deemed a success and seven stones 'large as nuts' were duly extracted, but when his carers entered his room on 6 May they found him dead. His body was taken to the Church of the Gesù and displayed there, where several Piarists visited to pay their respects.[40] Father Berro went to see his corpse, and noted bitterly that Pietrasanta – the Italian for 'holy stone' – should rather have been called '*Petra scandali*' ('scandal stone') for the things he had done to the order and the anger he had shown towards it. And not only one stone, he added, but seven for the seven members of Cherubini and Sozzi's circle whom he had supported. Three years of the Jesuit's apostolic visit had resulted in nothing but harm for the Piarists.

Further proof that the Society of Jesus was responsible for the downfall of the Piarists came a few months later. On the upper level of the façade of the Society's flagship church, the Gesù, were two large and beautiful statues, one signifying Religion, the other the Church. On 27 July, San Pantaleo's day – the feast day of the patron saint of the Piarists' mother church – a small puff of wind, which local shopkeepers later confirmed as being of trivial strength, blew down the statue of Religion. It detached itself from the façade and fell with a terrifying crash on the staircase below, reducing itself to dust, but injuring no one. According to Father Berro, this event proved that Pietrasanta and Jesuit machinations had played a key role in the downfall of the order. Just to be safe, the Society removed the other statue, the Church, from the façade, keeping the beautiful head and letting the rest smash to the ground.[41]

Father Cherubini, hearing the news of Pietrasanta's sickness in his hilltop exile, travelled hastily back to Rome, possibly hoping for a deathbed reunion. However, he arrived too late, and could only view the body displayed in the Gesù. As he walked around the streets of Rome, the gravity of his situation must have hit him hard, 'seeing himself abhorred by everyone in the Roman Curia, pointed at by everyone, called *destroyer of the Pious Schools* and realizing that not even the fathers of San Pantaleo wanted him, he had to wander around Rome all alone, like a failure'. And it was at this low point, wrote Father Berro, 'that everything was poisoned and his blood became so corrupted that it burst out in a sort of mange that neither purges, nor ointment could cure and the more remedies were applied the worse it got, so that the mange turned into the worst kind of leprosy, although it remained for some months in the parts [of the body] covered by clothing'.[42]

Cherubini took refuge – rather surprisingly – at the Nazarene College, where the new headmaster let him stay, after a personal intervention from Calasanz and given the threats of 'some act of desperation' from the sick man. Dr Giovan Maria Castellani, personal physician to Pope Gregory XV, professor of anatomy at the University of the Sapienza and a friend of Calasanz, confirmed the verdict of leprosy. According to Berro, the doctor said it was a particularly virulent form, and an obvious punishment from God for the traumas he had caused the founder. Cherubini's disease sounds remarkably similar to that of his close friend Sozzi four years earlier, though the fall from courtly favour for Cherubini meant that he did not have to suffer all the painful attempts that may have hastened Father Mario's death. Cherubini had always been a healthy man with a robust constitution but by October 1647 the disease had spread up his body and appeared on his hands and face, growing worse daily. Berro believed that the medicines and

unctions that Cherubini used once the disease was publicly visible probably contributed to his death by affecting his heart and inner organs.

As his sickness deepened Father Stefano sent a message via the head
of the Nazarene College to beg Father Calasanz for forgiveness. As
soon as he heard how ill Cherubini was, the old man set out on foot
with Father Berro to visit, a walk that – from near Piazza Navona
towards the church of Sant'Anna, not far from the Vatican – must have
taken more than an hour. On their arrival, the two priests met Flavio
Cherubini, Stefano's brother, weeping on the stairwell. 'Father General,'
he said, forgetting that his brother's actions had deprived Calasanz of
that title, 'Stefano is dying, the doctors have given him up for lost. But
Father, I beg you, don't frighten him by telling him any of this. It seems
he's resting now, let's leave him be.' But one of the lay brothers attending the sick man came out and told Calasanz that the patient was comatose rather than sleeping, so the old man decided to go in and pray
with him, reassuring his brother that, 'We must help his soul, even if we
cannot help his body.'

Calasanz sprinkled some holy water around the room and called out,
'Father Stefano, how are you?' Immediately the sick man regained con-
sciousness and seemed delighted to see his visitors. 'Father General,
help me, I'm very sick. I beg your pardon for all the troubles I have
caused you.' Calasanz immediately forgave him, and advised him to put
his faith in divine mercy and to make his confession, but he refused to
hear it himself, advising the dying man to use another priest instead,
Father Garzia Castiglia.

There is no mention whether Cherubini's good friend Monsignor
Albizzi ever visited during his illness. After confessing to Castiglia, he
fell into a delirium, and died on 9 January 1648. His body was briefly
put on show in the church and Father Berro grimly wrote that it was
the only way Father Stefano could attend San Pantaleo now, since 'he
could no longer have come there alive, after having been chased out by
the fury of the local population'. He was buried there, between the
chapels of Sant'Anna and Santa Caterina, without fanfare. Father

Calasanz wrote that his passing was a hopeful sign for the future of the organization.[43] Their contemporaries certainly felt that both Cherubini and Sozzi had received their just deserts.

But there were very few other hopeful indications left for the dismal group of fathers. That month, Father Calasanz, aged ninety-one, tripped and hurt his unshod foot returning from a visit to a nearby church. On 2 August he hobbled down the corridor to hear Mass in the domestic oratory, as every Sunday with the San Pantaleo schoolchildren. He managed to kneel while Father Berro held Mass, and it is this scene that Goya would later paint. It shows a hollow-cheeked old man, eyes closed receiving communion, while angelic-looking children peep out from behind him. His saintly halo is neatly in position.

Once more Dr Giovan Maria Castellani was summoned, along with Pietro Prignani, the house doctor to the community of San Pantaleo, and Dr Giovan Jacopo, the Borghese family doctor, who had attended Pope Paul V many years earlier. All agreed it was simply the weakness of old age. Father Calasanz insisted that the problem lay in his liver, which had been hurting for many years, and told Dr Prignani that when he came to do his autopsy, he should pay particular attention to this organ. The doctors seem to have had few remedies to suggest to the old man, although they agreed that marble slabs, refreshed with cold water and pressed to the relevant area would help ease the pain. These slabs have been kept and are still displayed within the small chapel at San Pantaleo dedicated to relics of Father Calasanz. Dr Castellani recommended bleeding the patient, although the others disagreed.

All the physicians did, however, agree that the patient should not drink, but as it was a hot summer in Rome he suffered terribly. Thomas Cook, a long-time English friend of his who had fled London after the 1605 Gunpowder Plot, and whose three sons had been pupils of Calasanz's, suggested a remedy. He claimed that he had worked for King James I of England, and that when forbidden to drink the king had put little slices of lemon sprinkled with sugar on his tongue. Father Angelo Morelli, who was in attendance that day, thought this an excellent idea and prepared some slices. But Father Calasanz, in an episode that Piarist historians see as a great example of 'his aversion to heresy and profound adherence to and reverence for the Catholic faith',[44] spat them out and declared that he did not wish to use a remedy invented by a heretic. Father Berro tried to reason with him, explaining, 'Father, the lemons are from Rome, the sugar is Spanish or Sicilian; the king is dead these many years; we, who are your sons, are giving it to you. What has it got to do with the king?' But Father Calasanz, obstinate to the last, replied, 'I don't want it, I don't want it, it's the invention of a heretic.' And he made Father Caputi throw the slices out of the window.[45]

The old father general weakened over the following days. Many visitors came to call, but no great cardinals, no papal representatives. On 23 August he received the last rites and the next night, around midnight, José Calasanz, surrounded by the community of fathers and brothers of San Pantaleo, quietly and peacefully expired, aged ninety-one, his life's work in ruins, his order suppressed and dishonoured.

Signs of sanctity were immediately evident. The body smelt of fresh roses and there was no sign of decomposition, a classic sign of future elevation. As the body was washed and prepared for burial, 'the right hand always moved to cover what should not in modesty be seen, and when they moved the body, the left hand repeated the gesture'.[46] During the autopsy his liver was indeed found to be too small and dense, while his heart was bigger than normal. This was placed in a great crystal container, while the brain, tongue, liver and spleen were preserved, covered in metal, and all were placed in a special walnut box, along with the reliquary containing the heart of Glicerio Landriani, which Calasanz had always treasured, and which Father Mario had removed from his desk.

His room was sealed up and retained as it was the day he died. It still exists, an austere and simple chamber with a chair and desk in one corner for the interminable letter-writing, and a simple bed with a rope suspended above it to help him to get up as he grew older. His enormous shoes – he was a tall man – still sit by the bed and the only luxury was a small stove for chilly winter letter-writing. In an adjoining chapel sit the relics retained after the autopsy.

For his funeral the bells rang out from San Pantaleo, until the neighbouring Palazzo Orsini sent a desperate message that the Duke of Bracciano was lying very ill and could not tolerate the sound of the bells. The communities of Rome (including the noviciate and the Nazarene College) as well as those of the neighbouring schools of Frascati, Moricone and Poli, attended. As the service began, a woman approached and, encouraged by Father Caputi, laid her crippled arm on the dead man's feet. Instantly she was cured and ran crying to the streets, 'A miracle, a miracle!'

Passers-by heard her call and rushed to the church. As the crowds pressed around the body, another cry went up. In the excitement, a woman's apron had been ripped in two. Picking up the torn shred, the woman bent to kiss the body, and then found, to her astonishment, that the apron had miraculously been reconstituted. Again the cry went up, 'A miracle, a miracle!' At that the crowd became dangerously over-excited, pressing around the inadequate guard provided by the Piarist fathers. People started to steal pieces, a shred of cassock, a tuft of hair, even a few toenails. It was turning into a riot with Calasanz's body at its centre. Teodoro Ameyden, the Dutch lawyer who had occasionally provided the Piarists with legal advice, wrote that 'his clothes were cut from around him, and the body barely saved, so easily can religion pass over into superstition'.[47] Monsignor Camillo de' Massimi, a papal secretary who lived nearby, raised the alarm, and the pope hastily sent a squad of Swiss guards to protect the body while it was re-clothed and repositioned behind a line of soldiers. He cannot have been very pleased to find such scenes of joy and wonderment at the funeral of a man whose life work he had destroyed. After several more miraculous events, Father José Calasanz was finally buried in his church of San Pantaleo, on 27 August 1648.[48]

CHAPTER TWENTY-ONE

'I only wish that the knowledge that we have today had been available to us earlier'

The last three governors of the Piarist Order, Fathers Calasanz, Sozzi and Cherubini, were dead. Pious Schools struggled on in towns throughout Italy and central Europe, but the order was no more, brought down by the machinations of two fathers, and the complicity of others. Monsignor Albizzi, close friend of Stefano Cherubini, assessor of the Holy Office of the Inquisition, and staunch supporter of Mario Sozzi, was elevated to the cardinalate in 1654. Innocent X died the following year. The order would remain dark for twenty years.

Stefano Cherubini, the priest who had finally fallen from grace, was unlamented. Likewise Mario Sozzi, the man who had dragged his own order before the Inquisition at every possible opportunity. José de Calasanz, meanwhile, who had initially covered up the scandal, was sanctified in 1767 and in 1948 was declared by Pope Pius XII to be Celestial Patron before God of all popular Christian schools in the world.

But if Father Calasanz had dealt with the initial accusation of child abuse when it was first made in Naples in 1629, by disciplining or expelling Father Stefano, instead of promoting him, it is possible that the course of events leading to the closure of the order would not have taken place. But under pressure from the influential Cherubini family, he had instead elevated Father Stefano, and tried to keep him away from young boys, when encouraging him to leave a teaching order and remove himself from all temptation would doubtless have been a sounder policy. Other potential child abuse scandals were also covered up and in each instance Calasanz's first priority was always the reputation of the order and the father concerned. This created a destabilizing secret at the heart of the order. The complications aroused by Father Mario Sozzi's friendship with Cherubini, and his accusations of disobedience and Galilean heresy, then threw the order further off-balance.

But as Cherubini moved to take over the whole order, the absolute lack of interest from Albizzi and the papacy in the accusations against him seem incomprehensible. Molesting children was a grave misdemeanour then, yet the authorities, despite innumerable protests, did nothing. It can only be that they did not consider the abuse of children by a priest to be a matter of enough gravity to prevent that priest becoming universal superior of a teaching order.

After intense lobbying, the Piarist Order was re-established as an independent congregation several decades later and, by the end of the seventeenth century the order was re-established with its original status. The following century saw a 'Golden Age', with some hundred colleges and schools spread throughout Italy, Spain and central Europe by 1776. Famous pupils through the centuries include musicians, statesmen and poets, such as Goya, Haydn, Mozart, Anton Bruckner, Franz Schubert, Emperor Ferdinand I, the Spanish King Ferdinand VII, Victor Hugo, the poets Giosuè Carducci and Giovanni Pascoli, the first president of the Italian Republic Luigi Einaudi, the 'father of modern genetics' Gregor Johann Mendel, architect Antonio Gaudí and gourmet writer Egon Ronay. Both Pope Pius IX, who is especially remembered for his declaration of papal infallibility, and Jose María Escrivá, the founder of Opus Dei, two men of particularly conservative tendencies, went to Piarist schools. Today the Piarist Order comprises nearly 1,500 priests, spread over nineteen provinces, with the bulk of its houses in Spain, followed by Italy, Mexico and Argentina.

While the modern Piarists have remained above scandal, perhaps having learned from their seventeenth-century experiences, the same cannot be said for the rest of the Catholic Church. During the 1990s, country after country discovered that some of its Catholic priests had been abusing those in their care, and that the hierarchy either looked away or implemented the same policy that Calasanz followed four hundred years earlier: *promoveatur ut amoveatur* – promotion to avoid the problem. Then and now the problem was simply ignored, on the grounds perhaps that the sexual misconduct with young boys was just not that important, and certainly not serious enough to be worth compromising a priestly career.

Various policies have been instituted to cope with the huge increase in claims of sexual abuse of children in recent years. Other institutions, such as state-run residential care homes in Wales and Islington in north London, have also experienced incidents of abuse, and it would be quite wrong to suggest that this is in any way a phenomenon limited to Catholic priests.[1] Similarities between the incidents in Islington and the Piarist experience include 'poor control of recruitment; confused administrative structures and weak, if autocratically disposed authority at the centre of the organization; poor victims without strong patrons and defenders; male victims and perpetrators'.[2]

In Catholic churches in England and Wales guidelines for child protection were introduced in 1994 but were not always followed. According to the *Daily Telegraph,* between 1995 and 1999 one in fifty of the 5,600 Catholic priests in England and Wales was investigated for child-abuse allegations, with twenty-one receiving convictions, and prosecutions pending at a rate of around one every three months.[3] Cardinal Cormac Murphy-O'Connor, Archbishop of Westminster and leader of the Church, appointed a priest he knew was suspected of paedophile activities, and who was later found guilty of nine sexual attacks, to the position of chaplain at Gatwick Airport, where he still had access to children.

In September 2001 an independent Review on Child Protection in the Catholic Church, led by Lord Nolan, was published and whole-heartedly accepted by the Catholic bishops of England and Wales. It recommended police checks on all staff, a new national protection unit, the creation of a database of all candidates for the priesthood, and immediate defrocking for clergy convicted of child abuse. That these measures were much needed, is shown by the case of the Archbishop of Cardiff, John Aloysius Ward, which came to light a month later.

Archbishop Ward had failed to act over not one but two paedophile priests, both of whom are serving jail sentences for crimes against children'.[4] He had ordained Father Joe Jordan, later jailed for eight years for sexually abusing boys, despite clear warnings from a fellow bishop that he was an unsuitable candidate, that he was already excluded from teaching and a potential abuser. Jordan stayed for a while at the archbishop's residence. In 1998 Ward's press officer, John Lloyd, also received a sentence of eight years for indecent assaults on children. When the scandal blew up, Archbishop Ward initially refused to resign, even when requested to do so by the papal nuncio to Britain. However, he was not sacked but permitted to resign, and complaints about his arrogance and obstinacy seem to have played at least as great a role in his downfall as his turning a blind eye to the abuse. The *Daily Telegraph*'s headline read: 'PAEDOPHILE ROW ARCHBISHOP QUITS: ROMAN CATHOLIC "FEELS AT PEACE" AFTER TALKS WITH POPE ON PRIESTS JAILED FOR CHILD ABUSE', whereas the *Guardian* blasted across its front page: 'SACKED: THE ARCHBISHOP JUDGED UNFIT FOR OFFICE'. The official website of the Catholic Bishops' Conference for England and Wales mentions none of this in its biography of the archbishop.[5]

In France, in the last few years, over thirty priests have been found guilty of raping or molesting children, with more prosecutions pending.[6] Monsignor Pierre Pican, Bishop of Bayeux and Lisieux, President of the Episcopal Committee for Childhood and Youth, and member of the Commission on the Family, appeared in court in June 2001 charged with 'non-denunciation of sexual attacks and poor treatment of minors' for failing to tell police of the crimes of Father René Bissey. Bissey was sent to prison for eighteen years for raping and molesting eleven boys in his congregation. Although he had admitted to the bishop, after complaints from parents, that he had been having sexual relations with several children, Bishop Pican had simply sent him to another parish, even leaving him to continue with his duties for Catholic Youth Action (*Action catholique à la Jeunesse*). In September 2001, for the first time ever, a bishop was called to answer for his actions before a civic court, found guilty and given a three-month suspended sentence and fined one franc symbolic damages. The French Church then created a consultative committee on sexual abuse against minors whose first action was to recommend the removal of a priest from Bordeaux, after his second conviction.[7]

In Belgium in 1998, the primate, Cardinal Godfried Daneels, was admonished in court for playing down the actions of a priest accused of sexual abuse. André Vander Lijn was jailed for raping ten children aged between ten and sixteen in his Brussels parish over thirty years. Even after legal proceedings were initiated against Vander Lijn, Daneels – often cited as a potential candidate for the papacy – had written to government officials asking them to 'exercise prudence' in their treatment of 'an excellent priest'.[8] It was far from a wholehearted condemnation of Vander Lijn's behaviour.

In Ireland by the end of 1999, over 150 priests had been accused of sexual abuse against children, 85 per cent of them from the Christian Brothers. In January 2002 the Church agreed to a landmark $110 million payment in settlement. Under the terms of an inquiry set up by the Irish government in September 2000 some 3,000 people came forward with accusations of physical and sexual abuse against members of the Christian Brothers, the Sisters of Mercy and the Oblates of Mary Immaculate.[9] In October 2003, the Irish government offered compensation to victims of child abuse from government-supported, religious-run institutions and was faced with a potential bill of 15 billion euros.[10] Before his death in 1997, Father Brendan Smyth had had a thirty-five-year career of abuse, being moved from parish to parish as his actions threatened to become known. The Irish attorney general delayed processing extradition requests from Northern Ireland where Smyth had been indicted in 1993 and Albert Reynolds's Fianna Fáil government became implicated in the resulting scandal. Bishop Brendan Comiskey turned a blind eye to the activities of one of his priests, the Reverend Sean Fortune, promoting him continually and placing him in positions of responsibility with easy access to children. His parishioners had written in vain to two bishops and to the papal nuncio. It was only when, eighteen years after the first complaint, one of his victims called in the police, leading to charges on sixty-six counts of sexual assault, indecent assault and buggery that the Church finally removed him from duties. Fortune committed suicide as his trial opened. Meanwhile Bishop Comiskey returned from six months' alcohol treatment at a clinic in the United States to face a critical BBC television documentary and was finally persuaded to resign in April 2002. As long ago as 1987, Irish Catholic bishops took out a special insurance policy to cover claims for clerical child abuse, even though Church spokesmen insist that the phenomenon was not acknowledged at that time. Cardinal Cormac Murphy-O'Connor, for instance, faced calls to resign in late 2002 over his re-appointments of suspected child abusers but claimed 'naivety and ignorance' over the behaviour of paedophiles to excuse his lack of effective action.[11] A recent book on child abuse scandals in residential homes noted that 'the Church authorities reacted as they have done everywhere, arguing that they, like the rest of the world, were ignorant of sexual abuse until very recently'.[12]

The claim that the church had only just become conscious of child abuse was called into question with the discovery by American lawyers in August 2003 of a document, apparently sent to all bishops throughout the world in 1962, and bearing Pope John XXIII's seal. The bishops were told to deal with matters concerning sexual abuse resulting from the confessional 'in the most secretive way' under pain of excommunication for all concerned. Church lawyers claimed the circular had been superseded by later guidelines and had been misrepresented, but the fact remains that there had been an awareness of the issue.[13]

The Archbishop of Vienna, Cardinal Hans Hermann Groer, the head of the Roman Catholic Church in Austria, was forced to retire in 1995 when, aged seventy-six, he was accused of sexual impropriety with students. In January 1999 he was again forced to retire, this time as abbot of a Benedictine monastery, for repeated acts of sodomy, mainly with novices. His biographer estimated he may have abused as many as 2,000 boys.[14]

The scandal even hit the Pope John Paul II's homeland of Poland. By late 1999 rumours were rife that the Archbishop of Poznań, Juliusz Paetz, a close colleague of the pope, had made improper advances to seminarians. He was accused of paying them night visits, of embracing young clerics in public and of using an underground tunnel to visit his victims. The rector of the seminary took the accusations seriously and banned the archbishop from entering the college. Finally, in February 2002, a daily newspaper, *Rzeczpospolita*, decided it had enough evidence to put the story on its front pages. For years seminarians had complained and Vatican emissaries had investigated, but silence had been enjoined on the complainants. On 28 March 2002 Paetz offered his resignation, which was accepted, although he denied the accusations and claimed that his 'kindness and spontaneity have been abused. My words, gestures and behaviour have been distorted and perversely interpreted.' But several priests refused to read out his last pastoral letter in their churches, and many of Poznań's clergy did not show up to hear his last homily, telling journalists they did not want 'to stand with evil'.[15]

Other countries such as Nigeria, Chile, Italy, Canada and Australia (where fifty-one priests were sentenced between 1993 and 2002) have also had their share of scandals, although as recently as 2001 when Pietro Forni, a Milan prosecutor, wrote about sexual abuse in Italy he was accused by Church authorities of writing fiction.[16]

In America, former altar boys who were sexually abused between 1981 and 1992 by Father Rudolph Kos, sentenced to life imprisonment in 1997, were awarded $119.6 million damages against the Roman Catholic Church in Dallas, Texas. But it was in spring 2002 that the issue finally dominated the headlines. In June 2001 Cardinal Bernard F. Law, Archbishop of Boston, admitted that seventeen years earlier he had given a priest, the Reverend John J. Geoghan, a job as a parish vicar, despite knowing of allegations that Geoghan had molested seven boys.[17] As the story began to unfold, nearly 200 people, the youngest of whom had been only four years old at the time, came forward with tales of molestation and rape by this father. It became clear that two cardinals and several bishops had aided the cover-up, always prioritizing Geoghan's career over any consideration for his victims. Despite years of abuse and many job transfers, Cardinal Law could still write to Geoghan on his enforced retirement, 'Yours has been an effective life of ministry ... On behalf of those you have served well, and in my own name, I would like to thank you. I understand yours is a painful situation.'[18] But Geoghan was just one of many. The archdiocese of Boston alone had secretly reached settlements involving at least seventy priests over the preceding decade. And throughout, Cardinal Law (described by the *Boston Globe* as 'indisputably the most influential American Catholic prelate and, more important, seen as such in the Vatican')[19] had known and had failed to ensure that Geoghan was kept away from children.

Public attitudes have changed over the last few decades, even in cities with a large Catholic poulation like Boston. In 1984 the Reverend Eugene M. O'Sullivan, the first priest in Massachusetts to be convicted of sexual abuse after admitting anally raping a thirteen-year-old altar boy, was given probation on condition that he did not continue to work with children. The following year Cardinal Law sent him to a new parish and a series of rapid moves over the following few years suggest he might well have continued to offend. But by February 2002, when Geoghan was convicted of squeezing the buttocks of a ten-year-old boy in a public swimming pool, there was no such leniency. The judge took into account 130 other allegations, including rape, and Geoghan was given a maximum ten-year sentence, only part of which he would serve. He was murdered by a fellow inmate eighteen months later.[20] Cardinal Law, who in 1992 had assured everyone that the case of James R. Porter, a priest who had attacked over one hundred children was 'an aberrant act' and blamed the media for their anti-Catholic bias, was put in the spotlight. He had covered up for Geoghan since the late 1980s and only finally defrocked him in 1998, four years after the criminal authorities had begun investigating him. In 1985, however, after one of the earliest sexual scandals in the American Catholic Church, when the Reverend Gilbert Gauthé molested eleven boys in Lafayette diocese, Louisiana, the newly created Cardinal Law had backed a confidential report on clerical sexual abuse of minors for the National Conference of Catholic Bishops. It was 'laced with clear and dire warnings – often in capital letters – about the incorrigible nature of priests who sexually molest youths', but when it was ready for publication Law withdrew his support for the report and the bishops filed it away.[21] In spite of that, the cardinal, as late as July 2001, could write: 'I only wish that the knowledge that we have today [on forces motivating child molesters] had been available to us earlier. It is fair to say, however, that society has been on a learning curve with regard to the sexual abuse of minors. The Church, too, has been on a learning curve.'[22] Had it paid more attention to its history, the Church could perhaps have had a headstart on the rest of society, rather than being left so far behind.

By 1999 the Roman Catholic Church in the United States had already agreed to pay out possibly as much as $1 billion in compensation to its victims. But with many more allegations surfacing, this was clearly just the beginning. The Church's cash cow, its wealthy American dioceses, was seriously threatened. The first time a jury had awarded punitive damages against the Church was in a 1990 case brought by a former altar boy. Although the initial $3.6 million was brought down on appeal to under $1 million, it sent a warning. The following year the

Santa Fe diocese was pushed to the verge of bankruptcy by a case cost-ing, at a conservative estimate, over $20 million. And as well as dam-ages, the Church's fundraising was badly hit. For instance, as the impact of the Boston cases began to sink in, the diocese's annual appeal fell on deaf ears, while a $350 million capital fundraising campaign ground to a halt. In March 2002, as the press coverage exploded, the Church in Boston settled an initial eighty-four lawsuits for between $15 and 30 million. But within two months, as some 500 people came forward and engaged lawyers to file their claims, the archdiocese was forced to renege on its deal, because of – in the words of Cardinal Law – a 'laud-able' concern that the growing numbers could leave the archdiocese penniless. By September the following year, the Archdiocese of Boston was offering the 500 alleged victims $85 million.[23]

Pope John Paul II was finally forced to accept the existence of the problem, but even the most sympathetic of commentators could not claim that the matter has been dealt with satisfactorily. A *motu proprio* (papal directive) was issued with so little fanfare it was almost secretive, published in January 2002, tucked into the Acts of the Apostolic See, the Vatican's official legislation record. It ordered that allegations of sexual abuse were to be reported secretly to the Congregation for the Doctrine of the Faith, the old Inquisition, where 'the hearing will be held in secret'.[24] But it would not be enough. In March the pope was finally forced to break his silence. In his annual letter to priests for Holy Thursday, he devoted paragraph thirty-eight (out of forty) to the sub-ject: 'At this time, too, as priests we are personally and profoundly afflicted by the sins of some of our brothers who have betrayed the grace of Ordination in succumbing even to the most grievous forms of the *mysterium iniquitatis* [mystery of evil] at work in the world.' But, fol-lowing centuries of tradition, his immediate concern was for the public scandal, which caused 'a dark shadow of suspicion' to fall 'over all the other fine priests'.[25]

Four days after the documents in another case, that of Father Paul Shanley, were ordered to be made public, Cardinal Law, under great pressure from the media and his lay constituents to resign, secretly flew out to Rome. The documents would show that Cardinal Law knew about Shanley's tendencies from as early as 1977 but continued to recommend him for positions as late as 1997, twenty years later. A week later, at the end of April 2002, all twelve American cardinals, including Law who was to remain in post, were summoned to Rome and convened in the Sala Bologna, the pope's private library, for what the Italian press dubbed 'the dirty linen summit'. Pope John Paul II finally offered some grains of comfort to the victims, expressing his 'profound sense of solidarity' with them. The communiqué pointed out that 'the sexual abuse of minors is rightly considered a crime by society and is an appalling sin in the eyes of God', but added in mitigation, 'Attention was drawn to the fact that almost all the cases involved adolescents and therefore were not cases of true paedophilia.' It went on to declare that 'people need to know that there is no place in the priesthood and religious life for those who would harm the young'. But there were no clear guidelines on whether suspected offenders would be immediately handed over to the civil authorities, whether offenders would be defrocked with greater urgency, or what the policy would be on those who had covered up for the offenders themselves.[26]

The wheels of the Vatican grind famously slowly. In an interview Cardinal Ratzinger once said, 'The art of *soprassedere*, of postponing ... can prove to be positive, can permit the situation to become less tense, to ripen and therefore to clarify itself.'[27] But it can also allow matters to putrefy and rot the heart. Meanwhile, members of the Vatican Curia have found scapegoats to blame for the succession of scandals. The pope's spokesman, Dr Joaquin Navarro-Valls, when asked about the abuse crisis in an interview, seemed to blame homosexuals, questioning whether the ordination of a man subsequently revealed to be gay was even valid; 'People with these inclinations just cannot be ordained.'[28] Cardinal Rodriguez Maradiaga of the Honduras told an interviewer that the whole issue had been blown up out of all proportion by the American media in an effort to distract attention from the Palestinian issue. For him, this level of persecution by the press recalled the worst days of 'Nero, Diocletian and more recently Stalin and Hitler'.[29] Behind the suggestion that the whole clerical abuse issue was predominantly an American problem, blown up by a scandal-seeking media, lay age-old accusations. John Allen, Vatican correspondent for CNN and journalist with the *National Catholic Reporter*, (an 'independent weekly' that 'works out of a Roman Catholic tradition and an ecumenical spirit') put his finger on it:

There is also a darker theory about the origins of the anti-Church temper in the American press currently making the rounds [in Rome]. It's something that so far only one prelate has dared to say out loud, and even then obliquely. Yet I have heard it come up repeatedly in private conversation, enough to convince me that it is fairly widely held. I should add that I am not talking about reactionaries who see a plot behind any criticism of the church, but about views expressed by several intelligent, cultured Catholic leaders of both left and right. To put the point more bluntly than these men ever would, in part they blame the Jews.[30]

The Vatican and important members of the Curia have sought to deflect responsibility for – and to downplay the significance of – the scandal. *The Times* described the Vatican's response as 'bafflingly slow, and dangerously obtuse'. The chair of theology at Boston College complained that 'sexual abuse was not given a high priority'.[31] In the context of two thousand years of Catholic Church history it was simply not seen as being of crucial importance. But the financial implications and the wider impact on the Catholic laity were not underestimated in Rome.

Cardinal Law did not attend the press conference that concluded the 'dirty linen summit' due to 'prior engagements', and perhaps showed that he had not moved very far on his return to America by including in his first legal response to charges that Father Shanley molested a six-year-old boy 'the assertion that the boy and his parents contributed to the abuse by being negligent'.[32] The American cardinals announced that as a result of their meeting with the pope they had outlined a preliminary policy to dismiss 'notorious' priests who had become guilty of the 'serial, predatory sexual abuse of minors'.[33] The less notorious priests – who presumably had not achieved notoriety by public exposure – would be subject only to the bishop's discretion, as in the past. *USA Today* was unimpressed and concluded it showed 'a church still in denial'.[34] By June 2002 a survey for the *Washington Post* showed that 218 American priests had been removed from their positions since the scandal broke in January. Thirty-four known offenders were still working in their parishes. That month American bishops met in Dallas to work out a proper strategy and decided that 'if a credible allegation of sexual abuse of a minor is made, the alleged offender will be relieved of any ecclesiastical ministry or function', but the onus still remained on the bishop to decide what policy to pursue.[35] Even that went too far for the Vatican, which, after several months of consideration, replied that this guidance would be vague, confusing and ambiguous and may prove 'difficult to reconcile with the universal law of the Church'. It was concerned that priests could be victimized and their careers destroyed by unfounded allegations. The new guidelines, voted in by an over-whelming majority of American bishops in November 2002, allow any priest accused of abuse to continue working while an investigation establishes if there was any truth in the allegation, and if the claim was deemed plausible he was then to be sent before a clerical tribunal. There was also a statute of limitations, so that crimes committed many years before no longer counted, even though in most of the recent cases the victims reached adulthood before they felt able to complain with enough authority to be taken seriously. The onus therefore remained, as it did before, with the bishop. There was no obligation to notify civil authorities.[36]

In December 2002 Cardinal Law's resignation was finally and belatedly accepted. Judicial investigations into priestly sexual abuse are still ongoing throughout much of the Catholic world. The problem clearly does not affect only isolated priests in distant rural communities. In several cases, cardinals and archbishops, who are direct deputies of the pope, have themselves been implicated. In others they have failed to act, have covered up for their priests, or failed to appreciate that the priests' actions have any relevance outside the confessional. The damage done to the pupils in their care has throughout taken second place to covering up embarrassment and ensuring the priest's own welfare and career, and thus the reputation of the Church. Faced with terrible publicity, a diminuation of trust among the faithful, and colossal compensation bills, in the last few years, in its guidelines and bishops' conferences, the Church has finally been forced to address the issue.

The example of the Piarist Order shows that abuse by priests is not a new problem. Modern perceptions of the gravity of the actions of paedophile priests are not anachronistic. In a period when far more importance was placed on strict morality and religious orthodoxy, when the rules of physical contact between adult priests and between teacher and child were far more tightly regulated for fear of anything untoward happening, known paedophile priests were moved around from school to school, and still permitted access to children. Calasanz knew what could happen if men and boys were left alone together: his writings and the school *Rules* show that. He knew what had happened, as did the cardinals, the bishops and, ultimately, the pope. The scandal was initially covered up to protect the reputation of an important cleric with influential family connections, but with the full knowledge of the pope the priest was raised to the overall governorship of a teaching order responsible solely for the education of children. The patron saint of Catholic schools covered up for the child abusers. It was only when the scandal became public and began to irritate the authorities too greatly that the order was suppressed, an unprecedented action in the history of the Church. It is time that the modern Catholic Church took a closer look at the history of the Order of Clerics Regular of the Pious Schools.

NOTES

Abbreviations

For full details, see Bibliography: Epistolaries and Other Primary Sources.

Annot: *Annotationi,* by Father Vincenzo Berro
EEC: Letters to Calasanz from central Europe
EHI: Letters to Calasanz from Spain and Italy
Ep.: Letters by Calasanz
Epco: Letters between contemporaries of Calasanz
Giner Guerri: The most recent biography of Calasanz by Severino Giner
  Guerri
Positio: The case for the beatification of Father Pietro Casani

A NOTE ON COINAGE AND TIME

1 EHI, p.2156, Father Pellegrino Tencani to Calasanz, 12 August 1639.
2 *Rome, Bologna, Perugia:*
  1 scudo = 100 baiocchi. The scudo d'oro contains 3.077 grammes of
    gold
  1 giulio = 10 baiocchi
  1 testone = 3 giuli
  1 piastre or silver scudo = 10 giuli
  1 grosso = ½ giulio
  1 mezzo-grosso = ¼ giulio
  1 baiocco = ¹⁄₁₀₀ scudo, ¹⁄₁₀ giulio, 4 quattrini, 16 denari. This is the price
    of a loaf of brown wheat bread

quattrino = ⅕ baiocco

10 florini = 6 scudi 25 baiocchi

Venice:

1 ducato = 124 soldi

1 lira = 20 soldi

Naples:

1 carlino = 10 grani = 100 centesimi

These tables rely on:

Christopher F. Black, *Italian Confraternities in the Sixteenth Century* (Cambridge: Cambridge University Press, 1989), p.286

Jean Delumeau, *Vie économique et sociale de Rome dans la seconde moitié du XVIe siècle*, (Paris: De Boccard, 1957), p.658

Laurie Nussdorfer, *Civic Politics in the Rome of Urban VIII* (Princeton: Princeton University Press, 1992), p.xvii

Monthly salaries:

A Vatican palace gardener earned 4 scudi; a priest 3½ scudi; a common sweeper earned 15 guili (though a confidential one, with access to restricted areas in the Vatican, earned 3 scudi); a serving girl earned ½ scudo. These figures are taken from Girolamo Lunadoro, *Relatione della corte di Roma, E de' riti da osservarsi in essa...* (Rome: Fabio de Falco, 1664).

PREFACE

1 See below, Chapter Twenty-One for more famous Piarist alumni.

2 *Catholic Encyclopaedia*, www.newadvent.org.

3 As examples picked at random, see www.catholic-forum.com/saints, which blames 'incompetence' and 'internal dissent', or the *Catholic Herald,* which cites 'bickering and backbiting' and 'skimming funds'.

4 Diario del Settimanni, Archivio di Stato, Firenze, MS 135, vol. IX, 4 April 1632.

5 *Guida dell'Archivio*, unpublished guide to the Inquisition Archive (Rome, 1998). John Tedeschi, 'The Dispersed Archives of the Roman Inquisition' in Gustav Henningsen and John Tedeschi (eds.) *The Inquisition in Early Modern Europe* (Illinois: Dekalb, 1986).

6 Pietro Redondi, *Galileo Heretic*, trans. Raymond Rosenthal (London: Allen Lane, 1987), p.8.

CHAPTER ONE

1 Quoted in Severino Giner Guerri, Sch.P., *San José de Calasanz: Maestro y Fundador. Nueva biografía crítica* (Madrid: Biblioteca de Autores Cristianos, 1992), p.287.

2 Quoted in Giner Guerri, p.210.

3 *The Diary of Montaigne's Journey to Italy in 1580 and 1581*, ed. and trans. E. J. Trechman (London: Hogarth Press, 1929), p.149.

4 Jean Delumeau, *Vie économique et sociale de Rome dans la seconde moitié du XVIe siècle* (Paris: De Boccard, 1957); bandits, vol.2, p.563; famine, vol.1, pp.172, 217, vol.2, p.624.

5 *The Diary of Montaigne's Journey to Italy in 1580 and 1581*, p.163.

6 Ep.V, L.1903, 28 October 1632.

7 *The Diary of Montaigne's Journey to Italy in 1580 and 1581*, p.149

8 Quoted in Helen Langdon, *Caravaggio: A Life* (London: Chatto & Windus, 1998), p.42.

9 Ep.VII, L.3393, 17 April 1640: 'Here there is good public health but great scarcity of alms for although there are no wars in the Papal States and grain is very cheap, there is great necessity among the common people. We are waiting, possibly in vain, for the Pope to create new cardinals after the current Easter holidays, in order to increase the number of important people in Rome so the poor can be helped more.'

10 *The Diary of Montaigne's Journey to Italy in 1580 and 1581*, pp.149, 162.

11 Annot, T.1, bk.1, ch.9.

12 Ludwig von Pastor, *The History of the Popes,* vol.22 (London: Kegan Paul & Co., 1952), p.317.

13 Ep.II, L.4, 25 November 1592.

14 Camillo Fanucci, *Trattato di tutte l'opere pie dell'alma città di Roma* (Rome, 1601), pp.70–1.

15 Angelo Grillo, quoted in Pastor, vol.22, p.295.

16 Quoted in Massimo Petrocchi, *Roma nel seicento* (Rome: Cappelli, 1970), p.148.

17 Langdon, p.56.

18 Gregory Martin, *Roma Sancta* (1581), ed. George Bruner Parks (Rome: Edizioni di Storia e Letteratura, 1969), p.208.

19 Martin, pp.210–14; Petrocchi, p.117.

20 109,729 in 1600, quoted in Langdon, p.39.

21 Vincenzo Berro, *Annotazioni*, ed. Osvaldo Tosti, in 'Come nacquero la prima volta le Scuole Pie in Trastevere', *Ricerche*, 47 (1996).

22 Ep.VIII, L.4185, 20 May 1644.

23 Except for French historians, who usually credit their own saint, Jean-Baptiste de la Salle, born in 1651, three years after Calasanz's death, with creating the first free public elementary school.

24 For example, letter from John Paul II, 24 June 1997, *Ricerche*, 53 (1997), p.7.

25 Annot, T.1, bk.1, ch.6.

26 Domenico Sella, *Italy in the Seventeenth Century* (London: Addison Wesley Longman, 1997), pp.212–13; Gaspar Schoppe on Bruno's interrogation and execution on www.positiveatheism.org/hist/bruno

27 Epco, p.1552, 20 July 1602; Giner Guerri, p.424.

28 Annot, T.1, bk.1, ch.13.

29 Giner Guerri, p.421. Ep.II, L.380a for the cardinals' visit, 13 March 1601.

30 Alessandro Bernardini, 'Delle croniche della congregatione', … written in 1614, reprinted in Positio, p.265; Giner Guerri, p.412 for the papal grant, August 1602; Giner Guerri, p.420 for the municipal grant.

31 Giner Guerri, p.456, n.148.

32 Quoted in Langdon, p.100.

33 Charles Nicholl, 'Screaming in the Castle', *London Review of Books*, vol. 20, No. 13 (2 July 1998); Maurizio Calò and Liliana Chiettini, 'Il Processo a Beatrice Cenci', *La Rivista dei Curatori Fallimentari*, at www.acfitalia.org/1998

34 Positio, p.264, Bernardini, 1614.

35 Annot, T.1, bk.1, ch.25; Positio, pp.248–9, August 1616.

36 With the brief 'Ad ea, per quae'.

37 Giner Guerri, p.576; Pastor, vol. 25, p.266.

38 Ep.II, L.71, 24 February 1621.

39 Sella, *Italy in the Seventeenth Century*, p.118.

40 'Memoriale al Cardinale Tonti', published in *Ephemerides Calasanctianae*, 36, nn.9–10 (1967), pp.120–5.

CHAPTER TWO

1 Epco, p.2835; letter from Francesco Castelli to the cardinals, 1644/5.

2 Positio, pp.172–3, 17 October 1614.

3 Ep.II, L.77, 13 August 1621.

4 'Breve relatione del modo che si tiene nelle Scuole Pie...' *Archivum Scholarum Piarum*, 3 (1938), pp.5–9; also republished in *Ricerche*, 43 (1995), pp.8–13.

5 Ep.III, L.1003, 29 November 1628.

6 Giner Guerri, p.445, n.108; Armando Petrucci, *Public Lettering: Script, Power and Culture* (Chicago: University of Chicago Press, 1993), p.42.

7 Ep.IV, L.1633, 22 June 1631; Ep. III, LL.535, 6 October 1626; 907, 23 July 1628.

8 EEC, p.32, 19 July 1632.

9 Most of this chapter is based on A. K. Liebreich, 'Piarist Education in the Seventeenth Century', *Studi Secenteschi*, 26 (1985), pp.225–78 and 27 (1986), pp.57–89.

10 Epco, p.1554, 31 August 1602.

11 Positio, pp.1312–13, Casani, 1645; Epco, pp.2499–500, 'Ad Cardinales deputatos', 1645.

12 Answer: $691\frac{3}{5}$. Padre Alessandro della Purificazion [Fantuzzi], *Arimmetica pratica* (1714), p.312.

13 Ep.VII, L.3753, 26 October 1641.

14 Sántha, p.485, n.4; 'Memoriale del Cardinale Paolucci', Reg. Cal. LXVIII; Calasanz on the importance of the classes, Ep.VI, L.2742, 18 June 1637.

15 Positio, pp.1312–13, Casani, 1645.

16 Epco, p.606, after 10 March 1644.

17 Silvio Antoniano, *Dell'educazione cristiana e politica dei figlioli*, ed. Leopoldo Pogliani (Turin, 1928).

18 Tommaso Campanella, *The City of the Sun*, trans. A. M. Elliott and R. Millner (London: Journeyman Chapbooks, 1981), n.7; 'Liber apologeticus contra impugnantes institutum Scholarum Piarum', ed. K. Jensen and A. K. Liebreich, *Archivum Scholarum Piarum*, 15 (1984), pp.29–76.

19 Annot, T.1, bk.1, ch.19.

20 Ottorino Calcagni, et al., *I regolamenti del Collegio Nazareno* (Rome, 1979), p.46.

21 Annot, T.2, bk.2, ch.27.

22 G.L. Moncallero and G. Limiti, *Il codice calasanziano palermitano (1603–1648)* (Rome: Edizioni dell'Ateneo, 1965), p.76, 1616–1620; Ep.IV, L.1631, 19 June 1631.

23 Tommaso Garzoni, *La piazza universale di tutte le professioni del mondo*

(Venice, 1595), p.726; on reading material, graffiti, performers, taverns, fighting, 'Breve relatione', p.9; on graffiti and wine, AGRome, Reg.Cal. XIII, 32 Ordini da osservarsi dalli scolari… di Campie (1630), f.2, parag.11 parag.15. Also EHI p.530 (1618), 'Ordini… Narni', parag.8; on graffiti and weapons, 'Leges … Littomisslii' (1644), in *Ricerche*, 47 (1996), document 12.

24 Positio, p.276, Alessandro Bernardini, 'Delle croniche della congregatione', 1617.

25 Giner Guerri, p.477, n.62; edict on children driving, no.813, 27 February 1648, in *Regesti di bandi, editti, notificazioni, e provvedimenti diversi relativi alla città di Roma e allo Stato Pontificio*, 7 vols. (Rome, 1920–58), vol.5.

26 Positio, p.276, Bernardini. Tourist comments, see, for example, Richard Lassels, *The Voyage of Italy*, c.1664, kindly shown me by Edward Chaney.

27 'Ritti comuni', original manuscript by Father Giacomo Graziani, AGRome, Reg. Cal. XIV, 74* (circa 1628), f.27v.

28 Sántha, p.410, n.12 for the Frascati ordinance; EHI pp.585–6, 10 November 1629; AGRome, Reg. Cal. XIV, 60/3, 'Discorso sulle Scuole Pie', AGRome, Reg. Cal. XIII, 32**, 'Ordini da osservarsi dalli scolari delle scuole pie di Firenza' (1630), parag.7; AGRome, Reg. Prov. 20, n.2, Fondazione in Firenze (1630–3).

29 Ep.IV, L.1429, 27 June 1630.

30 'Ritti comuni', Reg. Cal. XIV, 74, f.24v; spare pants in case of punishment, Annot, T.2, bk.1, ch.20; letter from Calasanz to Giovan Pietro Cananea in Frascati, 20 June 1624.

31 Ep.III, L.793, 21 February 1628; Ep.III, L.886, 30 June 1628.

32 Positio, p.193, letter from Bernardini to the Lucca Fathers, 31 December 1614.

33 Paul F. Grendler, 'The Organization of Primary and Secondary Education in the Italian Renaissance', *Catholic Historical Review*, vol. LXXI, 2 (1985), p.185.

34 Ep.V, L.1160, 20 July 1629.

CHAPTER THREE

1 Quoted in Domenico Sella, *Italy in the Seventeenth Century* (London: Addison Wesley Longman, 1997), p.112.

2 Ep.II, L.56, 6 December 1620; L.61, 6 January 1621.

3 Epco, p.516, 26 February 1624.

4 Ep.VII, L.3400, 27 April 1640; Ep.VII, L.3700, 10 August 1641; Ep.VII, L.3597, 27 June 1641; on chess, Moncallero and Limiti, p.185, L.30, 5 August 1633.

5 Annot, T.1, bk.2, ch.12.

6 Ep.III, L.1014, 9 December 1628.

7 Moncallero and Limiti, p.27.

8 Ep.VII, LL.3012, 3013, 15 January 1639.

9 Ep.III, L.971*, 21 October 1628.

10 Annot, T.1, bk.2, ch.11.

11 Epco, p.2723, October 1614; 'Ad tres Cardinales'.

12 Leonardo De Marco, 'L'abate Scolopio Glicerio Landriani 1588–1618', Ricerche, 59 (1999), pp.46–53; Epco, pp.2758–68, April/May 1630.

13 Annot, T.1, bk.3, ch.13; first request to go to Poland, Ep.VII, L.3475, 28 July 1640.

14 EEC, pp.27–9, 23 October 1631.

15 EEC, pp.14–22, 7 August 1631; also EEC, p.617, 6 August 1631; pp.22–7, 15 October 1631.

16 Epco, p.1368, 5 May 1633, Dietrichstein to Congregation de Propaganda Fide.

17 Epco, p.1169, 1644.

18 EEC, p.646, 4 May 1633, Ambrogio Leailth to Calasanz; Cardinal Barberini's prediction in Epco, p.568, 3 January 1637.

19 'Memoriale degli inconvenienti', Epco, pp.2771–5, July/August 1631.

20 Epco, pp.546–7, October 1631.

21 Ep.V, pp.23–4, 'Risposta al memoriale delli Inconvenienti'.

22 Ep.II, L.93, 3 November 1621; L.94, 13 November 1621; on stomach ache cures, Ep.III, 788, 19 February 1628.

23 Ep.IV, L.1235, 19 October 1629.

24 Ep.V, L.2027, 29 April 1633.

25 Filippo Scoma, 'Memorie cronologiche della fondazione e progressi della provincia di Sicilia delle Scuole Pie', Archivum Scholarum Piarum, 19–20 (1986), p.135.

26 Constitutiones S. Josephi Calasanctii a.1622 (Salamanca: Gráf. Ortega, 1979).

27 Annot, T.1, bk.1, ch.27.

28 EHI, p.1772, 1 March 1626.

29 'Good ones or nothing', Ep.V, L.1937, 25 December 1632; 'Half are

unfit…', Epco, p.76, 2 June 1643; from Genoa, EHI, p.2123, 22 December 1629; from Moravia, EEC, p.36, 5 October 1632.

30 Annot, T.3, bk.1, ch.19.

31 Annot, T.1, bk.2, ch.11.

32 Annot, T.1, bk.2, ch.11.

33 John Raymond, *An Itinerary Contayning a Voyage made through Italy in the yeare 1646, and 1647* (printed for Humphrey Moseley, and are to be sold at his shop at the Princes Armes in St Pauls Churchyard, 1648), p.113.

34 Scoma (1986), p.112; on Benedetto's battle, Ep.III, L.658, 15 July 1627.

35 Filippo Scoma, 'Memorie cronologiche della fondazione e progressi della provincia di Sicilia delle Scuole Pie', *Archivum Scholarum Piarum*, 17 (1985), p.124.

36 Scoma 17 (1985), p.107.

37 Fernand Braudel, *The Mediterranean and the Mediterranean World in the Age of Philip II*, trans. Siân Reynolds (London: HarperCollins, 1992), pp.250–2.

38 Peter Robb, *M* (London: Bloomsbury, 1998) on Cervantes, p.361; Salvator Rosa, quoted in Jonathan Scott, *Salvator Rosa. His Life and Times* (New Haven: Yale University Press, 1995), p.1; Ep.III, L.596, 20 March 1627; population estimate from Annot, T.2, bk.1, ch.17; Calasanz's comment in Ep.III, L.563, 11 December 1626; Salvator Rosa took the Piarist habit on 1 August 1630, according to a scribble on the back of Ep.IV, L.1448, 27 July 1630; on tendency of natives to return, Ep.V, L.2177, 14 January 1634.

39 Ep.III, L.560, 5 December 1626; Alberto Tanturri, 'Gli Scolopi nel Mezzogiorno d'Italia in età moderna', *Archivum Scholarum Piarum*, 50 (2001).

40 Annot, T.2, bk.2, ch.17.

41 Boris Behncke*, Italy's Volcanoes: The Cradle of Volcanology*, cited from www.geo.edu/~boris/VESUVIO; Ep.V, L.1731, 3 January 1632; L.1733, 10 January 1632.

42 Annot, T.1, bk.3, ch.27.

CHAPTER FOUR

1 Annot, T.1, bk.2, ch.7.

2 Epco, pp.1962–4, letter from Ottonelli to Pope Paul V, October 1620.

3 Positio, pp.500–502, letter from Ottonelli to Bishop Seneca and attached

list of accusations, 5 August 1625. The cardinals were carrying out the 1625 apostolic visit, a form of inspection for religious organizations.

4 Ep.II, L.396, 19 February 1626; Ep.X, 396/1, 21 February 1626.

5 Ep.III, L.587, 20 February 1627.

6 Filippo Scoma, 'Memorie cronologiche della fondazione e progressi della provincia di Sicilia delle Scuole Pie', *Archivum Scholarum Piarum*, 17 (1985), p.122. Scoma wrote this between 1724 and 1730 when he was assistant general of the Order. He had access to several works in the Sicilian archives, including Alacchi's own *Adnotationes Siculae*, which have since disappeared.

7 Description of drowning from Scoma, 17 (1985), p.122; EHI, p.567, 2 July 1627.

8 Ep.III, L.623, 29 May 1627, letter from Calasanz, Rome, to Cherubini, Naples; Ep.III, L.646, 28 June 1627, Calasanz, Rome, to Giovan Garzia Castiglia, Frascati.

9 Giner Guerri, pp.792–3.

10 Annot, T.3, bk.2, ch.15.

11 EHI, p.566, 2 July 1627, letter from Francesco Castelli, Genoa, to Calasanz, Rome.

12 EHI, pp.7–24, 1627, several letters from Alacchi to Calasanz.

13 Positio, p.565, 'Primo capitolo o congregatione generale fatta dell'anno 1627 adi xi ottobre'; cf.EHI, p.25.

14 Scoma, 17 (1985), p.128.

15 Ep.III, L.708, 7 October 1627.

CHAPTER FIVE

1 In 1627 the painting passed to the collection of Charles I, and on his fall was eventually acquired by Louis XIV, ending up in the Louvre; see Pamela Askew, *Caravaggio's Death of the Virgin* (New Jersey: Princeton University Press, 1990), pp. 3–13; also Peter Robb, *M* (London: Bloomsbury, 1998), pp.259, 290–3.

2 G.P.Caffarelli, *Famiglie romane, 1592*, f.274, Biblioteca Apostolica Vaticana, Ferr.282.

3 Domenico Sella, *Italy in the Seventeenth Century* (London: Addison Wesley Longman, 1997), p.112.

4 Ep.III, L.621, 22 May 1627.

5 Ep.III, L.623, 29 May 1627.

6 Ep.III, L.629, 30 June 1627.

7 EHI, pp.1222–8, 2 February 1629.

8 The term comes from a letter from Father Francesco Castelli, EHI, p.580, 3 November 1629, 'Mi dicono anco che tiene per suo [Cherubini's] individuo compagno Nicolò Maria Gavotti'.

9 Annot, T.1, bk.1, ch.23.

10 EHI, p.580, 3 November 1629.

11 April/May 1617, Regole, Positio, pp.332, 337.

CHAPTER SIX

1 Edward Stourton, *Absolute Truth. The Catholic Church in the World Today* (London: Viking,1998).

2 M. Mansio, *Vita del Letterato, Rome 1625*, quoted in Jean Delumeau, *Le catholicisme entre Luther et Voltaire* (Paris: Presses Universitaires, 1971), p.91.

3 Epco, p.2739, 6 September 1623.

4 On the percentage of men in Rome in 1598, see Giovanni Landucci, 'Il pauperismo del sec. XVII', *Ricerche,* 49 (1996), p.15; on Clement's anti-sex campaign, see Roberto Zapperi, *Eros e Controriforma: Preistoria della Galleria Farnese* (Turin: Bollati Boringhieri, 1994), pp.46–53; prostitutes banned from Borgo on 1 February 1592; confined to Ortaccio on 15 February; inns not allowed to rent to women, 9 November 1592; bull 'Cum in unaque bene', 15 December 1586, banned shirt sleeves and slippers; July 1600, quiffs (*ciuffi*) of hair banned; 7 June 1599, nude swimming banned.

5 Annot, T.1, bk.1, ch.9.

6 Ep.V, L. 2122, 7 October 1633.

7 Alan Bray, *Homosexuality in Renaissance England* (New York: Columbia University Press, 1995), p.13; John Boswell, *Christianity, Social Tolerance, and Homosexuality* (Chicago: University of Chicago Press, 1980), p.202.

8 Boswell, p.218.

9 David F. Greenberg, *The Construction of Homosexuality* (Chicago: University of Chicago Press, 1988), p.307.

10 Guido Ruggiero, *The Boundaries of Eros* (Oxford: Oxford University Press, 1985), p.145.

11 Ruggiero, pp.142, 144.

12 Helmut Puff, *Sodomy in Reformation Germany and Switzerland 1400–1600* (Chicago: University of Chicago Press, 2003), p.147.

13 Michael Rocke, *Forbidden Friendships: Homosexuality and Male Culture in Renaissance Florence* (New York: Oxford University Press, 1996), p.4.

14 Zapperi, p.50; Filippo Galletti writing on 28 January 1600, of the execution on 6 January; also a carter, Vincenzo Cappellari, on 31 August 1592.

15 Langdon, p.376.

16 Ep.V, L.1932, 18 December 1632.

17 Ep.VII, L.3008, 8 January 1639.

18 Ep.III, L.942*, 9 September 1628.

19 Richard P. McBrien, *Catholicism,* 3rd ed. (London: Geoffrey Chapman, 1994), p.995, the Congregation's Pastoral Letter to the world's bishops of 13 November 1986; Henry C. Lea, *Historia de la Inquisición Española,* vol. 3, ed. by Angel Alcala (Madrid: Fundación Universitaria Española, 1983), pp.775–8; statistic given in Channel 4 documentary *Abused and Catholic,* transmitted on 12 January 2003; see also John J. McNeill, *The Church and the Homosexual* (Kansas: Sheed Andrews and McMeel, 1976).

20 Puff, *Sodomy in Reformation Germany and Switzerland,* p.14.

21 *L'Alcibiade fanciullo a scuola,* cited in Rocke, *Forbidden Friendships,* p.95.

22 Paul F. Grendler, 'The Organization of Primary and Secondary Education in the Italian Renaissance', *Catholic Historical Review,* vol. LXXI, no. 2 (1985), p.197; Ruggiero, p.138.

23 On more modern sexuality, including paedophilia, see Jeffrey Weeks, *Sexuality and its Discontents* (London: Routledge, 1985).

24 Ep.III, L.942,* 9 September 1628.

25 Ep.III, L.1071, 3 March 1629.

26 Ep.III, L.1081, 23 March 1629; Gigli laconically notes: 'At 20 hours three suns in a circle were seen in the sky', Giacinto Gigli, *Diario di Roma,* vol.1, 1608–1644, ed. Manlio Barberito (Rome: Colombo, 1994), p.176.

27 Ep.IV, L.1160, 20 July 1629.

28 Ep.IV, L.1173, 4 August 1629; L.1184, 18 August 1629; on rain, Ep.IV, L.1196, 1 September 1629; L.1203, 10 September 1629.

29 EHI, p.1197, 13 October 1629.

30 Annot, T.1, bk.3, ch.18.

31 EHI, pp.540–1, 9 November 1629.

32 Annot, T.1, bk.3, ch.18.

33 EHI, p.636, 10 November 1629.

34 EHI, pp.637–8, 24 November 1629.

35 Mario Rosa, 'The World's Theatre: The court of Rome and Politics in the first half of the seventeenth century', in Gianvittorio Signorotto and Maria Antonietta Visceglia, *Court and Politics in Papal Rome, 1492–1700* (Cambridge: Cambridge University Press, 2002), pp.78–98.

36 Ep.IV, L.1267, 1 December 1629.

37 Ep.IV, L.1537, 30 September 1630.

38 Giner Guerri, p.799; an earlier father archivist, Claudio Vilá Palá, also mentioned it, calling the promotion 'a sad tactic', Positio, p.777.

39 Ep.IV, L.1556, 4 January 1631.

40 Ep.IV, L.1578, 20 February 1631.

41 Ep.V, L.1748, 13 February 1632.

42 Ep.IV, L.1560, 11 January 1631; L.1564, 18 January 1631.

43 Epco, p.701, 18 January 1631; Alacchi had returned from his pilgrimage to Spain, had annoyed everyone once more, and was again being sent off on pilgrimage. He made it as far as Venice, where he was awaiting embarkation to the Holy Land when plague struck and closed the port, which is where this letter reached him. See below, Chapter Seven.

44 Ep.IV, L.1603, 19 April 1631.

45 Positio, p.832, 31 October 1631.

46 Ep.IV, L.1602, 17 April 1631. '… voglio che sappia che quanto io fo in questo particolar che V.R. è andato a trattar è solo per cuprir questa vergogna grande accio non venga a notitia de Superiori nel che molto ci perderebbe la religione, che sin adesso sta in bonissimo concetto et sopito questo negotio, al resto di finirlo a rimediar vi si attenderà con prudenza et secretezza che sarà molto meglio che romperla di presente et quanto al restar tanto il Pre quanto li altri securi d'ogni contraditione io farò una declaratoria tanto grande che mostrarò che questa che ho fatto a favor di N. è stato per recuoprir questo negotio et che li Padri costi non si sono mossi da passione alcuna ma solo per il bene della religione et col ordine de superiori siche in questo particolar possono lasciar ogni timor e cooperar al rimedio di cuoprir questo negotio e se non le pare di stracciar costi le scritture le mandi per V.R. qui et per sodisfatione di cotesti secolari V.R. potrà far veder all'Aurilia al grossi la patente che io diedi a V.R. et assicurarli che io ho in tal concetto il Pre N. che penso servirmene per ben commune della religione. Insomma V.R. deve procurar costi che le cose si quietino et non se ne parli più tra secolari che qui poi accomodaremo il

. resto et sarà di maniera che ancora costì li Padri restino sodisfatti et sicuri et se li Padri costi nonostanti tutte queste cose non vorranno obedire me ne darà aviso.'

47 Ep.IV, L.1603, 19 April 1631.

48 Ep.IV, L.1609, 26 April 1631.

49 Epco, pp.702–3, 11 April 1631.

50 On de Totis's legal advice, EHI, p.869, 5 July 1627, de Totis to Calasanz; Laurie Nussdorfer, *Civic Politics in the Rome of Urban VIII* (New Jersey: Princeton University Press, 1992), p.90; *Regesti di bandi, editti, notificazioni, e provvedimenti diversi relativi alla città di Roma e allo Stato Pontificio*, 7 vols. (Rome 1920–1958), vol.4, p.1388, 2 January 1637.

51 Ep.IV, L.1682, 17 September 1631.

52 Annot,T.1, bk.3, ch.18.

53 Annot,T.1, bk.3, ch.18.

54 Epco, p.702, 11 April 1631.

CHAPTER SEVEN

1 On the Memorial of the Inconveniences, see above, Chapter Three.

2 Ep.IV, L.1115, 2 June 1629.

3 Filippo Scoma, 'Memorie cronologiche della fondazione e progressi della provincia di Sicilia delle Scuole Pie', *Archivum Scholarum Piarum*, 17 (1985), p.140; Ep.IV, L.1237, 20 October 1629.

4 Positio, p.565, 'Primo capitolo o congregatione generale fatta dell'anno 1627 adi xi ottobre'. See also above, Chapter Four.

5 Ep.IV, L.1226, 4 October 1629; L.1231, 13 October 1629; L.1242, 27 October.

6 Carlo M.Cipolla, *Cristofano and the Plague. A Study in the History of Public Health in the Age of Galileo* (London: Collins, 1973), p.15.

7 EHI, pp.590–1, 24 November 1629; EHI, pp.1211–2, 7 December 1629; Geoffrey Hawthorn, *Plausible Worlds: Possibility and Understanding in History and the Social Sciences* (Cambridge: Cambridge University Press, 1991), pp.39–80.

8 Ep.IV, L.1437, 13 July 1630.

9 Ep.IV, L.1395, 24 May 1630; L.1417, 15 June 1630.

10 Ep.IV, L.1486, 7 September 1630.

11 Moncallero and Limiti, p.133, L.45, letter of Calasanz, 16 August 1631.

12 Daniela Lombardi, '1629–1631: crisi e peste a Firenze', *Archivio storico italiano*, 137 (1979), pp.3–50; Laurie Nussdorfer, *Civic Politics in the Rome of Urban VIII* (New Jersey: Princeton University Press, 1992), p.145ff.; Marisa Brogi Ciofi, 'La peste del 1630 a Firenze con particolare riferimento ai provvedimenti igienico-sanitari e sociali', *Archivio storico italiano*, 142 (1984), p.47–77; Giulia Calvi, *Histories of a Plague Year: The Social and the Imaginary in Baroque Florence*, trans. Dario Biocca and Bryant T. Ragan, Jr. (Berkeley: University of California Press, 1989).

13 Moncallero and Limiti, pp.126–33, LL.37, 43, 5 July and 2 August 1631.

14 Ep.IV, L.1447, 27 July 1630; L.1539, 7 December 1630; also Moncallero and Limiti, pp.123–5, L.35, 28 June 1631.

15 Ep.IV, L.1503, 30 September 1630.

16 Ep.IV, L.1447, 27 July 1630, 'guardie esquisitissime'; this could also be translated as 'most perfect'.

17 EHI, p.25, 10 October 1629.

18 Brian Pullan, *Rich and Poor in Renaissance Venice. The Social Institutions of a Catholic State, to 1620* (Oxford: Blackwell, 1971), p.408; David Chambers and Brian Pullan, *Venice: A Documentary History 1450–1630* (Oxford: Blackwell, 1992), pp.26–7; on Alacchi's ladder, see Scoma, 17 (1985), pp.142–50.

19 Ep.IV, L.1365, 19 April 1630.

20 Moncallero and Limiti, p.111, L.22, letter from Calasanz, 1 March 1630, and pp.154–5, L.76, 10 January 1632.

21 Moncallero and Limiti, pp.142–3, L.49, 23 September 1631; Ep.IV, L.1715, 15 November 1631.

22 Moncallero and Limiti, pp.99–100, L.11, 4 January 1630; Ep.IV, L.1662, 9 August 1630.

23 Ep.V, L.1872, 11 September 1632; L.1910, 6 November 1632; Scoma, 18 (1985), pp.344, 346.

24 Ep.IV, LL.1729, 1763, 1768, etc.

25 Scoma, 18 (1985), p.309, 344.

26 Moncallero and Limiti, pp.145–6, L.53, 26 September 1631, and pp.147–8, L.58, 8 November 1631; Ep.IV, L.1711; gossip heard in Rome, Moncallero and Limiti, pp.150–1, L.68, 13 December 1631; more on Biagio's behaviour in Scoma, 18 (1985), p.324; Ep.IV, L.1715, 15 November 1631.

27 Scoma, 18 (1985), p.353.

28 Ep.IV, L.1715, 15 November 1631.

29 Ep.IV, L.1718, 22 November 1631.

30 Ep.V, L.1763, 20 March 1632.

31 Ep.V, L.1750, 14 February 1632.

32 Scoma, 18 (1985), pp.352–3.

CHAPTER EIGHT

1 Much of this material is from A. K. Liebreich, 'The Florentine Piarists', *Archivum Scholarum Piarum*, 12 (1982), pp.273–304.

2 EHI, p.1188, 1 April 1630.

3 EHI, pp.1211–2, 7 December 1629.

4 AGR, Reg. Prov. 20, Domus Florentiae, n.3.

5 Diario del Settimanni, Archivio di Stato, Firenze. MS 135, vol.IX, 4 April 1632.

6 Father Arcangelo cited in Giner Guerri, p.745, n.166; priests dying, in Marisa Brogi Ciofi, 'La peste del 1630 a Firenze con particolare riferimento ai provvedimenti igienico-sanitari e sociali', *Archivio storico italiano*, 142 (1984), p.68.

7 Leodegario Picanyol, SP, *Le Scuole Pie e Galileo Galilei* (Rome, 1942); Giovanni Giovanozzi, *Scolopi Galileiani* (Florence: Arte della Stampa, 1917); EHI, p.1212, 7 December 1629.

8 Eric Cochrane, *Florence in the Forgotten Centuries, 1527–1800* (Chicago: University of Chicago Press, 1973), p.188.

9 Pietro Redondi, *Galileo Heretic*, trans. Raymond Rosenthal (London: Allen Lane, 1987), p.14.

10 Redondi, p.37.

11 Redondi, p.38.

12 Redondi, p.45.

13 Redondi, p.59.

14 This is not the place to go into the details of the argument, which have been dealt with in great detail by many other historians. The bibliography on Galileo is vast and still expanding at a great rate. Antonio Favaro (ed.), *Le opere di Galileo Galilei*, 20 vols. (Florence: Tipografia di G. Barbèra, 1929–39) will keep most people going for a while. Far more accessible is Dava Sobel, *Galileo's Daughter: A Drama of Science, Faith and Love* (London: Fourth Estate, 1999).

15 Quoted in Mario Biagioli, *Galileo, Courtier: The Practice of Science in the Culture of Absolutism* (Chicago: University of Chicago Press, 1993), p.339.

16 Biagioli, pp.330–40; Sobel, p.290.

17 Sobel, p.362.

18 Tommaso Campanella, 'Liber apologeticus contra impugnantes institutum Scholarum Piarum', intro. and trans. K. Jensen, A. K. Liebreich, *Archivum Scholarum Piarum*, 15 (1984), pp.29–76.

19 Ep.V, LL.1878, 28 September 1632; L.1894, 14 October 1632; Calasanz in Frascati with Campanella.

20 Redondi, pp.40–1.

21 Michelini sends Galileo regards from Campanella, Epco, p.1866, 12 October 1634; on Campanella's escape, see Chapter Two.

22 Maurizio Torrini, 'Aspects de l'École Galiléenne', in Massimo Bucciantini and Maurizio Torrini (eds.), *Geometria e atomismo nella scuola Galileiana* (Florence: Olschki, 1992), pp.1–16.

23 'Castelli' by A.de Ferrari in *Dizionario biografico degli Italiani*; letter from Michelini to Galileo, 8 April 1634 in Antonio Favaro, *Le opere di Galileo Galilei*, vol. XVI, p.76, and Epco, p.1864; Castelli to Galileo, 8 April 1634, Favaro, vol.XVI, p.75, and Epco, p.2805; Benedetto Castelli, *Carteggio*, ed. Massimo Bucciantini (Florence: Olschki, 1988); letter from Michelini to Castelli, 2 September 1634, pp.134–5.

24 EHI, p.1434, 14 February 1634.

25 Favaro, vol. XVI, p.92.

26 Epco, p.1865, 12 October 1634.

27 Giovanni Giovanozzi, *Scolopi Galileiani* (Florence: Arte della Stampa, 1917), p.8.

28 Ep.VI, L.2358, 31 March 1635.

29 Castelli to Michelini, 10 February 1635, Favaro, vol. XVI, p.210.

30 Castelli to Galileo, 17 October 1635, Favaro, vol. XVI, p.322.

31 Osvaldo Tosti, SP, on 'Angelo Morelli', *Archivum Scholarum Piarum*, 40 (1996), pp.24–93.

32 Ep.IV, L.1342, 16 March 1630; Ep.VI, L.2443, 19 September 1635; Castelli, *Carteggio*, p.158, letter from Castelli to Borelli, 15 September 1636.

33 EHI, p.542, 24 November 1629; letter from Father Pietro Casani.

34 Favaro, vol. XVII, p.247, Galileo to Diodati, 2 January 1638.

35 Various letters between Barberini and Muzzarelli, March 1638, Favaro, vol.

XVII, pp.290–348. Allan Olney, *The Private Life of Galileo* (London: Macmillan, 1870), pp.284–5.

36 John Gribbin, *Science: A History* (London: Allen Lane, 2002), p.101; see also Sobel, pp.349–70.

37 Epco, p.1867, 12 December 1637. Also in Favaro, vol. XVII, p.235.

38 Favaro, vol. XVII, p.315, Peri to Galileo, February 1638.

39 Gian Carlo was appointed 'Generalissimo of the Spanish Seas' but showed very little enthusiasm for his new military career, being more interested in women, theatre and art. Leopoldo, the most sympathetic to the Piarists of the Medici princes, was born in 1617, the seventh and youngest of the Grand Duke Cosimo II's children. His father died when he was only three years old and the Grand Duchess Maria Maddalena of Austria organized his education, appointing as his first tutor Jacopo Soldani, one of Galileo's followers. With the eventual emergence of his brother Ferdinand from childhood to take over the reigns of government, Leopoldo became increasingly influential in Tuscan politics, taking a particular responsibility for manufacturing, agriculture and the economy. He always remained interested in scientific and literary affairs, being elected to the famous Accademia della Crusca in 1641, and in 1657 founding the equally renowned Accademia del Cimento, one of the great scientific institutions of the age, before being promoted to the cardinalate ten years later. See also http://info.crusca.fi.it/fabitaliano2/statiche/biografia.

40 Giovanozzi, p.13; letter of 25 July 1638.

41 Favaro, vol. XVIII, p.128; L.3948, 7 December 1639.

42 Favaro, vol. XVIII, p.130; L.3950, Galileo to Castelli, 18 December 1639.

43 Favaro vol. XVII, p.359, Galileo to Castelli, 25 July 1638; Favaro, vol. XVII, p.411, Michelini to Galileo, 11 December 1638; E. Ferroni, 'La tradizione scientifica dei Padri Scolopi della Toscana', *Ricerche*, 2 (1981), p.76.

44 Favaro, vol. XVIII, p.11, Galileo to Baliani, 7 January 1639. The book was Baliani's *De motu gravium solidorum*.

45 Olney, p.288.

46 Favaro, vol. XVIII, p.331, Torricelli to Galileo, 1 June 1641; Leodegario Picanyol, *Le Scuole Pie e Galileo Galilei* (Rome, 1942), pp.97–8.

47 Ep.VII, L.3074, 16 April 1639.

48 Explanatory note to Ep.VII, L.3074.

CHAPTER NINE

1 For example, on the endless legal problems of the Nazarene College, Ep.V, L.1842; building problems at Ancona, Ep.V, L.1883; the roof at Norcia, Ep.V, L.2113.

2 Ep.V, L.2073, 12 July 1633.

3 Scoma, 18 (1985), p.354.

4 Scoma, 18 (1985), p.359–60.

5 Scoma (1986), pp.99; number of pupils in Palermo, Moncallero and Limiti, p.202.

6 Moncallero and Limiti, pp.60–63; Scoma (1986), pp.51–8, 71, 111, 114; on his giggling, 18 (1985) p.353.

7 EHI, pp.30–1, 1 February 1635; p.33, May 1635; Scoma (1986), p.129.

8 Ep.X, L.2538(1), 29 May 1636, nomination to visitor.

9 Ep.VI, L.2594, 20 September 1636.

10 Ep.X, L.2608(1), 11 October 1636.

11 Ep.VI, L.2646, 13 December 1636.

12 EHI, pp.33–7, 8 January 1637.

13 On Brother Carlo's theft, Ep.VI, L.2739, 13 June 1637.

14 Ep.VI, L.2670, 29 January 1637.

15 Ep.X, L.2705(1), 18 April 1637.

16 Positio, p.933.

17 Ep.X, L.2784(1), 28 November 1637.

18 Ep.VI, L.2902, 11 July 1638.

19 Ep.VII, L.3123, 13 August 1639.

20 EHI, pp.43–6, 8 September 1641.

21 Ep.VII, L.3747, 5 October 1641.

22 Moncallero and Limiti, p.71, letter of 21 June 1642.

23 Annot, T.1, bk.3, ch.7.

CHAPTER TEN

1 See above, Chapter Three.

2 Rosario Villari, *The Revolt of Naples,* trans. James Nowell with assistance of John A. Marino (Cambridge: Polity Press, 1993), pp.75, 149.

3 Peter Burke, *The Historical Anthropology of Early Modern Italy: Essays on*

Perception and Communication (Cambridge: Cambridge University Press, 1987), p.197.

4   EHI, p.1067, 12 October 1638; Ep.VI, L.2924, undated; EHI, p.1070, 16 October 1638.

5   EHI, p.1059, 31 August 1638.

6   EHI, p.1070. 16 October 1638, Giuseppe Fedele, provincial of Naples, to Calasanz.

7   Ep.VI, L.2925, 21 August 1638.

8   EHI, p.1042, 10 August 1638; Calasanz's orders, Ep.VI, L.2917, 7 August 1638.

9   Ep.VI, L.2944, 25 September 1638; also Ep.VI, LL.2988, 11 December, etc.

10   EHI, p.1044, 15 August 1638, Fedele to Calasanz.

11   Ep.VI, L.2924, undated; EHI, p.1073, 19 October 1637.

12   Ep.VII, LL.3692 and 3708, 3 and 17 August 1641.

13   EHI, p.1289, for biography of Guarnotto; for his support of Cherubini, see Epco, p.1613, 19 December 1643.

14   Ep.VII, L.3151, 29 September 1639.

15   Ep.VII, L.3114, undated but assumed by Picanyol to be July 1639.

16   EHI, p.1099, 2 September 1639, womanizing; p.1094, 13 May 1639.

17   EHI, pp.1948–9, 8 September 1640.

18   Ep.VII, L.3063, 2 April 1639.

19   Ep.VIII, L.3949, 15 March 1642; the description of these events draws much from Father Osvaldo Tosti's introduction to Berro's *Annotationi, Archivum Scholarum Piarum,* 21 (1987), p.14.

20   EHI, p.681, 2 November 1641.

21   Cherubini's complaint, Epco, p.709, 21 October 1634; Ep.VI, L.2400, 4 July 1635; L.2408, 14 July 1635; L.2410, 18 July 1635, L.2432, 5 September 1635; L.2620, 1 November 1636.

22   Ep.VII, L.3790, 27 November 1641.

23   Epco, pp.826, 9, 19 and 23 March 1639; Ep.VII, L.3060, 26 March 1639.

24   e.g. Ep.VI, L.2549, 28 June 1636; Calasanz asks Cherubini to sell the cow because the baker is hassling for his debt of 79 scudi; L.2693, 14 March 1637, 'You must find me the money as soon as possible because there are many debts and I must pay 70 scudi to Sig.Caetano'.

25   Ep.VII, L.3065, 5 April 1639, to Lorenzo Ferrari della Nunziata.

26   Annot, T.2, bk.1, ch.1.

27   Annot, T.2, bk.2, ch.10 in a letter from Nikolsburg of 22 August 1644.

28 EHI, p.606, 12 February 1633.

29 Ep.V, L.2208, 18 March 1634.

30 Ep.V, L.2250, 22 July 1634.

31 Ep.VI, L.2534, 20 May 1636.

32 Annot, T.2, bk.1, ch.1.

33 Ep.VII, L.3192, 12 November 1639.

CHAPTER ELEVEN

1 Ep.VII, L.3287, 24 February 1640.

2 Ep.VII, L.3317, 16 March 1640.

3 Ep.VII, L.3410, 5 May 1640.

4 Ep.VII, L.3446, 2 June 1640.

5 Annot, T.2, bk.1, ch.2.

6 Annot, T.2, bk.1, ch.2.

7 Giner Guerri, p.929; letter from Clemente Settimi to Leopoldo de Medici, Epco, p.2467, 14 December 1641.

8 Annot, T.2, bk.1, ch.2.

9 Annot, T.2, bk.1, ch.3.

10 AGR, Reg. Cal. 69; letter from Padre Castelli. Much of this section is taken from A. K. Liebreich, 'The Florentine Piarists', *Archivum Scholarum Piarum*, 12 (1982).

11 Ep.VII, L.3287, 24 February 1640; L.3317, 16 March 1640; L.3446, 2 June 1640; L.3454, 16 June 1640; Giner Guerri, p.931.

12 Epco, p.252, 8 January 1643.

13 Annot, T.2, bk.1, ch.1.

14 Ep.VII, L.3454, 16 June 1640; L.3457, 23 June 1640.

15 Ep.VII, L.3457, 23 June 1640; Epco, pp.2528–9, January 1643, Sozzi's Calumnious Memorial to the Holy Office.

16 Cited in Giner Guerri, p.932.

CHAPTER TWELVE

1 Ameyden, quoted in Stefanie Walker and Frederick Hammond (eds.), *Life and the Arts in the Baroque Palaces of Rome: Ambiente Barroco* (New Haven: Yale University Press, 1999); on his legal work for the Order, see Epco, p.858, 14 January 1640; p.98, 15 February 1640; Ep.VII, L.3439, 26 May

1640. Ameyden acted on behalf of the rebel Genoese house, visiting the Pope on their behalf in February 1640.

2 Nussdorfer, pp.34–8; Biagioli, pp.315–18.

3 Pastor, vol. 29, pp.361–4.

4 *Dizionario biografico degli Italiani* (Rome: Istituto dell'Enciclopedia italiana, 1960–)

5 Nussdorfer, p.35.

6 Epco, p.650, 7 October 1624.

7 On Farfa, Ep.III, L.971, 21 October 1628; Ep.V, L.2136, 12 November 1633; Annot.T.1, bk.2, ch.25.

8 Nussdorfer, p.37. On the incident with the Venetian ambassador, see above, Chapter Seven.

9 Nussdorfer, p.36.

10 Niccolò Del Re, *La curia romana, lineamenti storico-giuridici* (Rome: Edizioni di storia e letteratura, 1970) p.92; Edward Peters, *Inquisition* (New York: Free Press, 1988); James B. Given, *Inquisition and Medieval Society: Power, Discipline, and Resistance in Languedoc* (New York: Cornell University Press, 1997).

11 Peter Robb, *M* (London: Bloomsbury, 1998), p.247.

12 Romano Canosa, *Sessualità e inquisizione in Italia tra cinquecento e seicento* (Rome: Sapere 2000, 1994), p.285.

13 Paul Collins, *Papal Power: A Proposal for Change in Catholicism's Third Millennium* (London: Fount, 1997).

14 Joseph Cardinal Ratzinger with Vittorio Messori, *The Ratzinger Report* (San Francisco: Ignatius Press, 1986), p.10.

15 Ratzinger with Messori, p.68.

16 Jean Delumeau, *Vie économique et sociale de Rome dans la seconde moitié du XVIe siècle*, 2 vols. (Paris: De Boccard, 1957), vol.1, p.143.

17 Eliseo Masini, *Sacro arsenale o'vero prattica dell'Officio della S. Inquisitione ampliata* (Rome: appresso gl'Heredi del Corbelletti, 1639), p.5.

18 Masini, p.13.

19 Masini, p.22.

20 Paul F. Grendler, *The Roman Inquisition and the Venetian Press 1540–1605* (New Jersey: Princeton University Press, 1977).

21 *The Assayer, Works*, VI, pp.219ff, quoted in Redondi, p.68.

22 Annot, T.2, bk.1, ch.4.

23 Epco, p.2529, January [?] 1643.

24 Ep.VII, L.3501, 8 September 1640.

25 Letters from Settimi, Epco, pp.2463–6, 30 March and 20 April 1641 to Galileo, 11 May 1641 to Leopoldo de' Medici.

26 Ep.VII, L.3737, 7 September 1641.

CHAPTER THIRTEEN

13 Epco, pp.2525–6, October 1641. I would like to thank Dr Dilwyn Knox of University College, London, for his advice on this translation.

2 Redondi, pp.237–40.

3 Redondi, pp.56–9.

4 Redondi, p.163.

5 Redondi, p.221.

6 Galileo to N.Fabri de Peiresc, 21 February 1635, in Favaro, XVI, p.215ff. quoted in Redondi, p.24.

7 Epco, pp.2523–4, October 1641.

8 Cited in Giner Guerri, p.938.

9 Cited in Giner Guerri, p.939.

10 Epco, pp.2466–7, 14 December 1641; Diario del Settimani, Archivio di Stato, Firenze, MS135, vol. IX, 24 November 1641, 'in the refectory of Santa Croce Pandolfo Ricasoli and Faustina Mainardi …were condemned to perpetual prison'.

CHAPTER FOURTEEN

1 Epco, p.2467, 14 December 1641.

2 Epco, p.2530, February/March 1644; Ep.VIII, L.3824, 14 December 1641.

3 Ep.VII, L.3795, 30 November 1641.

4 Ep.VIII, L.3908, 2 February 1642; L.3951, 15 March 1642.

5 Ep.VII, L.3832, 14 December 1641; L.3841, 21 December 1641; L.3839, 17 December 1641.

6 Ep.VIII, L.3912, 7 February 1642.

7 Ep.VIII, L.3999, 31 May 1642; L.4003, 7 June 1642.

8 Ep.VIII, L.3854a, 1 January 1642.

9 Giner Guerri, p.942.

10 Ep.VIII, L.3816, 7 December 1641.

11 Epco, p.2470, 16 January 1642.

12 Cited in Lucien Ceyssens, *Le Cardinal François Albizzi (1593–1684): Un cas important dans l'histoire du jansénisme* (Rome: Pontificium Athenaeum Antonianum, 1977), p.82. Documents in the Inquisition Archive relevant to Albizzi's work include St.St.D3–f, Epitome ... del Cardinal Francesco Albizzi; St.St.D3–g.h, St.St.D3–i. St.St.F1–F7 on Jansenism. See also Rainer Decker, 'Spee und Tanner aus der Sicht eines römischen Kardinal-Inquisitors', *Spee-Jahrbuch* 6 (1999), pp.45–52.

13 Ceyssens, pp.85, 184.

14 Pastor, vol. 29, p.152.

15 Albizzi, *De Iurisdictione quam habent S.R.E. Cardinales in Ecclesiis suorum Titulorum* (Romae Ex Typographia Reu. Camerae Apostolicae, 1666).

16 Ceyssens, pp.255–9.

17 Ceyssens, p.259.

18 Ceyssens, p.265; Alexander VII, quoted by anonymous contemporary, Ceyssens, p.256.

CHAPTER FIFTEEN

1 Ceyssens, p.84.

2 Ep.VIII, L.3980, 26 April 1642.

3 Annot, T.2, bk.1, ch.9.

4 Epco, p.2530, February/March 1643.

5 Ep.VIII, L.3873, 11 January 1642; L.3909, 2 February 1642.

6 Ep.VIII, L.3850, 28 December 1641.

7 Epco, p.2939, 22 February 1642.

8 Epco, p.2943, 29 March 1642.

9 'An Account of Philaretus during his Minority by Robert Boyle', in *Robert Boyle by Himself and Friends*, ed. M. Hunter (London: W. Pickering, 1994), p.20. The effect on his future sex life is from John Gribbin, *Science: A History* (London: Allen Lane, 2002), p.130.

10 Ep.VIII, L.3917, 8 February 1642.

11 Epco, p.2941, 23 March 1642.

12 Ep.VIII, L.4018, 12 July 1642.

13 Epco, p.2530, February/March 1644.

14 Annot, T.2, bk.1, ch.10.

15 Annot, T.2, bk.1, ch.10.

16 Annot, T.2, bk.1, ch.10.

17 Ep. X, L.4157(1), 23 February 1643.

18 Annot,T.2, bk.1, ch.11.

19 Annot,T.2, bk.1, ch.11; the following descriptions are mostly supplied by Berro, who was told them by eyewitnesses.

20 Masini, p.19.

21 Ep.VIII, L.4125, 29 August 1643.

22 Annot, T.2, bk.1, ch.12.

CHAPTER SIXTEEN

1 Annot, T.2, bk.1, ch.12; most of the following description is taken from this vivid source.

2 Annot,T.2, bk.1, ch.13.

3 Ep.X, L.4028(1), 8 August 1642.

4 Positio, pp.1187–9, 14 August 1642.

5 Epco, p.2531; Giner Guerri, pp.956–7.

6 Nussdorfer, pp.195ff.

7 Giacinto Gigli, quoted in Nussdorfer, p.214.

8 Epco, p.2697, 20 August 1642.

9 Giacinto Gigli, quoted in Nussdorfer, p.216.

10 Ep.VIII, L.4049, 18 [?] October 1642.

11 Epco, pp.2898–9, 22 October and 6 November 1642.

12 Epco, p.200, 8 November 1642, 'suo parziale amico'.

13 Epco, p.200, 8 November 1642.

14 Annot, T.2, bk.1, ch.14.

15 Epco, p.64, [?] December 1642.

16 Ep.VIII, L.4082, 10 January 1643, Calasanz has heard rumours of the brief; Epco, p.2534, Sozzi complains that Calasanz sees the title as honorific.

CHAPTER SEVENTEEN

1 Annot, T.2, bk.1, ch.15.

2 Ep.VIII, L.4096, 28 March 1643; Epco, p.2608, 26 March 1643.

3 Annot, T.2, bk.1, ch.16.

4 Annot, T.2, bk.1, ch.16.

5 Annot, T.2, bk.2, ch.9.

6   Epco, p.2900, 3 March 1643.

7   *Constitutiones Societatis Iesu, anno 1558* (London: 1838), p.38; *Constitutiones S. Josephi Calasanctii a.1622* (Salamanca: Gráf. Ortega, 1979), p.13.

8   Moncallero and Limiti, p.55.

9   Annot,T.2, bk.3, ch.25.

10 Redondi, p.35.

11 Biagioli, p.252.

12 'Contro gl'ipocriti', cited in Giovanni Calò, 'Campanella e gli Scolopi', *La voce del Calasanzio* (Oct.1935), p.10.

13 Annot, T.2, bk.1, ch.18.

14 Annot, T.2, bk.2, ch.8.

15 Annot, T.2, bk.2, ch.9.

16 In *Symbola Heroica* (Amsterdam, 1634), quoted in Erwin Panofsky, 'Galileo as a Critic of the Arts: Aesthetic Attitude and Scientific Thought', *Isis*, vol.47, issue 1 (March 1956), pp.3–15, cited from www.compilerpress.atfreeweb.com.

17 Epco, pp.2065–6, 15 May 1643; Epco, p.184, 15 [13?] May 1643.

18 Annot, T.2, bk.1, ch.19.

19 Annot, T.2, bk.1, ch.21, 'mali portamenti'; Ep.IX, p.175, 11 February 1644 in Latin.

20 Annot, T.2, bk.1, ch.21.

21 Annot, T.2, bk.1, ch.24; from the German province, Annot, T.2, bk.2, ch.10.

22 Ep.VIII, L.3858, 3 January 1643, wrongly ascribed to 1642.

23 Epco, pp.2078–9, 19 June 1643; Epco, p.2098, 7 February 1644.

24 From Nikolsburg, 22 August 1644, quoted in Annot, T.2, bk.2, ch.10.

25 Annot, T.2, bk.1, ch.19.

26 EHI, p.1149, 24 March 1640; on Sacchetti, Irene Fosi, *All'ombra dei Barberini. Fedeltà e servizio nella Roma barocca* (Rome: Bulzoni, 1997).

27 Ep.VII, L.3032, 29 January 1639; L.3037, 5 February 1639.

28 Epco, p.672, 10 August 1639, letter from Castiglia to Panello; cf.Ep.VII, L.3509, 29 September 1640, letter from Calasanz to Rapallo in Genoa.

29 Ep.VII, L.3141, 17 September 1639; L.3175, 22 October 1639.

30 Ep.VII, L.3620, 5 July 1641.

31 EHI, p.675, 19 October 1641.

32 EHI, p.2191, 26 October 1641, 'se non vuol sentire disgusti et grandi'.

33 EHI, p.2195, 9 November 1641.

34 EHI, p.1229, 29 November 1641.

35 Ep.VIII, L.3865, 4 January 1642; L.3913, 8 February; EHI, p.126, 18 January 1642.

36 Epco, p.2214, 5 March 1644.

37 Epco, p.2208, 2 January 1644.

38 Annot, T.2, bk.1, ch.25.

39 EP.VI, L.2985, 4 December 1638.

40 Annot, T.2, bk.1, ch.25; 'in sandals', literally 'discalced' or barefoot, although in fact they supposedly wore open sandals.

41 EHI, pp.1868–9, 22 November 1643 and 5 December 1643; and Annot, T.2, bk.3, ch.22.

42 Annot, T.2, bk.2, ch.9.

43 EHI, pp.1868–9, 22 November 1643.

44 EHI, p.1869, 5 December 1643.

45 Epco, p.2214, 5 March 1644; pp.1046–7, 2 April 1644.

46 Annot, T.2, bk.2, ch.22.

47 Annot, T.2, bk.1, ch.25.

48 Epco, p.1615, 10 January 1644 to the apostolic visitor.

49 Epco, p.1613, 19 December 1643, Guarnotto to the apostolic visitor.

50 Epco, p.1296, 19 May 1643.

51 Epco, p.1299, 25 May 1643.

52 Epco, p.1303, 6 June 1643.

53 Epco, p.1339, 31 October 1643.

54 Epco, p.1358, 18 June 1644.

55 Epco, p.2130, 5 May 1644.

56 Annot, T.2, bk.1, ch.25; Ep.V, L.1906, 28 October 1632.

57 EHI, p.302, 15 July 1645.

58 Annot, T.2, bk.1, ch.21.

59 Annot, T.2, bk.1, ch.24.

60 Annot, T.2, bk.1, ch.25; interrogatorii da essi intitolati 'Circumstantiae servandae', Epco, p.2079, 19 June 1643.

61 EHI, pp.302–3, 15 July 1645.

62 Ep.VIII, L.4131, 19 September 1643.

63 Annot, T.2, bk.1, ch.27.

64 With grateful thanks to Dr Tony Chu, consultant dermatologist at Hammersmith Hospital, London.

65 Annot, T.2, bk.1, ch.29.

66 ProcIn, pp.615–7, cited in Giner Guerri, p.981.

67 Annot, T.2, bk.1, ch.29.

68 Annot, T.2, bk.1, ch.29.

69 Annot, T.2, bk.1, ch.3; literally 'per essere stato mio molto familiare e con-sigliero', which could be translated as 'very familiar with me', 'part of my family', 'very close to me', 'my familiar and adviser'.

70 Positio, p.1793, n.183; Annot, T.2, bk.1, ch.30.

71 Annot, T.2, bk.1, ch.31; Father Berro quotes a Piarist acquaintance of Muzzarelli who came from the same village for this suspiciously pro-Piarist account of Muzzarelli's disease and repentance.

CHAPTER EIGHTEEN

1 Epco, p.2085, 1 October 1643.

2 Rumours, e.g. Epco, p.1438, 14 October 1643; letter to the Cardinals' Commission, Epco, p.197, [?] February 1644, but probably earlier.

3 Epco, p.66, 11 November 1643, Albizzi to Pietrasanta. It seems suspiciously convenient for the Inquisition assessor that the cardinals, busy men sitting on many committees and with many other interests, should be able to meet so rapidly and come to so unanimous a decision, a decision moreover which they failed to announce officially for several months. It is more likely that Albizzi bypassed the committee altogether, and decided on the appointment by convincing only Cardinal Roma, the president of the Commission.

4 Cherubini throws himself at Calasanz's feet, Annot, T.2, bk.2, ch.2; letter from Pietrasanta, Epco, p.2094, 11 November 1643; letter from Cherubini, Epco, p.896, 14 November 1643.

5 Annot, T.2, bk.2, ch.3 and 5.

6 Annot, T.2, bk.2, ch.9, 'chi ha cervello'.

7 Epco, p.2495, February 1644; Ep. X, L.4149(1), after 2 January 1644.

8 Annot, T.2, bk.2, ch.2; protest memos, e.g. from Narni, Epco, p.1218, 30 January 1644; Fanano, Epco, p.1027, 5 February 1644; Moricone, p.1051, Carcare, p.1011, Genoa, p.1043, Naples, p.1062, etc.

9 Epco, p.2097, 7 February 1644; Epco, p.2104, 6 February 1644.

10 Epco, p.899, 6 February 1644.

11 Annot, T.2, bk.2, ch.7.

12 Epco, p.196, 3 February 1644.

13 Ceyssens, p.262.

14 Giner Guerri, p.1005.

15 Epco, p.216, 18 August 1644; also in Annot, T.2, bk.2, ch.9.

16 Annot, T.2, bk.2, ch.11.

17 'Il regestum Calasanctianum 68 dell'Archivio Generale (Documenti Paolucci)' ed. Father Osvaldo Tosti, *Archivum Scholarum Piarum*, 26 (1989), pp.95–6, 106.

18 Epco, p.900, 6 February 1644; Epco, pp.902, 20 February 1644.

19 Ep.X, L.4157(1), 23 February 1644. 'Io infrascritto fo fede che, essendo il p.Pietro della Natività prov.le delle Suole Pie di regno di Napoli, fui avvisato più volte della cattiva prattica che con alcuni scolari teneva il p.Stefano degl'Angeli, all'hora ministro delle Scuole Pie della Duchesca, e per evitar li scandali, che ne potevano seguire se li parenti delli giovanetti ne havessero havuto notizia, lo levai di Napoli e lo feci venire a Roma con titolo honorato per rispetto della sua casata; [...] et io vedendo la cosa scoperta, per evitar maggiori inconvenienti, se si publicasse simil cosa, feci per riverenza di sua casa una scrittura, nella quale dichiaravo che, per detto processo, non fusse molestato detto p.Stefano in maniera alcuna, o altre parole simili, non però affermavo che non fussero vere le cose contenute in detto processo; et un'altra volta diedi per scritto di mia mano, che insino all'hora non si era proceduto contro detto Pre giuridicamente per non fare dishonore alla sua famiglia ...'

CHAPTER NINETEEN

1 Annot, T.2, bk.2, ch.10, letter from Nikolsburg, 22 August 1644.

2 Annot, T.3, bk.3, ch.35.

3 Giner Guerri, pp.1014–6.

4 Epco, pp.2106–9, approx March 1644.

5 Epco, p.211, 18 August 1644.

6 Pastor, vol. 29, p.399.

7 Nussdorfer, pp.230–48; 'Avviso di Roma', 30 July 1644 in Pastor, vol. 29, p.573.

8 Nussdorfer, pp.234–46.

9 Ep.VIII, L.4212, 6 August 1644.

10 Epco, p.906, 30 July 1644.

11 Ep.VIII, L.4224, 24 September 1644.

12 Epco, pp.202–20, 18 August 1644.

13 Torgil Magnuson, *Rome in the Age of Bernini*, vol. 2 (New Jersey: Humanities Press, 1986), p.3.

14 Catholic Encyclopaedia, cited at www.newadvent.org/cathen

15 Conversation between Calasanz and Pamphilij from Annot, T.1, bk.3, ch.31.

16 Annot, T.2, bk.3, ch.2.

17 Stefanie Walker and Frederick Hammond (eds.), *Life and the Arts in the Baroque Palaces of Rome: Ambiente Barroco* (New Haven: Yale University Press, 1999), p.118.

18 Quoted in Magnuson, p.26.

19 Annot, T.2, bk.2, ch.16 and 17.

20 Epco, p.1994, 19 July 1645.

21 Epco, p.1993, 17 June 1645 and 15 July 1645.

22 Ep.IX, p.139; Calasanz in Annot. T.2, bk.3, ch.7, 20 October 1645; also Annot, T.2, bk.3, ch.10, 16 December 1645; Ep.VIII, L.4230, 18 October 1644.

23 Annot, T.2, bk.2, ch.17; Ep.VIII, L.4253, 18 February 1645.

24 Pastor, vol.29, p.29.

25 Epco, pp.2912–3, 18 December 1645.

26 Ep.VIII, L.4236, 11 November 1644.

27 Epco, p.3034, wrongly dated [?] February 1646; also in Annot, T.2, bk.2, ch.19, January 1645; Ep.VIII, L.4253, 18 February 1645; on relations between Warsaw and Rome, Pastor, vol. 29, p.166.

28 Epco, p.2951, 21 January 1645; Epco, pp.2952–3, 28 January 1645.

29 Annot, T.3, bk.3, ch.5, memo from Pietrasanta.

30 Annot, T.3, bk.2, ch.7.

31 EHI, p.1599, 26 May 1646.

32 Annot, T.2, bk.2, ch.17.

33 Pastor, vol.29, p.3.

34 Andrea Leonetti, *Memorie del Collegio Nazareno eretto in Roma da S.Giuseppe Calasanzio* (Bologna, 1882); Pasquale Vannucci, *Il Collegio Nazareno* (Rome, 1930); Ottorino Calcagni et al, *I regolamenti del Collegio Nazareno* (Rome, 1979).

35 Annot, T.1, bk.1, ch.30 and bk.3, chs.2–4.

36 Niccolò Del Re, *La curia romana, lineamenti storico-giuridici* (Rome: Edizioni di storia e letteratura, 1970), pp.244–8.

37 Ep.VI, L.2472, 10 November 1635.

38 Annot, T.2, bk.3, ch.15; Calasanz on theatre in Ep.V, L.1983, 2 March 1633 and Ep.VI, L. 2509, 27 February 1636.

39 Annot, T.2, bk.3, ch.19; on the debts, see for instance, Annot, T.3, bk.2, ch.7.

40 Annot, T.2, bk.2, ch.17.

41 Annot, T.2, bk.3, ch.1.

42 Epco, p.2981, 4 September 1645.

43 Epco, p.2984, 23 September 1645.

44 Epco, p.2681, 28 September 1645; Riccardi's response, Epco, p.2986, 7 October 1645.

45 Epco, pp.352–3, 10 January 1646; Annot, T.2, bk.3, ch.14.

46 Epco, p.118, 6 March 1646.

47 Annot, T.2, bk.3, ch.20, letter from Pietrasanta, 9 February 1646, also Epco, p.2121.

48 Epco, pp.2505–6, 16 February 1646 and Annot, T.2, bk.3, ch.21.

49 Ep.IX, pp.216–20, 16 March 1646; Positio, pp.1329–33.

CHAPTER TWENTY

1 Annot, T.2, bk.3, ch.31.

2 Annot, T.3, bk.1, ch.3.

3 Ep.VIII, L.4337, 3 March 1646; L.4347, 22 March 1646.

4 Epco, p.2966, 9 June 1646.

5 Ep.VIII, L.4366, 28 April 1646.

6 Annot, T.2, bk.3, ch.29.

7 Ep.VIII, L.4357, 12 April 1646.

8 Ep.VIII, L.4341, 17 March 1646.

9 Annot, T.2, bk.3, ch.33; Ep.VIII, L.4357, 12 April 1646.

10 Epco, pp.918–9, [?] March 1646.

11 Annot, T.3, bk.1, ch.10 and ch.11.

12 *Regesti di bandi, editti, notificazioni, e provvedimenti diversi relativi alla città di Roma e allo Stato Pontificio*, 7 vols. (Rome, 1920–58), Edict 169, 3 July 1625.

13 Annot, T.3, bk.1, ch.11.

14 Annot, T.3, bk.1, ch.12.

15 Moncallero and Limiti, p.320, 3 September 1646; Ep.VIII, L.4416, 20 October 1646; L.4422, 3 November 1646.

16 Ep.VII, L.3749, 12 October 1641.

17 EHI, p.2198, 23 November 1641.

18 Francis Haskell, *Patrons & Painters. A Study in the Relations Between Italian Art and Society in the Age of the Baroque*, (revised ed.) (New Haven: Yale University Press, 1980), p.22.

19 Annot, T.3, bk.1, ch.30.

20 F. Saxl, 'The Battle Scene without a Hero: Aniello Falcone and his Patrons', *Journal of the Warburg Institute*, 3 (1939–40), pp.70–87.

21 Annot, T.3, bk.1, chs.26–7.

22 Annot, T.3, bk.1, ch.41.

23 Annot, T.3, bk.1, chs.19 and 20.

24 Annot, T.3, bk.3, ch.1, letter from Ladislaw IV, Warsaw to Abbot Orsi, resident in Rome, 16 June 1646.

25 Annot, T.3, bk.3, ch.12, letter from Martiniz, Prague to Calasanz, 13 December 1646.

26 Annot, T.3, bk.3, ch.13, letter from Ossoliński, Warsaw to Panciroli, 15 June 1647; description by Berro from same section.

27 Annot, T.3, bk.3, ch.22.

28 Epco, p.2974, 9 May 1648.

29 Epco, p.2987, 14 April 1646.

30 Epco, p.2907, 5 March 1648; p.2972, 4 April 1648.

31 Giner Guerri, pp.1067–72.

32 Epco, p.354, 4 August 1646; EHI, p.1615, 21 July 1646.

33 EHI, pp.1618–19, 28 July 1646.

34 EHI, p.352, 28 July 1646.

35 Caputi, cited in Giner Guerri, p.1092.

36 EHI, p.358, 1 September 1646.

37 Ep.VIII, L.4396, 25 August 1646.

38 Giner Guerri, p.1083.

39 Epco, pp.69–71, 2 November 1646.

40 Giner Guerri, p.1092; Annot, T.3, bk.2, ch.3.

41 Annot, T.3, bk.2, ch.12.

42 Annot, T.3, bk.2, ch.8.

43 Annot, T.3, bk.2, ch.6; Ep.VIII, L.4522, 10 January 1648.

44 Giner Guerri, p.1101, though he does admit it is 'a bit exaggerated'.

45 Giner Guerri, p.1101.

46 Caputi, quoted in Giner Guerri, p.1107.

47 A. Teodoro Ameyden Bastiaanse (1586–1656). *Un neerlandese alla corte di Roma* ('s-Gravenhage: Staatsdrukkerij, 1967), from Avvisi, Diario di Roma, bibl.Casanat.ms 1833, ff.126v–127r, 29 August 1648.

48 See also Giacinto Gigli, *Diario di Roma*, a cura di Manlio Barberito, vol. 1 (1608–44) (Rome: Colombo, 1994), p.532.

CHAPTER TWENTY-ONE

1 The 1995 independent report into the events in Islington showed several similarities with the Piarist case; for instance it reported that 'such a chaotic organization breeds the conditions for dangerous and negligent professional practices in relation to child care'. (*Evening Standard*, 30 June 2003) The head of Islington council at the time was Margaret Hodge, appointed to the position of Minister for Children in June 2003.

2 Letter of 2 May 2003 from Professor David d'Avray to the author, University College London.

3 *Daily Telegraph,* 18 September 2001.

4 *Guardian*, article by Stephen Bates, 26 October 2001.

5 *Catholic Church in England and Wales,* http://217.19.224.165/CN/01/ Ward.htm, checked on 22 August 2003.

6 Stanislas Lalanne, spokesman for the Bishopric of Bayeux, cited in www.radicalparty.org/belgium/presse/liberation_6.htm, checked on 15 June 2003.

7 *Time*, 1 April 2002.

8 Quoted from BBC News, 9 April 1998 at http://news.bbc.co.uk.

9 *Time*, 1 April 2002.

10 *Daily Telegraph*, 2 October 2003. The estimate of 15 billion euros is based on 150,000 victims claiming, although the government anticipates only 10,000 coming forward, at a cost of one billion euros, just over £725 million.

11 Interview with the Cardinal on BBC TV's *Newsnight*, also reported on http://news.bbc.co.uk, 6 December 2002.

12 Christian Wolmar, *Forgotten Children: The Secret Abuse Scandal in Children's Homes* (London: Vision, 2000).

13 *Observer*, 17 August 2003; http://news.bbc.co.uk, which printed substantial extracts; *Irish Times*, 26 August 2003. The Vatican site has no reference to the document, *Crimine solicitationes*, which was discovered in the Vatican

archives. It apparently dealt mainly with the issue of priests who may solicit sex in the confessional but also included what it referred to as 'the worst crime', sex acts perpetrated by clergymen with youths or animals.

14 Obituary by Felix Corley in the *Independent*, 27 March 2003, citing *Das Buch Groer* by Hubertus Czernin.

15 *Warsaw Voice*, 7 April 2002, at www.warsawvoice.pl.

16 *New York Times*, 28 April 2002.

17 The main source for this is a book by the investigative staff of the *Boston Globe, Betrayal: The Crisis in the Catholic Church* (Boston: Little, Brown & Co., 2002).

18 *Betrayal: The Crisis in the Catholic Church*, p.14.

19 *Betrayal: The Crisis in the Catholic Church*, p.141.

20 *Betrayal: The Crisis in the Catholic Church*, p.125.

21 *Betrayal: The Crisis in the Catholic Church*, p.36.

22 *Betrayal: The Crisis in the Catholic Church*, p.36.

23 *Betrayal: The Crisis in the Catholic Church*, p.49; BBC News, 10 September 2003 at http://news.bbc.co.uk.

24 Quoted from BBC News, 8 January 2002 at http://news.bbc.co.uk.

25 *Time*, 1 April 2002. Cited on the official site of the Holy See at www.vatican.va.

26 www.vatican.va.

27 Joseph Cardinal Ratzinger with Vittorio Messori, *The Ratzinger Report* (San Francisco: Ignatius Press, 1986), p.69.

28 Interview with *New York Times*, 3 March 2002.

29 www.30giorni.it, May 2002. 'È un argomento doloroso strumentalizzato dai mass media. Quando si mischiano denaro, politica e giustizia, la giustizia diventa ingiusta. Noi tutti sappiamo che Ted Turner è apertamente anticattolico, ed è lui il padrone non soltanto della *Cnn* ma anche di *Time Warner*. Per non parlare degli altri quotidiani, come il *New York Times*, il *Washington Post* e il *Boston Globe,* che si sono resi protagonisti di quella che non esito a definire una persecuzione contro la Chiesa. Mi fa molto pensare il fatto che in un momento in cui tutta l'attenzione dei mass media era focalizzata su quanto succedeva in Medio Oriente, con le tante ingiustizie che si sono fatte al popolo palestinese, stampa e tv Usa si sono ossessivamente fermati su scandali sessuali che sono accaduti quaranta anni fa, trenta anni fa... Un accanimento che mi ricorda i tempi di Nerone, Diocleziano e, più recentemente, di Stalin e Hitler.'

30 19 July 2002, http://nationalcatholicreporter.org. He repeated his allegations on British TV, in *Abused and Catholic*, presented by Mark Dowd,
transmitted by Channel Four on 11 January 2003. 'One of the things
I heard consistently [from members of the Curia off the record] is the
theory that part of the energy for what a lot of the people in the Vatican
saw as an exaggerated hostility from the American press on the sex abuse
issue, part of the fuel for it, comes from the fact that the American press is
disproportionately Jewish ... I know there is a class of people in the
Catholic world that is instinctively suspicious of Jews.' Quote about the
National Catholic Reporter from www.natcath.com.

31 Richard Owen in *The Times*, 24 April 2002; Stephen Pope, Boston
College, quoted in *Abused and Catholic*.

32 *Betrayal: The Crisis in the Catholic Church*, p.162.

33 *New York Times*, 25 April 2002.

34 *USA Today*, 25 April 2002.

35 *The Times*, 10 June 2002; *International Herald Tribune*, 10 June 2002; BBC
News on http://news.bbc.co.uk, 15 June 2002.

36 *Guardian*, 19 October 2002; BBC News on http://news.bbc.co.uk, 18
October 2002 and 13 November 2002.

NOTE ON THE SOURCES

The history of the Piarist Order has remained unexplored by lay historians. The Piarist fathers themselves have produced a wealth of material, much of it hagiographical, although in recent years a succession of excellent clerical archivists have edited and published the essential documents relating to the seventeenth century. None of this is easily available outside the archives and libraries of the order itself.

My main sources of information were the collections of contemporary letters published by the order, and original documentary material from the archives of the order, especially those at Rome and Florence, as well as from the Vatican library and archives. In spite of my hopes, not a great deal of new material emerged from the Inquisition archive. More detail is provided in the notes.

The chroniclers Vincenzo Berro (1603–65) and Gian Carlo Caputi (1608–81) provided the basis for most of the early biographies of Calasanz, and I have drawn heavily on Berro's *Annotationi*, which were published in 1987–8 in the order's internal magazine, *Archivum Scholarum Piarum*. In the second half of the eighteenth century two hagiographical biographies were published, Vincenzo Talenti's *Vita del Beato Giuseppe Calasanzio* (1753) and Urbano Tosetti's *Compendio storico della vita di San Giuseppe Calasanzio* (1767). The latter coincided with Calasanz's sanctification and was translated into English in 1850, as well as being translated and rearranged by a French canon, Timon-David, in 1884. In 1949 Calasanz Bau wrote his important, though also hagiographical, *Biografía crítica*, which was horribly translated into English in 1974.

The 1930s, 1940s and 1950s were dominated by the figure of the general archivist Leodegario Picanyol, and several of the basic tools for further research owe their existence to him. His most important contribution was his nine-volume edition of the *Epistolario di San Giuseppe Calasanzio*, the letters of the founder. In spite of some reservations about their accuracy – accusations first levelled in 1965 by historians Moncallero and Limiti, who checked them against new letters discovered in Palermo – I have used these extensively. Since the original letters are no longer in any condition to be handled (though I have seen and used some), there is currently no alternative.

The next major historian to emerge within the Piarist Order was the Hungarian general archivist, György (Georgio) Sántha. His book, *San José de Calasanz: su obra. Escritos*, published in 1956 and reissued in 1984, was immaculately documented. His affection and respect for Calasanz, although always evident, did not cloud his objective presentation. His central European background facilitated his work on the *Epistulae ... ex Europa Centrali* (1969), letters to Calasanz from central Europe, which was followed by a similar two-volume edition of letters from Spain and Italy (1972). He died before completing a six-volume edition of letters exchanged between Calasanz's contemporaries. This was completed (1977–82) by the next general archivist, Claudio Vilá Palá. Vilá Palá also subjected Pietro Casani, one of Calasanz's closest associates, to searching enquiry while preparing the case for his beatification. However, this investigation (published as the *Positio super virtutibus*) proved critical in some respects of the role of the founder himself, and Vilá Palá was sent to live out his days in Barcelona. The next archivist, Osvaldo Tosti from Florence, proved a safe pair of hands and under his curatorship many important documents, such as Berro's *Annotationi*, were published, albeit with little critical analysis. *Archivum Scholarum Piarum* became a journal for documentary reproduction, not for analytical investigation.

The most recent biographer of Calasanz is Severino Giner Guerri, historian general of the order since 1985. His doctoral thesis was on Calasanz's beatification process, but his most important book to date is *San José de Calasanz: Maestro y fundador*, published in 1992, which I have consulted extensively. He too deals with 'The lamentable case of Father Cherubini' and 'Serious accusations against Father Alacchi', although I attach more importance to these events than he does.

BIBLIOGRAPHY

Epistolaries and Other Primary Sources

Berro, Vincenzo, *Annotationi*, ed. P. Osvaldo Tosti in *Archivum Scholarum Piarum*, 21–2 (Rome: 1987), 23 (1988), 24 (1988)

Constitutiones S.Iosephi Calasanctii a.1622 (Salamanca: Gráf. Ortega, 1979), also translated into Italian, *Ricerche*, 45 (1995)

Epistolario di San Giuseppe Calasanzio, [Ep.], ed. Leodegario Picanyol, 9 vols. (Rome: Editiones Calasanctianae 1950–6); vol. 10, ed. Claudio Vilá Palá (1988)

Epistolarium Coaetaneorum S.Iosephi Calasanctii, 1600–1648 [Epco], ed. Georgio Sántha and Claudio Vilá Palá, 7 vols, (Rome: Monumenta Historica Scholarum Piarum, 1977–82)

Epistulae ad S.Iosephum Calasanctium ex Europa Centrali, 1625–1648 [EEC], ed. Georgio Sántha, 2 vols (Rome: Monumenta Historica Scholarum Piarum, 1969)

Epistulae ad S. Iosephum Calasanctium ex Hispania et Italia 1616–1648, [EHI] ed. Georgio Sántha, 2 vols (Rome: Monumenta Historica Scholarum Piarum, 1972)

'Il regestum Calasanctianum 68 dell'Archivio Generale (Documenti Paolucci)', *Archivum Scholarum Piarum*, 26 (Rome: 1989)

Romana seu Lucana Beatificationis et Canonizationis Servi Dei Petri Casani: Positio super virtutibus ex officio concinnata [Positio], ed. Claudio Vilá Palá, 2 vols (Rome: Sacra Congregatio pro causis sanctorum officium historicum, 99, 1982)

Journals of the Order

Archivum Scholarum Piarum
Ricerche, Rivista trimestrale degli Scolopi in Italia

Archives

Archive material has been cited in the relevant footnote.

SCOLOPI ARCHIVES

Archivio Generale delle Scuole Pie, Rome
Archivio Provinciale delle Scuole Pie, Florence
Archivio Provinciale delle Scuole Pie, Genoa

OTHER ARCHIVES

Archivio della Congregazione per la Dottrina della Fede, Rome
Archivio di Stato, Florence
Archivio Segreto Vaticano

Bibliography

Abetti, G. *Amici e nemici di Galileo* (Milan: Bompiani, 1945)

Acton, Harold, *The Last Medici* (London: Methuen, 1932, revised 1958)

Adamson, J. W., *Pioneers of Modern Education* (Cambridge: Cambridge University Press, 1905)

Amerio R., 'Di un punto meno noto del periodo romano del Campanella', *Rivista di filosofia neo-scolastica* (Milan: Università del Sacro Cuore, July 1932)

Antoniano, Silvio, *Dell'educazione cristiana e politica dei figlioli*, ed. by Leopoldo Pogliani (Turin, 1928)

Apa, Giovan Francesco, *Principii della lingua latina praticati in Firenze nell'Accademia degli Sviluppati* (Rome: Domenico Marciani, 1643)

Apa, Giovan Francesco, *Teatro della Latinità* (Naples: per il Gaffaro, 1655)

Ariès, Philippe, *Centuries of Childhood: A Social History of Family Life* (London: Jonathan Cape, 1962)

Askew, Pamela, *Caravaggio's Death of the Virgin* (New Jersey: Princeton University Press, 1990)

Asor Rosa, A., *La cultura della Controriforma* (Bari: Laterza, 1974)

Baigent, Michael and Richard Leigh, *The Inquisition* (London: Viking, 1999)

Baldini, A. Enzo, *Puntigli spagnoleschi e intrighi politici nella Roma di Clemente VIII: Girolamo Frachetta e la sua relazione del 1603 sui cardinali* (Milan: Franco Angelo, 1981)

Balducci, Ernesto, 'I 350 anni degli Scolopi a Firenze', *Ricerche*, 1, (1981)

Bastiaanse, A. Teodoro Ameyden (1586–1656), *Un neerlandese alla corte di Roma* ('s-Gravenhage: Staatsdrukkerij, 1967)

Bau, Calasanz, *Biografía crítica de San José de Calasanz* (Madrid, 1949)

Biagioli, Mario, 'The Social Status of Italian Mathematicians, 1450–1600', *History of Science*, 27 (1989)

Biagioli, Mario, *Galileo, Courtier: The Practice of Science in the Culture of Absolutism* (Chicago: University of Chicago Press, 1993)

Black, Christopher F., *Italian Confraternities in the Sixteenth Century* (Cambridge: Cambridge University Press, 1989)

Blunt, Anthony, *Guide to Baroque Rome* (London: Granada, 1982)

Boston Globe (investigative staff), *Betrayal: The Crisis in the Catholic Church* (Boston: Little, Brown & Co., 2002)

Boswell, John, *Christianity, Social Tolerance, and Homosexuality* (Chicago: University of Chicago Press, 1980)

Boswell, John, *The Marriage of Likeness: Same Sex Unions in Pre-modern Europe* (London: Fontana, 1995)

Bowen, James, *A History of Western Education*, vol.3 (London: Methuen, 1981)

Boyle, Robert, 'An Account of Philaretus during his Minority by Robert Boyle', *Robert Boyle by Himself and Friends*, ed. M. Hunter (London: W. Pickering, 1994)

Braudel, Fernand, *The Mediterranean and the Mediterranean World in the Age of Philip II*, trans. Siân Reynolds (London: Harper Collins, 1992)

Bray, Alan, *Homosexuality in Renaissance England* (New York: Columbia University Press, 1995)

Brizzi, Gian Paolo, *La formazione della classe dirigente nel sei-settecento* (Bologna: Il Mulino, 1976)

Brizzi, Gian Paolo, 'Strategie educative e istituzioni scolastiche della Controriforma', *Il letterato e le instituzioni*, ed. A. Asor Rosa (Turin: Einaudi, 1982)

Brogi Ciofi, Marisa, 'La peste del 1630 a Firenze con particolare riferimento ai provvedimenti igienico-sanitari e sociali', *Archivio storico italiano*, 142 (1984)

Bucciantini, Massimo and Maurizio Torrini (eds.), *Geometria e atomismo nella scuola Galileiana* (Florence: Olschki, 1992)

Bulgarelli, Tullio (ed.), *Gli avvisi a stampa in Roma nel Cinquecento* (Rome: Istituto di Studi Romani Editore, 1967)

Burg, B. R., *Sodomy and the Perception of Evil: English Sea Rovers in the Seventeenth-century Caribbean* (New York: New York University Press, 1983)

Burke, Peter, *The Historical Anthropology of Early Modern Italy: Essays on Perception and Communication*, (Cambridge: Cambridge University Press, 1987)

Calcagni, Ottorino *et al.*, *I regolamenti del Collegio Nazareno* (Rome: 1979)

Calò, Giovanni, 'Campanella e gli Scolopi a proposito dell'Apologia delle Scuole Pie', *Atti della Regia Accademia dei Lincei*, ser.VI, vol. xi, fasc.5–6 (Rome: Accademia nazionale dei Lincei, 1935)

Calò, Giovanni, 'Campanella e gli Scolopi', *La voce del Calasanzio*, October 1935

Calvi, Giulia, *Histories of a Plague Year: The Social and the Imaginary in Baroque Florence*, trans. Dario Biocca and Bryant T. Ragan, Jr. (Berkeley: University of California Press, 1989)

Campanella, Tommaso, 'Liber apologeticus contra impugnantes institutum Scholarum Piarum', eds. K. Jensen and A. K. Liebreich, *Archivum Scholarum Piarum*, 15 (1984)

Campanella, Tommaso, *The City of the Sun*, trans. A. M. Elliott and R. Millner (London: Journeyman Chapbooks, 1981)

Campanelli, A., *La pedagogia Calasanziana* (Rome: Campitelli, 1925)

Canosa, Romano, *Sessualità e inquisizione in Italia tra cinquecento e seicento* (Rome: Sapere 2000, 1994)

Castelli, Benedetto, *Carteggio*, ed. Massimo Bucciantini (Florence: Olschki, 1988)

Ceyssens, Lucien, *Le Cardinal François Albizzi (1593–1684): Un cas important dans l'histoire du jansénisme* (Rome: Pontificium Athenaeum Antonianum, 1977)

Chambers, David and Brian Pullan, *Venice: A Documentary History 1450–1630* (Oxford: Blackwell, 1992)

Cipolla, Carlo M., *Literacy and Development in the West* (London: Penguin, 1969)

Cipolla, Carlo M., *Cristofano and the Plague. A Study in the History of Public Health in the Age of Galileo* (London: Collins, 1973)

Clementi, Filippo, *Il carnevale romano nelle cronache contemporanee*, 2 vols (Rome: Tipografia Tiberina 1899)

Cleugh, James, *The Medici: A Tale of Fifteen Generations* (New York: Doubleday, 1975)

Cochrane, Eric, *Florence in the Forgotten Centuries, 1527–1800* (Chicago: University of Chicago Press, 1973)

Cochrane, Eric, *Italy 1530–1630*, ed. Julius Kirshner (London: Longman 1988)

Collins, Paul, *Papal Power: A Proposal for Change in Catholicism's Third Millennium* (London: Fount, 1997)

Cygan, Jerzy, O. F. M. Cap., 'Der Anteil Valerian Magnis an der Verteidigung des Piaristenordens', *Collectanea Franciscana*, 38 (1968)

de Dainville, F., 'L'enseignement des mathématiques au XVIIe siècle', *Dixseptième siècle*, 30 (1956)

de Dainville, F,. 'Collèges et fréquentation scolaire au XVIIe siècle', *Population*, 12 (1957)

Decker, Rainer, 'Spee und Tanner aus der Sicht eines römischen Kardinal-Inquisitors', *Spee-Jahrbuch*, 6 (1999)

Delumeau, Jean, *Vie économique et sociale de Rome dans la seconde moitié du XVIe siècle*, 2 vols (Paris: De Boccard, 1957)

Delumeau, Jean, *Le catholicisme entre Luther et Voltaire* (Paris: Presses Universitaires, 1971)

De Rosa, Peter, *Vicars of Christ: The Dark Side of the Papacy* (London: Bantam Press, 1988)

de Vivo, F. 'Indirizzi pedagogici ed istituzioni educative di ordini e congregazioni religiose nei secoli XVI–XVII', *Rassegna di Pedagogia* (1960)

Del Col, Andrea and Giovanna Paolin (eds.), 'L'Inquisizione romana:

metodologia delle fonti e storia istituzionale', *Atti del seminario internazionale*, (Trieste: Università di Trieste, 2000)

Del Re, Niccolò, *La curia romana, lineamenti storico-giuridici* (Rome: Edizioni di storia e letteratura, 1970)

Diaz, F., *Il granducato di Toscana*. vol. 1, *I Medici* (Turin: UTET, 1976)

Dizionario biografico degli Italiani (Rome: Istituto dell'Enciclopedia italiana, 1960–)

Duffy, Eamon, *Saints and Sinners: A History of the Popes* (New Haven: Yale University Press, 1997)

Ehrle, F. and H. Egger, *Piante e vedute di Roma e del Vaticano dal 1300 al 1676*, Biblioteca Apostolica dal 1300 al 1676 (Venice: Biblioteca Apostolica Veneta, 1956)

Farrell, Allan P., *The Jesuit Code of Liberal Education* (Milwaukee: Bruce, 1938)

Fantini, R., *L'istruzione popolare a Bologna fino al 1860* (Bologna: Zanichelli, 1971)

Fanucci, Camillo, *Trattato di tutte l'opere pie dell'alma città di Roma* (Rome, 1601)

Favaro, Antonio (ed.), *Le opere di Galileo Galilei*, 20 vols (Florence: Tipografia di G. Barbèra, 1929–39)

Ferroni, E., 'La tradizione scientifica dei Padri Scolopi della Toscana', *Ricerche*, 2 (1981)

Firpo, L., *Lo stato ideale della Controriforma* (Bari: Laterza, 1957)

Fosi, Irene, *All'ombra dei Barberini. Fedeltà e servizio nella Roma barocca* (Rome: Bulzoni, 1997)

Frijhoff, W. and D. Julia, *Ecole et société dans la France d'Ancien Regime: Quatre exemples – Auch, Avallon, Condom, Gisors* (Paris: Colin, 1975)

Gamba, C. M., 'Il poligrafo tedesco gaspare Scioppio e il suo programma di riforma degli studi', *Annali del corso di lingue e letterature straniere*, 1 (1951)

Garin, E., *L'educazione in Europa, 1400–1600* (Bari: Laterza, 1976)

Garzoni, Tommaso, *La piazza universale di tutte professioni del mondo* (Venice, 1595)

Gigli, Giacinto, *Diario di Roma*, ed. Manlio Barberito, vol. 1 (Rome: Colombo, 1994)

Giner Guerri, Severino, Sch.P., *San José de Calasanz: Maestro y Fundador. Nueva biografía crítica* (Madrid: Biblioteca de Autores Cristianos, 1992)

Giordano, F., *Il Calasanzio e l'origine della scuola popolare*. (Genoa: A.G.I.S., 1960)

Giovanozzi, Giovanni, *Scolopi Galileiani* (Florence: Arte della Stampa, 1917)

Given, James B., *Inquisition and Medieval Society: Power, Discipline, and Resistance in Languedoc* (New York: Cornell University Press, 1997)

Greenberg, David F., *The Construction of Homosexuality* (Chicago: University of Chicago Press, 1988)

Grendler, Paul F., *Schooling in Renaissance Italy: Literacy and Learning 1300–1600* (Baltimore and London: Johns Hopkins University Press, 1989)

Grendler, Paul F,. 'The Organization of Primary and Secondary Education in the Italian Renaissance', *Catholic Historical Review*, vol. LXXI, no. 2 (1985)

Grendler, Paul F., *The Roman Inquisition and the Venetian Press 1540–1605* (New Jersey: Princeton University Press, 1977)

Grendler, Paul F., 'The Schools of the Christian Doctrine in 16th century Italy', *Church History*, 53 (1984)

Grendler, Paul F., 'What Zuanne Read in School: Vernacular Texts in Sixteenth-Century Venetian Schools', *The Sixteenth Century Journal*, 13, 1, (1982)

Gribbin, John, *Science: A History, 1543–2001* (London: Allen Lane, 2002)

Haskell, Francis, *Patrons and Painters. A Study in the Relations Between Italian Art and Society in the Age of the Baroque* (revised ed.) (New Haven: Yale University Press, 1980)

Hawthorn, Geoffrey, *Plausible Worlds: Possibility and Understanding in History and the Social Sciences* (Cambridge: Cambridge University Press, 1991)

Henningsen, Gustav and John Tedeschi (eds.), *The Inquisition in Early Modern Europe* (Illinois: Dekalb, 1986)

Hughes, Steven C., 'Fear and Loathing in Bologna and Rome: The Papal Police in Perspective', *Journal of Social History*, 21 (1987)

Hutchinson, Robert, *When in Rome: An Unauthorised Guide to the Vatican* (London: HarperCollins, 1998)

Imbert, G., *Seicento fiorentino*, 2nd ed. (Milan: Athena 1930)

Landucci, Giovanni, 'Il pauperismo del sec.XVII', *Ricerche*, 49 (1996)

Lane, Frederic C., *Venice. A Maritime Republic* (Baltimore: Johns Hopkins University Press, 1973)

Langdon, Helen, *Caravaggio: A Life* (London: Chatto & Windus, 1998)

Lea, Henry C., *Historia de la Inquisición Española*, ed. Angel Alcala. vol. 3 (Madrid: Fundación Universitaria Española, 1983)

Lecointre, Claire, 'Caspar Schoppe et les Ecoles Pies. Un exemple de collaboration scientifique et pédagogique au 17e siècle', *Archivum Scholarum Piarum*, 18 (1985)

Leonetti, Andrea, *Memorie del Collegio Nazareno eretto in Roma da S. Giuseppe Calasanzio* (Bologna, 1882)

Liebreich, A. K., 'The Florentine Piarists', *Archivum Scholarum Piarum*, 12 (1982)

Lombardi, Daniela, '1629–1631: crisi e peste a Firenze', *Archivio storico italiano*, 137 (1979)

Lucchi, Piero, 'Leggere, scrivere e abbaco: L'istruzione elementare agli inizi dell'età moderna', in *Scienze credenze occulte livelli di cultura* (Florence: Convegno Internazionale di Studi, 1982)

Lunadoro, Girolamo, *Relatione della corte di Roma, E de' riti da osservarsi in essa* ... (Rome: Fabio de Falco, 1664)

Lutterbach, H., 'Gleich geschlechtliches sexuelles Verhalten. Ein Tabu zwischen Spätantike und Früher Neuzeit', *Historische Zeitung*, 267 (1998)

Magnuson, Torgil, *Rome in the Age of Bernini*, vol. 2 (New Jersey: Humanities Press, 1986)

Martin, Gregory, *Roma Sancta (1581)*, ed. George Bruner Parks (Rome: Edizioni di Storia e Letteratura, 1969)

Masini, Eliseo, *Sacro arsenale o'vero prattica dell'Officio della S. Inquisitione ampliata* (Rome: appresso gl'Heredi del Corbelletti, 1639)

Maugain, G., *Etude sur l'évolution intellectuelle de l'Italie environ 1657 à 1750* (Paris: Hachette, 1909)

McBrien, Richard P., *Catholicism*, 3rd ed. (London: Geoffrey Chapman, 1994)

McNeill, John J., *The Church and the Homosexual* (Kansas: Sheed Andrews and McMeel, 1976)

Menniti Ippolito, Antonio, *Il tramonto della curia nepotista* (Rome: Viella, 1999)

Moncallero, G. L. and Giuliana Limiti, *Il codice calasanziano palermitano (1603–1648)* (Rome: Edizioni dell'Ateneo, 1965)

Montaigne, Michel de, ed. and trans. E. J. Trechman, *The Diary of Montaigne's Journey to Italy in 1580 and 1581* (London: Hogarth Press, 1929)

Neveu, Bruno, *L'erreur et son juge; Remarques sur les censures doctrinales à l'epoque moderne* (Naples: Bibliopolis, 1993)

Nussdorfer, Laurie, *Civic Politics in the Rome of Urban VIII* (New Jersey: Princeton University Press, 1992)

Nutton, Vivian (ed.), *Medicine at the Courts of Europe, 1500–1837*, esp. Richard Palmer, 'Medicine at the Papal Court in the 16th Century' (London: Routledge 1990)

Olney, Allan, *The Private Life of Galileo* (London: Macmillan, 1870)

Panciroli, Ottavio, *I tesori nascosti nell'alma città di Roma* (Rome: Luigi Zannetti, 1600)

Erwin Panofsky, 'Galileo as a Critic of the Arts: Aesthetic Attitude and Scientific Thought', *Isis*, vol. 47, issue 1 (1956)

Passerini, L., *Storia degli stabilimenti di beneficenza e d'istruzione gratuita della città di Firenze* (Florence: Le Monnier, 1853)

Pastor, Ludwig von, *The History of the Popes*, trans. dom Ernest Graf, 39 vols (London: Kegan Paul and Co., 1952)

Peters, Edward, *Inquisition* (New York: Free Press, 1988)

Petrocchi, Massimo, *Roma nel seicento* (Rome: Cappelli, 1970)

Petrucci, Armando, *Public Lettering: Script, Power and Culture* (Chicago: University of Chicago Press, 1993)

Picanyol, Leodegario, *Brevis Conspectus historicus-statisticus* (Rome, 1932)

Picanyol, Leodegario, 'La Scuola dei Nobili nelle Scuole Pie Fiorentine e il suo Fondatore P. Giovan Francesco Apa', *Rassegna di storia e bibliografia scolopica* (1939)

Picanyol, Leodegario, *Le Scuole Pie e Galileo Galilei* (Rome: Scuole Pie, 1942)

Poutet, Y., 'L'enseignement des pauvres dans la France du XVIIe siècle', *Dixseptième siècle*, 90–1 (1971)

Prosperi, Adriano, 'Vicari dell'Inquisizione fiorentina alla metà del Seicento. Note d'archivio', *Annali dell'Istituto storico italo-germanico di Trento*, 8 (1982)

Puff, Helmut, *Sodomy in Reformation Germany and Switzerland 1400–1600* (Chicago: University of Chicago Press, 2003)

Pullan, Brian, *Rich and Poor in Renaissance Venice: The Social Institutions of a Catholic State, to 1620* (Oxford: Blackwell, 1971)

Quazza, Romolo, *Preponderanza spagnola (1559–1700)* (Milan: Vallardi, 1950)

Ratzinger, Joseph Cardinal with Vittorio Messori, *The Ratzinger Report* (San Francisco: Ignatius Press, 1986)

Raymond, John, *An Itinerary Contayning a Voyage made through Italy in the yeare*

1646, and 1647 (Printed for Humphrey Moseley, and to be sold at his shop at the Princes Armes in St Pauls Churchyard, 1648)

Redondi, Pietro, *Galileo Heretic*, trans. Raymond Rosenthal (London: Allen Lane, 1987)

Regesti di bandi, editti, notificazioni, e provvedimenti diversi relativi alla città di Roma e allo Stato Pontificio, 7 vols (Rome, 1920–58)

Robb, Peter, *M*, (London: Bloomsbury, 1998)

Rocke, Michael, *Forbidden Friendships: Homosexuality and Male Culture in Renaissance Florence* (New York: Oxford University Press, 1996)

Ruggiero, Guido, *The Boundaries of Eros* (Oxford: Oxford University Press, 1985)

Ruggiero, Guido, *Violence in Early Renaissance Venice* (New Jersey: Rutgers University Press, 1980)

Sántha, Jorge, *Ensayos críticos sobre S.José de Calasanz y las Escuelas Pías* (Salamanca, 1976)

Sántha, György, C. Aguilera, J. Centelles, *San José de Calasanz. Su obra escritos* (Madrid: Biblioteca de Autores Cristianos, 1956)

Saxl, F., 'The Battle Scene without a Hero: Aniello Falcone and his Patrons', *Journal of the Warburg Institute*, 3 (1939–40)

Schwickerath, R., *Jesuit Education – Its History and Principles* (St Louis: Herder, 1903)

Scoma, Filippo, 'Memorie cronologiche della fondazione e progressi della provincia di Sicilia delle Scuole Pie', *Archivum Scholarum Piarum*, 17 and 18 (1985), 19–20 (1986)

Scott, Jonathan, *Salvator Rosa. His Life and Times* (New Haven: Yale University Press, 1995)

Sella, Domenico, *Italy in the Seventeenth Century* (London: Addison Wesley Longman, 1997)

Signorotto, Gianvittorio and Maria Antonietta Visceglia, *Court and Politics in Papal Rome, 1492–1700* (Cambridge: Cambridge University Press, 2002)

Sindoni, Angelo, 'Le scuole pie in Sicilia', *Rivista di storia della Chiesa in Italia*, xxv(2) (1971)

Snyders, G., *La pédagogie en France aux XVIIe et XVIIIe siècle* (Paris: Thèse lettres, 1965)

Sobel, Dava, *Galileo's Daughter: A Drama of Science, Faith and Love* (London: Fourth Estate, 1999)

Spinelli, Mario, *Giuseppe Calasanzio, il pioniere della scuola popolare* (Rome: Città Nuova, 2001)

Stourton, Edward, *Absolute Truth: The Catholic Church in the World Today* (London: Viking, 1998)

Tacchi-Venturi, P., *Storia della Compagnia di Gesù in Italia*, 2nd ed. (Rome, Milan, 1931–50)

Talenti, V., *Vita del Beato Giuseppe Calasanz* (Florence, 1917)

Tanturri, Alberto, 'Gli Scolopi nel Mezzogiorno d'Italia in età moderna', *Archivum Scholarum Piarum*, 50 (2001)

Tedeschi, John, *Il Giudice e l'Eretico. Studi sull'Inquisizione romana* (Milan: Vita e pensiero, 1997)

Tosti, Osvaldo, 'Angelo Morelli 1608–1685', *Archivum Scholarum Piarum*, 40, (1996)

Vannucci, Pasquale, 'Il Campanella e il Calasanzio', *La Cultura*, XII (1933)

Vannucci, Pasquale, *Il Collegio Nazareno* (Rome, 1930)

de Viguerie, Jean, *Une œuvre d'education sous l'Ancien Régime. Les Pères de la Doctrine Chrétienne en France et en Italie, 1592–1792* (Paris: La Sorbonne, Nouvelle Aurore, 1976)

Vilá Palá, C., 'El Padre Mario Sozzi. I', *Archivum Scholarum Piarum*, 5 (1979), 7–8 (1980)

Vilá Palá, C., 'Influencia de Campanella en la Pedagogia Calasancia?' *Suplemento de Revista Calasancia I*, 1 (1959)

Vilá Palá, C., 'P. Silvestro Pietrasanta, S. J. Datos biograficos y bibliograficos', *Archivum Scholarum Piarum*, 1 (1977)

Villari, Rosario, *The Revolt of Naples*, trans. James Nowell with assistance of John A. Marino (Cambridge: Polity Press, 1993)

Walker, Stefanie and Frederick Hammond (eds.), *Life and the Arts in the Baroque Palaces of Rome: Ambiente Barroco* (New Haven: Yale University Press, 1999)

Weeks, Jeffrey, *Sexuality and its Discontents* (London: 1985)

White, Michael, *The Pope and the Heretic* (London: Little Brown & Co., 2002)

Christian Wolmar, *Forgotten Children: The Secret Abuse Scandal in Children's Homes* (London: Vision, 2000)

Zapperi, Roberto, *Eros e Controriforma: Preistoria della Galleria Farnese* (Turin: Bollati Boringhieri, 1994)

INDEX

Abbate, Brother Pier Agostino, 50

Abruzzo, 12

Aids, 63

Alacchi, Father Melchiorre: training methods, 40–1, 121; new foundations, 42–5, 47, 49, 55, 61, 81, 83, 89–94, 112–14, 118, 120; criticized by Ottonelli, 48–9; appointed visitor general, 49, 76; accusations of sexual misconduct, 50, 52–3, 55, 76, 83, 105, 116, 118; accused of breaking confessional seal, 50, 53, 83, 105, 118; enemies, 50, 52, 85, 96; dogged by scandal, 50–1; returned to classroom, 51; questioning of novices, 52, 55, 118; denies charges, 53; hostility towards, 53–4, 82; pilgrimage to Spain, 54–5, 77, 81, 82; intended exile, 79; return to Italy, 81; licensed to travel to Holy Land, 83, 85, 89; in Venice, 83–5, 88–93, 95, 112; scandalous behaviour, 90–3; expelled from Venice, 93–4, 112; in Sicily, 112–17; temper, 114, 115, 118; appointed

consultor general and procurator general, 118; banished from Rome, 118, 129; cancer and death, 119–20, 129; accusations against Cherubini and Ambrogi, 119–20; opposition from Sozzi, 132, 133

Alba, 51

Albizzi, Monsignor Francesco: assessor to Inquisition, 139, 160–2; Roman inquisitor, 157; character, 162–4, 165; interest in money, 163; support for Sozzi, 165, 169, 171, 172, 180–2, 184, 189; *Autobiography*, 165; arrests Calasanz, 173–4, 175–6; alliance with Cherubini, 177; associated with Jesuits, 187–8; visits Sozzi's deathbed, 203; supports Cherubini's succession, 206–7, 209–10; acceptance of bribes, 210–12, 245; probable author of attack on Piarists, 216, 231; opposed to reinstating Calasanz, 222–3, 230; role in destruction of Piarist order, 231–2, 234–5; continued support for Cherubini, 246–7, 248, 252, 257;